LYING FOR MONEY

LYING FOR MONEY

HOW LEGENDARY FRAUDS
REVEAL THE WORKINGS
OF THE WORLD

DAN DAVIES

PROFILE BOOKS

First published in Great Britain in 2018 by
PROFILE BOOKS LTD
3 Holford Yard
Bevin Way
London
WC1X 9HD

www.profilebooks.com

10 9 8 7 6 5 4 3 2

Typeset in Fournier by MacGuru Ltd
Printed and bound in Great Britain by Clays Ltd, Elcograf S.p.A.

The moral right of the author has been asserted.

A CIP catalogue record for this book is available from the British Library.

ISBN 978 1 78125 965 8
eISBN 978 1 78125 967 2

To Tess

CONTENTS

A scandal in Mayfair   1

1. The basics   26
2. Long firms   43
3. The snowball effect   84
4. Counterfeits   120
5. Cooked books   142
6. Control fraud   163
7. The economics of fraud   198
8. Cold cases   216
9. Market crimes   239
10. Defrauding the government   263
11. The bottom line   283

Acknowledgements   302
Index   303

A SCANDAL IN MAYFAIR

'Guys, you've got to hear this,' I said. I was sitting in front of my computer, with one eye on a screen of share prices and the other on a live stream of the House of Commons Treasury Select Committee hearings. As the Barclays share price took a graceful swan dive, I pulled the headphones out of the socket and turned up the volume. My colleagues left their terminals and came around to watch BBC Parliament with me. It didn't take long to realise what was happening. 'We've got to get hold of Tom.' We all agreed. 'Bob's getting murdered.'

Bob Diamond, the swashbuckling chief executive of Barclays, had been called before the committee to explain exactly what his bank had been playing at in the LIBOR scandal. The day before his appearance, he had made things very much worse by seeming to accuse the Deputy Governor of the Bank of England of ordering him to fiddle an important benchmark, then walking back the accusation as soon as it was challenged. He was trying to turn on his legendary charm in front of a committee of angry MPs and it wasn't working.

On our trading floor, calls were coming in from all over the City. Investors needed to understand what was happening and whether the damage was repairable. Tom was our designated expert on Barclays Bank but he was asleep five time zones away in New York. Without waiting to ask him I called his clients, a pretty serious breach of stockbroking etiquette. But it had to be done. The world was changing. Later that day, as Tom tried to keep in touch between meetings, he and I would exchange some harsh words, some of the only ones between us in a long working friendship.

A couple of weeks later, the damage was done. The money was gone, Bob Diamond was out of his job and the market, as it always does, had moved on. Over a glass or two of beer, Tom and I were repairing our fences and asking ourselves the unavoidable question: how did we get it so wrong?

He was the market's top analyst of British banks. I was the team's regulation specialist. Both of us had been aware of 'the LIBOR affair' and had written about it on several occasions over the previous months. But we had assumed that it would be the typical kind of regulatory risk for the banks – a slap on the wrist, a few hundred million dollars of fines, no more than that.

The first puzzle was that, to start with, it looked like we were *right*. By the time it caught the attention of the mainstream media, the LIBOR scandal had reached what would usually be the end of the story – the announcement on 27 June 2012 of a regulatory sanction. Barclays had admitted a set of facts, made undertakings not to do anything similar again, and agreed to pay a fine of £59.5m to the UK's FSA and $160m to the US Department of Justice. That's how these things are usually dealt with. If anything, it was considered quite a tough penalty.

But the LIBOR case marked the beginning of a new process for the regulators. As well as publishing their judgement, they gave a long summary of the evidence and reasoning which led to their decision. In the case of the LIBOR fines, the majority of that evidence took the form of transcripts of email and Bloomberg chat.*

Ahhh, the transcripts.

> Trader C: 'The big day [has] arrived ... My NYK are screaming at me about an unchanged 3m libor. As always, any help wd be greatly appreciated. What do you think you'll go for 3m?'
> Submitter: 'I am going 90 altho 91 is what I should be posting.'
> Trader C: '[...] when I retire and write a book about this business your name will be written in golden letters [...]'.
> Submitter: 'I would prefer this [to] not be in any book!'

Perhaps it's unfair to judge the LIBOR conspirators on their chat records; few of the journalists who covered the story would like to see their own Twitter direct message history paraded in front of an angry public. Trading is, for all its bluster, basically a service industry, and there is no service industry anywhere in the world whose employees don't blow off steam by acting out or insulting the customers behind their backs. But traders tend to have more than the usual level of self-confidence, bordering on arrogance in much the same way that the USA borders on Canada. And in a general climate in which the public was both unhappy with

---

*Bloomberg terminals, the $50,000/year news and financial data servers that every trader uses, have a chatroom function as well as being able to give you prices and transmit news. Financial market professionals are vastly more addicted to this chat than tween girls are to Instagram and many of them failed to realise that if you discussed illegal activity on this medium you were making things easy for the authorities.

the banking industry and unimpressed with casual banter about ostentatious displays of wealth, the LIBOR transcripts appeared crass beyond belief. Every single popular stereotype about traders was confirmed. An abstruse and technical set of regulatory breaches suddenly became a morality play, a story of swaggering villains who fixed the market as if it was a crooked horse race. The politicians could hardly have failed to get involved.

It is not a pleasant thing to see your industry subjected to criticism which is at once overheated, ill-informed and entirely justified. In 2012, the financial sector finally got the kind of enemies it deserved. The popular version of events might have been oversimplified and wrong in lots of technical detail, but in the broad sweep it was right. The nuanced and technical version of events which the specialists obsessed over might have been right on the detail, but it missed one utterly crucial point: a massive crime of dishonesty had taken place. There was a word for what had happened and that word was fraud. For a period of months, it seemed to me as if the more you knew about the LIBOR scandal, the less you understood it.

That's how we got it so wrong. We were looking for incidental breaches of technical regulations, not systematic crime. And the thing is, that's normal. The nature of fraud is that it works outside your field of vision, subverting the normal checks and balances so that the world changes while the picture stays the same. People in financial markets have been missing the wood for the trees for as long as there have been markets. And bankers have ended up in worse swamps than I did.

The Cazique of Poyais

It is common for young men in a hurry to make rash career decisions. Few of us, though, have screwed it up quite as badly as a London banker by the name of Gauger.* In 1822 he was making a career in the City. A good chap from a good family, nevertheless promotion was arriving slowly in the house of Thomas, Jenkins & Co., and so Gauger decided to do what bankers have done for generations: jump a few rungs up the ladder by taking a higher-risk opportunity in an emerging market. The job in question was the role of General Manager of the Bank of Poyais, a new British colony in Central America being established by Sir Gregor MacGregor, the war hero and minor Scottish nobleman. Gauger paid a considerable sum of his family's money to purchase this commission. His trust seemed to have been reciprocated when he took delivery of a chest full of $5,000 worth of newly printed Poyais Dollars to transport to the colony's capital, the fair city of St Joseph.

Several weeks later, up to his knees in a foreign swamp, Mr Gauger must have been having second, if not third thoughts. He would never be the man to run the central bank of Poyais, for there was no such country as Poyais. Despite the engraved pictures of it that had decorated all of MacGregor's marketing material, there was no city of St Joseph. There wasn't even a trading post. The Poyais Dollars in his chest

---

* Or possibly Gouyer, or possibly Mauger. His name only appears in court records of the litigation arising from this episode, by which time he no longer lived in England (spoiler: this story doesn't end happily for him). I have gone for 'Gauger' as it looks more like a Huguenot name, which would make sense for a banker.

weren't completely worthless: the local Miskito children quite liked the pretty pictures on them. But that wouldn't have been much comfort to Gauger, who had encouraged many other colonists to exchange this absurd scrip for their valuable English and Scottish currency. He had been made the victim of, and party to, one of early capitalism's first and most audacious investment frauds.

Similar disappointments were felt by the other passengers of the *Honduras Packet* and *Kennersley Castle*, which between them had carried around 250 families from Britain to the mouth of the Black River, located in modern Honduras. The voyagers included cobblers (who were never going to be official shoemakers to the Princess of Poyais), musicians (never going to direct the national opera of Poyais) and soldiers (never going to take up their officers' commissions in the army of Poyais). In an even worse plight were the unskilled and agricultural colonists, who quickly realised that their dreams of an idyllic retirement running sugar plantations farmed by Native American labour were unlikely to be realised without significant unplanned work on a patch of land known as the Mosquito Coast. There was real land, but Poyais was not a real country – no capital city, no fertile plains, not much of anything except swamp and thick local rainforest.

The colonists did not take the revelation well. Those who could hitched lifts to Belize. Mr Gauger headed off to seek his fortune in the USA, where he disappears from the records; it is not known what subsequently happened to him, but if he stayed in America, he did not live long enough to appear in the 1850 census under any of his possible names. Many of the other colonists just died from heat, malnutrition, bad rum and suicide.

In London, meanwhile, the self-styled Cazique (from a local native American word meaning 'chief') of Poyais was hard at work, hustling with his bankers for a bond issue on behalf of the Government of Poyais. Sir Gregor MacGregor* was in fact preparing for the *second* London flotation of an issue of Poyais bonds, the proceeds of a previous issue already having been largely wasted. The Cazique was a descendant of Rob Roy who had, like many ambitious officers after the Napoleonic Wars, joined in the independence struggles of Spain's South American colonies and failed to gain either fortune or honour. He returned to London with a highly embellished account of his service and the claim that he had been asked by the Poyais tribe of Native Americans to become their king. On this basis, he appointed brokers to raise sovereign debt and started selling parcels of land and passages on the *Kennersley Castle* and *Honduras Packet*.† We

---

* Or to give him his full official noble rank, Mr Gregor MacGregor; the knighthood was meant to be a Portuguese order granted during the Peninsular War but was every bit as bogus as the Cazique title. He was a genuine member of the clan and related to Scottish nobility, but his only earned titles were military – a Captain in the British Army (forced to resign for disrespecting superiors) and various titles from Colonel to General in various versions of the Venezuelan and Colombian armies in which he had served as a mercenary. 'General' doesn't mean all that much – Simón Bolívar and Francisco de Miranda tended to hand out promotions instead of pay to officers when times were thin.

† It is more complicated than this. In fact, as far as anyone can tell, MacGregor provided so many assisted places to colonists and advances against their wages in the non-existent thriving Poyaisian economy, that he probably lost money on sales to colonists, which was partly what the funds raised by the sovereign loans were meant to cover. It was not wholly clear, either to his contemporaries or to us with the benefit of hindsight, what he thought he was playing at.

haven't heard the last of him. For now, though, we need to ask the question: how did this fantasist manage to take anyone in?

The shallow answer explains the Poyais fraud historically. In fact, there were plenty of countries raising money on the London market which didn't, in the modern sense, exist. It was the early 1800s and the Spanish possessions in the Americas (which, at the time, still included modern Florida) were going through a series of independence struggles. The revolutionary governments of New Granada and Venezuela, among others, had not been recognised by the British Crown. Their loans were sold at significant discounts to speculators who could expect a windfall if the state lasted long enough to redeem the principal. These were high-risk, high-return investments, generally bought by gamblers who knew what they were getting into.

So much for the financial backers. But even the colonists deserve some slack, incredible as their naïvety sounds at first. If they had checked in the library, they would have found a book called *Sketch of the Mosquito Shore* in which the fertile plains of Poyais and its bustling capital were described – MacGregor had faked it, under the pseudonym 'Thomas Strangeways', copying out all the most favourable bits from almanacs of the West Indies and Latin America and then exaggerating them. He claimed that the soil was so fertile that three or four plantings of rattan would have to be made before it was sufficiently impoverished to be good for sugar cane, and that the native Miskito tribe wanted nothing more in the world than to work for British settlers, preferring to be paid in cheap textiles rather than cash. Presumably in order to sound credible, he restricted himself to saying that the Black

River was full of golden nuggets, rather than claiming they grew from the trees.

If they had gone to the Court of Chancery, they would have found official documents certifying the ownership of the land – MacGregor had sworn false affidavits to have the claim 'inrolled' there, based on a much more limited letter of intent (which did not include the granting of any titles of nobility like 'Cazique', by the way) which he had extracted from the tribal leader of all the Mosquito Coast peoples including the Poyais, 'King George Frederick', whom he had treated to copious amounts of whisky one night while on the run from a previous adventure.* The Poyais bonds were sold and traded on the London Stock Exchange and quoted in the newspapers alongside those of the Bank of England.

Even the usual protection against scams – that if something seems too good to be true, it is – would not necessarily have protected anyone. The small territories of Latin America were at the time often giving substantial incentives to attract

---

* This also was not necessarily as weird as it seems. Tribal societies did make land deals, and these sometimes involved the granting of royal or equivalent status in the tribal society to foreign land promoters. The ability to sell one's land is an important benefit of owning it, and in the absence of a developed society with land registries and law courts, strange things sometimes have to be done. This sort of consideration was a major part of the motivation for the Treaty of Waitangi, for example, as agreed between colonists and the Māori of New Zealand. By establishing that property rights in land were assigned to chiefs, and that transactions between Maori and colonists would be governed by statute law (at the time, that of New South Wales), the treaty aimed to tackle what was becoming a fairly serious problem whereby small Maori family groups would draw up 'sale' agreements for huge tracts of land with passing opportunistic explorers, who would then demand that the colonial administration enforce their claims.

settlers, particularly Europeans with capital and skills. If it seems fanciful that you could buy valuable land for a pittance and then commandeer nearly costless labour to get incredibly rich developing it, bear in mind that this is exactly what the plantation fortunes of Jamaica and the United States were based on. So it wasn't as easy to see through this mirage as one might think. It was just more difficult to find things out in those days.

That, in my view, is the shallow explanation of how it happened.

The deeper explanation is that it only looks ridiculous to us because we have different blind spots today to the ones that people had at the start of the nineteenth century. And the troubling corollary of that is: there are always blind spots.

The Canadian Paradox

Some places in the world are what they call 'low-trust societies'. The political institutions are fragile and corrupt, business practices are dodgy, debts are rarely repaid and people, rightly, fear being ripped off on any transaction. In the 'high-trust societies', conversely, businesses are honest, laws are fair and consistently enforced and the majority of people can go about their day in the knowledge that the overall level of integrity in economic life is very high. With that in mind, given what we know about the following two countries, why is it that the Canadian financial sector is so fraud-ridden that Joe Queenan, writing in *Forbes* magazine in 1985, nicknamed Vancouver the 'Scam Capital of the World', while ship owners in Greece will regularly do multimillion-dollar deals on a handshake?

We might call this the 'Canadian Paradox'.* There are different kinds of dishonesty in the world. The most profitable kind is commercial fraud, and commercial fraud is parasitical on the overall health of the business sector on which it preys. It is much more difficult to be a fraudster in a society in which people only do business with relatives or where commerce is based on family networks going back for centuries. It is much easier to carry out a securities fraud in a market where dishonesty is the rare exception rather than the everyday rule.

The existence of the Canadian Paradox suggests that there is a specifically *economic* dimension to a certain kind of crime of dishonesty. Trust – particularly between complete strangers, with no interactions beside relatively anonymous market transactions – is the basis of the modern industrial economy. And the story of the development of the modern economy is in large part the story of the invention and improvement of technologies and institutions for managing that trust. In other words, many things about the way the business world is organised make a lot more sense when you realise that they exist because of the constant drive for countries to become less like Greece and more like Canada.

And as industrial society develops, it becomes easier to be a victim. In *The Wealth of Nations*, Adam Smith described how prosperity derived from the division of labour – the eighteen distinct operations that went into the manufacture of a pin,

---

* Am I being unfair to the Canadians? Is this kind of fraud really more prevalent in Canada than in other countries? Criminological and statistical issues with respect to defining, detecting and categorising fraud as a crime more or less guarantee that a proper answer to this question is impossible. But Canada, and particularly its regional stock exchanges, does have a reputation.

for example. While this was going on, the modern world also saw a growing *division of trust*. In previous eras when people set out across continents to discover new worlds, they had known that they were stepping out into the unknown, but Mr Gauger was at the cutting edge of a new reality. Already, he belonged to a class of people whose natural assumption was to take things on trust, to assume that the fact that an offer was extended publicly meant that it was probably legitimate. Nearly 200 years later, his equivalents in the City of London were no more likely to expend personal effort on checking things for fraud than to throw their own pots and sew their own trousers. The more a society benefits from the division of labour in checking up on things, the further you can go into a con game before you realise that you're in one. In the case of Mr Gauger, he ended up to his knees in brackish water. In the case of several dealers in the LIBOR market, by the time anyone realised something was crooked, they were several billions of dollars in over their heads.

The LIBOR Scandal

With the perspective of a few years' hindsight, the system was always a shoddy piece of work. Some not-very-well-paid clerks from the British Bankers' Association called up a few dozen banks and asked 'If you were to borrow, say, a million dollars in [a given currency] for a 30 day deposit,* what would you expect to pay?'. They would throw away the

---

*A short-term loan from one bank to another. Due to the inconvenient habit of customers to borrow from one bank and put the money in an account at another, banks are always left either with surplus customer deposits, or short

highest and lowest outliers and calculate the average of the rest, which would be recorded as '30 day LIBOR' for that currency. The process would be repeated for three-month loans, six-month loans and any other periods of interest, and the rates would be published. You would then have a little table recording the state of the market on that day – you could decide which currency you wanted to borrow in and how long you wanted the use of the money, and the LIBOR panel would give you a good sense of what high-quality banks were paying to do the same.

Compared to the amount of time and effort that goes into the systems for nearly everything else banks do, not very much trouble was taken over this process. Other markets rose and fell, stock exchanges mutated and were taken over by super-fast robots, but the LIBOR rate for the day was still determined by a process that could only slightly unfairly be termed 'a quick ring-around'. Nobody noticed until it was too late that hundreds of trillions of dollars* of the world economy rested on a number compiled by the few dozen people in the world with the greatest incentive to fiddle it.

It all fell apart in the immediate aftermath of the collapse of Lehman Brothers in 2008, when banks were so scared that they effectively stopped lending to each other. Although the market was completely frozen, the daily LIBOR ring-around still took place, and banks still gave, almost entirely

---

of funds. The 'London Interbank' market is where they sort this out by borrowing from and lending to each other, at the 'Offered Rate' of interest.
* Yes hundreds, and yes trillions. LIBOR, as a measure of 'the general state of short-term interest rates' was an incredibly useful number to have, and so it became the industry standard benchmark for floating rate loans, of which there are a lot.

speculatively, answers to the question 'If you were to borrow a reasonable size, what would you expect to pay?'.

But the daily quotes were published, and that meant everyone could see what everyone else was saying about their funding costs. And one of the tell-tale signs of a bank in trouble is that its funding costs start to rise. If your LIBOR submission is taken as an indicator of whether you're in trouble or not, you really don't want to be the highest number on the daily list. Naturally, then, quite a few banks started using the LIBOR submission process as a form of false advertising, putting in a lowballed quote in order to make it look like they were still obtaining money easily when they, in fact, could hardly borrow at all. And so it came to pass that several banks created internal message trails saying, in effect, 'Dear Lowly Employee, for the benefit of the bank and its shareholders, please start submitting a lower LIBOR quote, signed Senior Executive'. This turned out to be a silly thing to do.

All this was known at the time. There was an article in the *Wall Street Journal* about it. I used to prepare PowerPoint slides with charts on them that had gaps for the year 2008 because the data was 'somewhat hypothetical'. The regulators held a 'liaison committee' meeting so that representatives from the banks could discuss the issue of LIBOR reporting, and even published its minutes on the Bank of England website. What nobody seemed to realise is that an ongoing crime was being committed, and the name of that crime is fraud. There was a conspiracy to tell a lie (about the bank's true cost of funding, to the LIBOR phone panel), in order to induce someone to enter into a bargain at a disadvantage to themselves. If one looks back to the Ten Commandments or to the oldest common law, it's in the book – thou shalt not bear false witness. This was, in fact, how the majority of the LIBOR offences were eventually tried. And the general public caught onto all this a lot quicker than the experts did, which put the last nail in the coffin of the already weakened trust in the financial system. You could make a case that a lot of the populist politics of the subsequent decade can be traced back to the LIBOR affair.

As I found myself reflecting over coffee in Maddox Street, LIBOR teaches us a valuable lesson about commercial fraud – that unlike other crimes, it has a problem of denial as well as one of detection. There are very few other criminal acts where the victim not only consents to the criminal act, but voluntarily transfers the money or valuable goods to the criminal. And the hierarchies, status distinctions and networks which make up a modern economy also create powerful psychological barriers against seeing fraud when it is happening. White-collar crime is partly defined by the kind of person who commits it: a person of high status in the community, the kind of person who is always given huge helpings of the benefit of the doubt.

Trust and its abuses

In terms of financial damage, LIBOR was massively worse than Poyais, although nobody directly died from it. But the thread that links the two of them is that the blind spots are built into the system, and only become glaringly apparent once the whole thing has collapsed and people are watching the sun set over a pestilent swamp where a capital city ought to be. The problem is that whenever you're creating an economic institution like the LIBOR market or the colonial system of the nineteenth century, you have to make decisions about what checks and balances you need to put into the system. And every decision about what you're going to check up on is also a decision about what you're *not* going to check up on. And when you've decided what you're not going to check up on, then those are the things you're going to have to take on trust.

We can see now that the earlier statement – that white-collar executives are given the benefit of the doubt – is not really something we should regret or regard as an invidious fact about social class. It's pretty much the definition of what it is to be a high-trust society. If you want to be like Canada, you more or less have to accept that you're going to be the kind of place where people assume that a guy in a suit is probably honest. If you're going to build the kind of society that Britain grew into in the nineteenth century, you might have to accept that every now and then you're going to send hundreds of colonists and investors to a country that doesn't exist.

The way we might describe this is to say that fraud is an *equilibrium* quantity. We can't check up on everything, and we can't check up on nothing, so one of the key decisions that an economy has to make is how much effort to spend on checking. This choice will determine the amount of fraud.*

---

*Although probably not in any particularly predictable way. Anti-fraud protections aren't like sausage machines or steam looms with a straightforward relationship between input and output, and fraudsters have their own decisions to make too. But all we really need is for there to be a broad relationship that more control most likely means less fraud, and a

And since checking costs money and trust is really productive, the optimal level of fraud is unlikely to be zero.

This, then, is a book about trust and betrayal. But not all kinds of trust and not all kinds of betrayal. In popular culture, the fraudster is the 'confidence man', somewhere between a stage magician and the trickster gods of mythology. In films like *The Sting* and *Dirty Rotten Scoundrels*, they are master psychologists, exploiting the greed and myopia of their victims, and creating a world of illusion. People like this do exist (albeit rarely), and we will meet some of them later on. But they are not typical of white-collar crime.

The interesting questions are never about individual psychology. There are plenty of larger-than-life characters. But there are also plenty of people like Enron's Jeff Skilling and Baring's Nick Leeson: aggressively dull clerks and managers whose only interest derives from the disasters they caused. And even for the real craftsmen the actual work is, of necessity, incredibly prosaic. Even a master fantasist like Sir Gregor spent a lot of his time calculating agricultural yield tables and dealing with land claim documentation. The way in which most white-collar crime works is by manipulating *institutional* psychology. That means creating something which looks as much as possible like a normal set of transactions. The drama comes later, when it all unwinds.

Fraudsters don't play on moral weaknesses, greed or fear; they play on weaknesses in the system of checks and balances, the audit processes which are meant to supplement an overall environment of trust. One point which will come up again

---

broad assumption that people will make decisions which work for them and ensure the long-term stability and viability of the overall system.

and again as we look at famous and large-scale frauds is that in many cases, everything could have been brought to a halt at a very early stage if anyone had taken care to confirm all the facts.*

But nobody does confirm all the facts. There are just too bloody many of them. Even after the financial rubble has settled and the arrests been made, this is a huge problem. It is a commonplace of law enforcement that commercial frauds are difficult to prosecute. In many countries, proposals have been made, and sometimes passed into law, to remove juries from 'complex fraud trials', or to move the task of dealing with them out of the criminal justice system and into regulatory or other non-judicial processes. Such moves are understandable. There is a need to be seen to get prosecutions and to maintain confidence in the whole system. However, taking the opinions of the general public out of the question seems to me to be a counsel of despair.

When analysed properly, there isn't much that is truly difficult about the proverbial 'complex fraud trial'. The underlying crime is often surprisingly crude; someone did something dishonest and enriched themselves at the expense of others. What makes white-collar trials so arduous for jurors is really their *length*, and the amount of detail which needs to be brought for a successful conviction. Such trials

---

* Another thing which will come up again and again is that it is really quite rare to find a major commercial fraud which was the fraudster's first attempt. An astonishingly high proportion of the villains of this book have been found out and even served prison time, then been placed in positions of trust once again. 'Sir' Gregor MacGregor had tried a version of his land and currency scam in Amelia Island, previously a Spanish possession off the coast of Florida.

are not long and detailed because there is anything difficult to understand. They are long and difficult because so many liars are involved. And when a case has a lot of liars, it takes time and evidence to establish that they are lying.

This state of affairs is actually quite uncommon in the criminal justice system. Most trials only have a couple of liars in the witness box, and the question is a simple one of whether the accused did it or not. In a fraud trial, rather than denying responsibility for the actions involved, the defendant is often insisting that no crime was committed at all, that there is an innocent interpretation for everything.

In order to promote this innocent explanation, a crooked businessman* might employ the services of crooked lawyers, crooked accountants, even crooked bankers. Crucial documents will turn out to be ambiguously worded or lost altogether. And the question of guilt may turn on having to judge what was in the businessman's mind at the time – was this an unfortunate series of deals, or an attempt to steal? The goal of the prosecution in a fraud case is to construct a straightforward framework, fitting all the disputed deals into a pattern. The goal of the defence is usually to insist on looking at every piece of evidence individually and burying the pattern in a mass of contradictory detail.

Not everyone accused of fraud is guilty. But if you want to understand how white-collar crime works – to protect

---

*A note on pronouns. Most of the time this book will follow modern usage of generic 'they' and so on. However, it cannot be overlooked that commercial fraud is overwhelmingly a male affair; it occupies the intersection between the structural sexism of business management, and the structural sexism of crime. Sometimes it feels much more sensible to refer generically to both crooks and victims as 'he'.

yourself, enrich yourself or just to understand the way of the world – you need to think like a prosecutor. Financial frauds might be presented as masses of overlapping documents and witnesses, but they are created from simple plans following basic principles. Stick to the broad sweep. Don't get bogged down in the detail.* Under the blizzard of paperwork, the chances are that you're dealing with one of four basic manoeuvres.

The four types of white-collar crime

The most basic kind of fraud is simply to borrow some money and not pay it back, or alternatively buy some goods and not pay for them.† In a modern economy, business people are forced to trust each other to pay invoices and deliver goods as promised. This feature of real-world commerce is surprisingly absent from economics textbooks, but it is absolutely fundamental. Most industries would be very different – almost unrecognisable, and certainly unable to operate at their actual scale – if all transactions had to take place on a cash-on-delivery basis. Every single stage in the production of this book, from the author's advance to the printers' payment terms to the retailers' sale-or-return, depends on the fact that businesses extend credit to each other to let payment be made when the money has arrived to make it.

---

* I will occasionally admit 'it's more complicated than that' in a footnote when I'm doing something really horrific in terms of skating over detail.
† 'There's only one thing that's worse than selling something that isn't there to sell, and that's buying something and not paying for it', as Mr Gruber said in *Paddington at Work*. The description of a securities promotion fraud in the chapter 'Paddington Buys a Share' is surprisingly accurate and detailed and a very good introduction to the subject.

Strangely, the credit extended between businesses, from suppliers to their customers and vice versa, is not systematically measured in official statistics. Yet any sensible estimate of it would dwarf the size of the banking system – probably less than 10 per cent of commercial credit is directly financed by a bank loan. And it is the practice of intentionally running up a lot of credit, and then defaulting on it, which is the basis of the fraud known as a **long firm.** This is our first lesson in commercial crime. It also introduces the key problem of detecting and prosecuting frauds. Even after it has been completed and the money stolen, a long firm often looks just like an honest business that went bust. Unlike most other kinds of criminal, white-collar fraudsters do exactly the same basic stuff as their honest counterparts. What makes the crime is the intent to deceive.

Another way of stealing money through commercial fraud is to abuse people's trust in the ways by which ownership and value are verified. Again, the fraudster exploits the fact that a world in which every single document was checked, every claim of ownership verified and every certificate of quality audited, would be a world in which a huge proportion of the business world's time and effort was wasted by checking up on each other. The only practical way to do many types of business is to trust that, for the most part, documents are what they appear to be, and that they prove what they claim to prove. Abusing this trust by creating false documents to verify false claims is **counterfeiting.** We can see at this stage that, just as different types of trust relationships reinforce each other to make commerce profitable, different types of fraud can also reinforce each other. In order to carry out a long firm fraud, for example, you might want to counterfeit a document which shows you to be more financially sound than you actually are.

As an economy gets more sophisticated, it tends to separate the function of providing capital to a business from the activity of managing one. In such an economy, it is usually impossible (or at least highly inefficient) for the ultimate owners and creditors of a company to monitor everything that is done by the managers they have employed. Like everyone else, they have to rely on trust. And this trust opens up the possibility of a **control fraud**. A control fraud differs from the simpler kind because the means by which the value is extracted to the criminal is generally legitimate – high salaries, bonuses, stock options and dividends, but the legitimate payments are made on the basis of fictitious profits and unreal assets, and the manager tends to take vastly higher risks than those which would be taken by an honest businessman.

It is also unique in that it is, at least potentially, a *subjunctive* crime – if things turn out well for the underlying business, and the wild risks which the control fraudster takes pay off, the victims never know they have been had and the crime never exists. It is even possible to create a ***distributed control fraud***, in which the mechanism of fake profits, high risk and value extraction arises without the necessary involvement of a single legally culpable actor, by assembling a set of perverse, 'criminogenic' incentives which make the distortions happen independently.

Finally, we reach the highest level of abstraction. These frauds exploit the general web of trust which makes up a modern economy, rather than a single relationship. There are plenty of actions which are not even really crimes at all in the traditional sense – they are not obviously or intrinsically dishonest activities. Nevertheless, experience has shown us that a market economy works better if people are able to assume that they won't be done. Cartels, for example, or insider dealing rings, might be examples of **market crimes**, where the victim is the market itself rather than a particular person who has lost an identifiable sum of money. Market crimes can be very lucrative, but they make other users of the market more reluctant to extend the trust that makes the system work. More than any other, this kind of crime is a matter of judgement, local convention and practice, rather than one of cut and dried criminality. A blatant market crime in one jurisdiction could be considered aggressive but legal practice in another and the definition of good business somewhere else. A long firm clearly falls under 'Thou shalt not steal', and a counterfeit under 'Thou shalt not bear false witness', but where's the commandment 'Thou shalt not trade securities while in possession of material non-public information'? The investigation of market crimes takes us into some profound questions about the workings of the modern economy itself. It also takes us to some of the biggest frauds: because market crimes can only arise in a market big and important enough to need its own legal framework, the sums of money are often eye-watering.

Don't get too hung up on the terminology in any of these cases – in particular, don't expect it to match up too closely to the criminology literature. We're less interested at this stage in the details than in the broad structure and the type of breach of trust that's involved. This gets more abstract at every stage. A long firm makes you question whether you can trust anyone. A counterfeit makes you question the evidence of your eyes. A control fraud makes you question your trust in the institutions of society and a market crime makes you question society itself. Since it's impossible to run a modern economy without all four levels of trust, fraud is an insidious crime.

Diversionary tactics

So how does this book work? We will alternate stories of famous frauds (with digressions into the underlying structures which they exploited) and examinations of the trust mechanisms which underpin the modern world (with digressions into how some famous fraudsters exploited them). Commercial fraud is the evil twin of the modern economy. Understanding one gives us powerful insights into the other.

By the end of this journey into corruption, you will be better placed to understand how frauds work, and even to manage – one can never quite eliminate – the risks to your own business or employer. You will also get a useful glimpse into the way that the honest commercial system works. Like the human brain, the market economy is an information processing system. Like the human brain, we get our best looks at its hidden mechanisms when it breaks down. Just as neurologists study the consequences of head injuries, we can learn about the economy by looking at currency forgers and pyramid schemes.

You might, of course, choose to use this book instead as an instruction manual. There are enough case studies and schematics for you to work out how to do one. But bear this in mind. Almost all of the fraudsters discussed in this book got caught. Some of them enjoyed a high lifestyle before they did. But many of them greeted their inevitable discovery with tears of joy that the whole wretched, stressful business had come to an end. The time, effort and commercial acumen that goes into almost any fraud would nearly always have been better spent on doing something productive.

Nearly always.

THE BASICS

'The aim of crime as a business is to acquire wealth. There are broadly two ways of doing this: by taking it without the owner's consent, or by persuading him to part with it voluntarily even if afterwards he does not want you to keep it. The first kind accounts for most of what people think of as "crime" but it is a self-limiting business. It cannot be disguised. A blown safe can't be passed off as a safe the accountant lost his temper with.'

Leslie Payne, The Brotherhood: My Life With the Krays

In any of the dozens of mid-budget British movies that have been made about the Kray twins and the gangland of Swinging London, one of the pivotal scenes is always the murder of Jack 'the Hat' McVitie by Reggie Kray. Along with the shooting of George Cornell in the Blind Beggar pub in Whitechapel, it's one of the cornerstones of the Kray legend. Given that, it's curious that so few people know what the motive was. In fact, Reggie was angry with McVitie because he had failed to carry out a £500 contract killing; he had been commissioned to murder the Krays' accountant, a man called Leslie Payne. Leslie makes a good teacher for an introductory course in commercial fraud; he was responsible for a variety of scams, all of them at a comprehensible scale, and most of them in a reasonably straightforward manner. Like his tailors in Savile Row, he liked things to be kept simple and classic without too many distracting frills.

The Kray brothers wanted Leslie dead because they thought he was about to turn them in, and they were right; he did, and got away to write a very readable if morally bankrupt autobiography. It's full of tips on how he carried out the frauds which bankrolled their empire.* On his own account of the 'board meetings' which the brothers held in pubs, the average take from a week's villainy consisted of about two thousand pounds in cash, of which no more than a quarter came from robberies. The rest was from protection payments from gambling clubs, and from Leslie's speciality – the 'long firms'.

Payne wasn't the Krays' accountant in the sense of keeping books for their crime syndicate – Reggie did that himself, writing 'Protection from club in Walthamstow – £30' and 'Bribe to Dalston Police – £40' in expensive ledgers that he had purchased despite Leslie begging him not to. Leslie Payne was rather an accountant by trade, who worked for the twins and who used his considerable business talent to create illusions of prosperous and honest businesses in order to extract trade credit.

Payment terms and trade credit

If you're selling sandwiches on the platform at the railway station, you get cash at lunchtime, but you need to buy bread

---

*It has a much more joyless last chapter, co-authored with a lawyer and presumably included at the insistence of the publisher, in which he explains how he has gone straight and makes a number of surprisingly astute recommendations about how company law should be changed to prevent similar crimes in the future.

and cheese in the morning. You could take out a bank loan to buy your supplies, but it's more common to ask the food suppliers to give you the bread and cheese on credit. In general, in almost every industry, there is some general recognition of the fact that trade customers need to make and sell their product before they have cash to pay for their inputs, and that their suppliers are often in a better position to provide credit to bridge this gap than the financial system is.

Why is supplier credit so common? Because of the convenience factor. As Payne the Brain put it, 'one could imagine a system of commerce where every transaction was made with cash and nothing was paid for in advance or in arrears … but it would mean every time you wanted to light a fire you had to go out and buy a shovel-full of coal'.

In the first place, it is comparatively cheap to provide. If the alternative to making a sale on credit is letting the goods hang around until the customer can raise the cash, there is a saving to be made by getting them moved out of your warehouse and into the customer's. This is particularly the case for things like fresh bread, which has a limited shelf life. Second, and related to this, it drives sales. Being prepared to deal 'on terms' means that you can sell to start-up businesses and to customers who happen to be short of cash that week, rather than restricting yourself to only selling to people with ready money. And finally, it's likely that a supplier will see somewhat less credit risk than a bank. For one thing, the supplier has an up-to-date picture of how the customer's business is faring, simply by looking at the customer's orders. And for another, when you provide bread and cheese on credit, you know that credit is being used to buy ingredients – a bank which lends cash is taking the risk that the loan might be used for a purpose other than the one for which it was intended.

Payment terms span a range of 'maturities' and the convention for charging interest on them also varies. You can be asked to pay cash on delivery (COD) or '7 days net', going as far as '30 days net' or even 90 days. Beyond 90 days, people tend to refer to 'vendor financing' rather than 'payment terms', and there tends to be more in the way of formal loan documentation; vendor finance is provided on expensive capital equipment like computer servers and jet engines and can last for years.

Whatever the period, though, there will come a day when the payment has to be made. If, on that day, it isn't, then the supplier has parted with goods or services and not been paid for them, just as if they had been lost or stolen in the ordinary way. Stealing things by getting them on credit and then not making the payment is the essence of the long firm.

Who bears the risk? Of course, everyone has cash flow problems to manage, and everyone would rather be paid up front and deal with their suppliers on credit. So the question of who gets what sort of terms from whom is always a complicated one, and reflects patterns of bargaining power, supply and demand and competition. You can tell more about the structure of any industry by looking at patterns of payment terms than you can from any 'five forces' or 'SWOT' analysis.

There is one other kind of credit extended in a similar manner to payment terms, which Leslie and his gang used to take advantage of, although it's harder to do so today. This is the credit which was created by the banking system due to the time needed to handle the paperwork for cheques. Particularly if a cheque was drawn on a foreign bank, or a small one with inefficient business practices, it could take quite a few days, during which period it would not necessarily be clear to the victim of a fraud that they had received a worthless payment. The practice of 'kiting cheques' (writing cheques on a bank account which didn't have enough money in it to honour the cheque, and where no overdraft facility had been agreed), used to be a way of getting a short-term interest-free loan, which you could then default on. This kind of cheque fraud was usually a smalltime crime of desperation (there are obvious disadvantages to a method of theft which requires you to provide the victim with your name and address). But if you had a ready supply of co-conspirators who were prepared to take the risk, you could go through a chequebook pretty quickly and very lucratively.

Credit control

So what did a typical Leslie Payne work of art look like? He describes one in quite disturbing detail in his book, right down to the specifics of the accounts and even includes some helpful templates for letters that anyone wishing to emulate him might want to use. The system is designed around two vital features of the modern economy – the practice of credit control, and the institution of bankruptcy.

When a company goes bust, you often find that its biggest creditors are its suppliers, and when a big customer fails to pay, the resulting loss can often be enough to drive its supplier under as well. So companies have to have 'credit controllers', as part of the process of managing their 'accounts receivable'. This credit control function can be quite informal – as a newly opened restaurant, you will probably have to pay cash on delivery for your fish,* with terms extending as you build up a record of payment. Or in larger companies there can be a whole credit control department which takes and reviews formal credit references. Or the accounts receivable team might subscribe to one of the agencies which provide credit assessments. Whatever the specific form, there is almost always someone there whose job it is to be unpopular with the sales force, earning a nickname like 'the abominable NO-man', 'Chief Business Prevention Officer' or similar. This person is the main obstacle that a crook needs to overcome.

Leslie's first step was to recruit some idiots. If you were an associate of the Kray gang there were usually quite a few of these on hand, and all he needed from them was their names as company directors. It was considered desirable if not essential that they were able to put on a suit and tie and sit down in one place for the duration of a bank or supplier meeting; otherwise the less they knew, the better. The main idiot would be taken down to a bank to sign a loan agreement for some working capital on his new cloth retail company, based out of a warehouse owned by the Krays. Then Leslie would go down to a printers' shop and order some new company letterhead in the names of half a dozen newly formed companies.

One of these companies – call it X&Y Ltd – might place an order with a reputable cloth wholesaler such as 'Legitimate

---

*As the chef and author Anthony Bourdain said, 'if you ever have any question about the viability of your operation, ask your fish purveyor; he probably knows better than you. You may be willing to take it in the neck, but he isn't'.

Trading Ltd' for a few hundred pounds worth of stretchy bri-nylon fabric in various colours. In opening up their account, they might send a letter to the merchant telling him that he could take references from A&B Ltd,* with whom they had a long trading relationship. Sure enough, once inquiries were made, the letter would come back to Legitimate Trading from A&B, saying that X&Y was a thoroughly reputable company and its directors were men of quiet thrift and virtue. Leslie had written both the initial letter and the subsequent references, as both companies were ultimately controlled by him.

While it was building up a good name with its suppliers, X&Y would be building up a great name with its customers. It not only sold bri-nylon cloth for 25 per cent below the normal wholesale price, it issued receipts showing a sale at 5 per cent *above* the wholesale price, allowing purchasing managers to lower their taxable profits, take backhanders for themselves or both. The rationale for doing this was simple – X&Y needed ready cash, because it wanted to keep growing and to keep getting more and more supplier credit. For about six months, it would pay all its bills promptly. As Leslie put it, 'the accounts are immaculate, the cash flow through the bank is impressive – this young company is the apple of everyone's eye'.

By now, what credit controller is going to cause trouble when X&Y Ltd puts in a truly massive order? In order to

---

* These are the pseudonyms that Leslie uses in the instructional section of his book, to obscure the actual fraud, which he got away with. The classroom atmosphere is rather jarred by his offhand comment that the managing director of A&B 'later took his own life when it all came to court'.

disguise the underselling and the cash taken out by Leslie Payne, the company will have been doubling its total trade credit every month for six months. So having started out with trial orders of around £1,000, by the sixth month it will be in a position to buy £60,000 of stretchy nylon on credit, sell it for £45,000 and move on to the next stage. The directors of X&Y Ltd (and potentially A&B, C&D, E&F and G&H, all of which were doing the same thing and providing references for one another) will now be called on to put the thing into bankruptcy.

Bankruptcy

'Going bankrupt' is not quite the same thing as 'going bust'. If you are bust, all that means is that you owe money and are not able to pay it back. If you are bankrupt, that has the specific meaning that you have entered into a legal process to manage the process of going bust.*

It was not always this way. For a large period of the history of debt, there was nothing which very much resembled a bankruptcy code, and the law was that – outside of occasional 'jubilee' episodes of overall debt forgiveness

---

*It's a distinction that makes a big difference in some cases, although not to many cases of fraud. Some of the biggest borrowers in the world are sovereign nations, raising money to finance their budget deficits. And although countries can go bust, there is no supranational law to govern them, so they can't go bankrupt. There are all sorts of piecemeal legal structures whereby investors can sue sovereign states and sometimes even take possession of their overseas assets. But there is no proper well-defined legal process of bankruptcy. Anyone who thinks this might mean less work for lawyers rather than more doesn't understand lawyers.

– borrowers had to pay what they could and debts would never be extinguished. In ancient societies, defaulting debtors could be stripped of their citizenship and sold as slaves for the benefit of their creditors (Athens was considered quite liberal in limiting the period of debt slavery to five years). The contract imposed by Shylock in *The Merchant of Venice* was an extreme example and the pound of flesh a metaphor, but it reflected an underlying reality. Even into the nineteenth century, debtors' prisons still existed. As time went on and debt became a more central part of the economy, however, it was gradually realised that this was unfair and inefficient, and that the law ought to provide a way in which it could be acknowledged that there was a limit to what could be asked of a debtor.

The next big innovation in bankruptcy law was the concept of 'limited liability', gradually brought in from the maritime world and firmly entrenched in Anglo-Saxon commercial law by the middle of the nineteenth century. A company is allowed to have an existence separate from the people who make it up and to take on debts (among other legal obligations) in its own name rather than theirs. The liability is 'limited' because when a company you own goes bankrupt, the lenders cannot pursue you for their losses, unless they have explicitly signed a guarantee agreement with you. Obviously, pretty much as soon as it came into existence, this legal concept began to be abused by fraudsters.

Economists, accountants and lawyers all agree that there are two kinds of insolvency, although not always on the terminology. You are 'commercially insolvent' (or 'legally insolvent' or 'cash-flow insolvent') if you have a payment come due and are not able to pay it. At this point, the person who you are meant to be paying has the right to make an application to a court to have you declared bankrupt. On the other hand, a company is 'technically insolvent' (or 'factually insolvent' or 'balance sheet insolvent') if the total of its liabilities are greater than the total of its assets.* The two concepts do not necessarily imply each other; it's quite common to be cash-flow insolvent while owning lots of valuable assets.

More relevant to our current case, though, is the opposite possibility: a company which has debts much bigger than its assets, but which is not legally insolvent yet because it has not had a payment fall due that it is unable to make. This is called 'wrongful trading' if it means that you are running up bigger and bigger debts and making the eventual losses in bankruptcy bigger for your creditors. It is also rather like what a long firm fraudster does. So, if you have been in charge of a bankrupt company, you can expect to get investigated. You can also expect (and this was why Leslie Payne wanted other people to sit on his boards) that you will not be allowed to be a director of any more companies for a while.

In the matter of the bankruptcy proceedings for A&B Ltd (and the rest of the alphabet soup), it would usually be found that there was very little available for the creditors. So Legitimate Trading Ltd and the other suppliers would be forced to take the commercial loss. By putting five or six long

---

* To expand on this a little, a profitable company which has negative net assets can act like a solvent one, and even trade its way back to solvency in a reasonably orderly fashion. Economists tend to deal with this by pretending 'the value of being able to operate a profitable business' is an asset, and accountants by shrugging and noting that there are worse things in the world than technical insolvency.

firms through the cycle at once, Leslie was able to maximise the use of the warm bodies who were put in as directors. This also minimised the possibility of a defence against charges of wrongful trading and made it more or less certain that the poor idiots would end up in jail, but that's the sort of thing you have to expect if you hang around with gangsters. None of them grassed.*

Collateral and the Golden Boos

Not all of Leslie's fiddles involved the ownership of a warehouse, nor the need for a fire or a robbery to shut things down at the end. He also took part in rather more white-collar operations, taking money from the Square Mile as well as the East End. The 'hire purchase scam' and the 'insurance scam' were also reliable money makers for the Krays† and their brainy friend.

The hire purchase scam was not particularly sophisticated – at heart, it was a fake collateral operation, which is a very old scam, of really quite general application. A hundred and fifty years before Leslie Payne, one of history's few really

---

*Leslie did.

† Another way in which the Kray gang exploited the financial system of the day was by simply stealing share certificates and bonds. Financial instruments were traded in paper form in those days, and although there were usually registers of who was the legal owner, the practice was inefficient enough that people who showed up with the paperwork would usually be given the benefit of the doubt. Leslie got heavily involved in the international market for bonds and oil companies of dubious provenance, something which seemed to require frequent flights to Nigeria in the company of unreliable hired muscle.

famous female fraudsters had carried out a version of it against the hotel trade. The Golden Boos scam works on the large amounts of 'trade credit' that it's possible to run up by means of the simple convention that hotel bills are paid on departure, and the innkeepers' favourite means of protecting themselves against defaulting guests.

If you spend a night in Boston, for example, you might see a notice which state law requires in every hotel room. It warns guests that it is an offence to 'make a show of leaving baggage in order to acquire credit'. This went into the state legal code because of the practice of 'making a show' – ostentatiously leaving a trunk full of valuables with an innkeeper while running up a large bill, then doing a moonlight flit before he realises it contains nothing but stones or rags.* The uncontested mistress of 'making a show' was Barbara Erni, the scourge of Liechtenstein, nicknamed 'Golden Boos' for her red-blonde hair.

Golden Boos used to travel around in the southern German Alps, carrying with her a trunk of unusual size and weight (as well as her hair, Barbara Erni was renowned for her physical strength). She would stay in the finest hotels, running up a large tab for food and drink with hoteliers who were reassured by the fact that her trunk was full of valuable goods and jewellery – so valuable, in fact, that she always demanded that it be locked up in the safest room in the house overnight. On the afternoon of her surprise departure, however, the trunk was usually found not to be full of rocks

---

* The plot of one *Fawlty Towers* episode turns on a similar point, as the fake 'Lord Melbury' deposits a suitcase full of bricks in Basil's safe then borrows £100 from him.

or junk, but to be entirely empty. Ms Erni had taken the scam a step further by using her luggage to store either a child or a small man (accounts differ) who would wait until midnight and then crawl out of the trunk to steal any other valuables in the same room before running away. Golden Boos and her partner would regroup at a safe distance and use part of their ill-gotten gains to buy another trunk. Although she was caught and beheaded in 1784 – the last person to be executed in Liechtenstein – her intriguing story passed into local folklore: there is a 'Golden Boos Lane' in her home village of Eschen.

As the Liechtensteinian innkeepers knew, holding onto a customer's valuables (otherwise known as taking collateral) makes it a lot easier to extend a loan to a business or a person. It reduces your risk in two ways. In the first place, it is usually easier to check out the quality of things than people, so if your main risk is the collateral, this is easier to manage than if your main risk is a debtor's ability and willingness to pay. And in the second, when your collateral is more valuable than the amount of your loan, the debtor stands to lose more by defaulting on the loan than by paying it back. So you can be reasonably sure that the debtor is going to make an effort to repay you. The limiting case here is where you have established a legal right to repossess the house that the debtor lives in, which makes mortgage loans one of the safest forms of credit. As the bankers' proverb goes:

> Mortgage lenders have no cares
> Whatever happens
> They get theirs

Collateral is a substitute for trust. It relies, however,

on strong legal institutions to make sure you can actually 'realise' it by taking possession of it when a debtor defaults. The activity of 'perfecting an interest', 'establishing security' and similar euphemism forms a large part of what lawyers send bills to bankers for, because the law on this is tricky.

It's even more tricky, though, if there is a problem with the collateral itself – it doesn't exist, or it's a suitcase full of rocks, or if the same item has been pledged to several lenders. Even the strongest legal institutions might not help if you trust somebody who is systematically setting out to abuse that trust. And some people do. Some make a career out of it.

The hire purchase scam and the insurance scam

Leslie Payne's version of the collateral scam involved hire purchase agreements for automobiles. You went to Europe and bought a very old second-hand Mercedes. You then took it back to your car dealership in London and re-registered it in the UK. With a new log book showing the current year, what you had was a £250 car with paperwork very similar to a brand-new one worth £2,000. You could give it away for free to one of the Krays' tame goons, who would sign a hire purchase agreement for the full £2,000. This hire purchase agreement could be sold by the car dealership to a finance company for close to its face value. The financiers would take the first few payments, then get a nasty surprise when the hirer lost interest and the nearly worthless car was repossessed.

A step up in profitability was achieved in the hire purchase scam when Leslie realised that you could buy crashed cars for £50, and that the hire purchase company wouldn't necessarily be able to prove that the accident had happened before the hire purchase agreement was signed. This offered the tantalising prospect of making money on both ends: taking the finance company with the hire purchase scam and claiming the car's value back from the insurer. And this in turn led him to start thinking about the insurance industry itself.

The insurance scam was simple in concept – set up Payne the Brain Insurance Limited,* take in a load of premiums for car insurance policies, transfer the money into an offshore account and then disappear before the claims started coming in. There was only one snag – since this fraud was very obvious, and had been around since the earliest days of the insurance industry itself, the authorities tended to be pretty snooty about who they would allow to set up an insurance company. You had to demonstrate that you had a large sum of capital in the bank.

Luckily, the banking regulators were a lot less snooty. Setting up a bank in London was tricky and involved a lot of intrusive questions about your criminal record and whether your business partners were gangsters. But in the Caribbean, you could hang a sign saying 'Bank' outside a coffee shop and the local registrars would be happy to record your ownership of the European Exchange Bank of the Bahamas.†　And then your island bank could open a London branch. The staff of your London branch would be happy to confirm to the Board of Trade that you had the money,‡ and from then

---

*He didn't actually use this company name.

†He did use this name.

‡In actual fact (because you would need to recruit clerks with a clean criminal record to run the London end rather than gangsters), you would

on, the scam was straightforward. Of all the loopholes that Leslie Payne exploited, this is the only one that has since been closed down.

Crime without punishment

Leslie ended up falling out with the Krays over some sour business deals and a failed attempt to establish a relationship with the American Mafia. The attempt to have him killed by Jack 'the Hat' McVitie was the only one that took place; the next year the twins were both convicted of murder and the gang began to roll up, not least because of the information provided by Payne the Brain to the police in exchange for his own escape to a more or less legitimate business career. He died peacefully in Croydon in 1990. His own exit from the criminal world echoes his description of how one of his long firms ended:

> The actual collapse is naturally not spectacular. People just don't turn up for work. A couple of manufacturers' representatives knock on the door and go away puzzled but they don't realise for a few days that the firm no longer exists. There is nothing much anyone can do. Bloggs [the front man] might be recognised by the accountants, the bank manager and the representatives of the firms who sold to him, but he probably came from Manchester and he has gone back there. No one knows

------

need to fly out to the Bahamas, hold a board meeting, agree that your bank would make you a loan and then transfer the loan amount into your account with the London branch. Same effect.

his real name or anything about him. The men who work in the warehouse are 'just as surprised as anyone else' – supposing they are ever traced.

Leslie Payne did a lot better than many long firm men. He more or less got away with it – often appearing at the Old Bailey but always leaving the court by the front steps. He knew when to wind up his scams and he made sure someone else took the blame. His book, by the standards of fraudsters' autobiographies, is short on self-pity* and long on practical details. But he was really quite small-time as things go. The big commercial frauds, the ones which create newspaper headlines and sometimes affect entire economies, tend to be a bit more grandiose, even in the world of long firms.

---

*It is also short on pity for anyone else. Even leaving aside the passing references to his victims ruining their lives and committing suicide, *The Brotherhood* is full of somewhat ridiculous attempts to claim that the beatings, stabbings and torture carried out by other members of 'The Firm' were nothing to do with him.

2

LONG FIRMS

*'There's only one thing that's worse than selling something
that isn't there to sell, and that's buying something and
not paying for it.'*

Michael Bond, Paddington at Work

Exit fraud

I am sorry guys but I have scammed you. I am not going
to try to justify it with my reasons, I am just a terrible
person. I am sorry for each and every person affected. I
am ashamed about the way I have deceived so many
people for my own personal gain. For what it is worth,
the money is not going to stupid lifestyle enriching purposes. Even though I could likely go on for a few more
days making fake promises and feedback I have reached
my goal and will lock myself out of my account.

For anyone interested. This started on 19–22 Decem-
ber. After that I have not had a single gram of weed or
hash in stock. That is all I had to say.

That was the message received by customers of '9THWON-
DER', an online drug dealer on a marketplace known as
'Evolution' when they logged on in January 2015 to check
why their merchandise hadn't arrived. The apology and confession were unusual but the scam wasn't. The unlisted

websites where contraband is bought and sold over confiden-
tial web browsers (known as 'dark markets', because online
criminals are addicted to science-fiction language), have been
absolutely rife with long firm frauds from the start. On the
one hand, this might be seen as predictable – if you are
looking for ideal targets to steal from, participants in illegal
drug markets have the attractive property that they can't
report you to the police without raising lots of awkward
questions about themselves. On the other hand, this obvious
fact was not lost on the original designers of the Silk Road
(the first such site to get real traction) and its competitors, and
the aim of these entrepreneurs was to build fraud protection
into the architecture of the system. Many of them produced
long and windy political manifestos on this very point, claiming that their virtual online realm was a techno-libertarian
paradise which did not need conventional laws.

So how did they all get ripped off?

The mechanics of the scam are almost so simple as to
need no explanation; you take money (in this case, electronic
money systems such as bitcoin*) on the basis of a promise
to send someone illegal drugs, and then you don't send the

---

*Bitcoin and similar crypto-currencies have been designed specifically to
emulate the anonymity of cash. They don't fully succeed in doing so – you
have to take lots of precautions to make sure that a bitcoin address or 'wallet'
cannot be linked to you as an individual, and if you make mistakes then the
bitcoin architecture will expose your full record of transactions. This is how
the proprietor of Silk Road was tracked down and arrested. But tracing a
bitcoin address to a human being is generally a task that requires the
resources of a law enforcement agency making a special effort to do so. It's
not feasible for an ordinary customer. Which, of course, is how the traders
in dark markets want it to be; they don't want anyone knowing who they are.
This does mean you sacrifice a lot of potential fraud controls though.

drugs. The interesting bit is that the controls which were put into the system to rule out this absurdly obvious possibility didn't work.

The way that things were meant to happen is that payments were meant to go through 'escrow'. You sent your bitcoins to a central address associated with the marketplace itself, so that the vendor could see that you had paid. Then, when your goods arrived, you sent a confirmation message and 'released' the payment, allowing it to be sent on to the vendor. Or, if your goods didn't arrive, you submitted a complaint to the marketplace, which via its dispute arbitration service* took evidence from you and the vendor about who was likely to be lying, and if it thought you were in the right, gave you your money back. All of this signing and acknowledgment was carried out on an anonymous basis via clever cryptographic protocols that don't need to be discussed here because for the most part they worked – there was no *technical* weakness worth speaking of.

The escrow system would seem to be a pretty solid protection against long firms; the illegal marketplaces actually had the sort of central credit bureau that is sometimes used in legitimate businesses, and the escrow service was available even for comparatively small deals, whereas normal trading companies only use the comparatively expensive escrow services provided by lawyers and banks when the size of the transaction warrants doing so. And for the most part, the escrow service worked. The vulnerability to long firm frauds came in because people didn't use it.

---

*As far as I can tell, these criminal markets provided surprisingly good and responsive customer service.

Why didn't they use it? It turns out that there was not (and is not yet) a technological solution powerful enough to overcome the economic fact we identified earlier – that the conventions of who gives trade credit to whom reflects the buyer and supplier power in the market. The escrow system was highly inconvenient for vendors. They had the normal cashflow problems associated with extending trade credit, in that they had to finance their inventories before getting paid.* Against this, they had somewhat more protection from deadbeat customers, through the escrow system. But they could still be made the victim of fraudulent or frivolous customer disputes; it was not uncommon for unscrupulous dealers to send in dozens of orders to a rival and then dispute them all, to drive one of their enemies out of business.

The biggest problem for the vendors, though, was that the dollar value of bitcoin was incredibly volatile, and they were faced with a typical small business dilemma – revenues in one currency (bitcoin) and costs in another (mainly US dollars). Since the market was competitive and transparent, mark-ups were somewhat less than those available to street dealers, and could easily be wiped out by weekly fluctuations in the bitcoin/dollar 'exchange rate'. Various means of allowing the vendors to hedge these currency movements were attempted, but they were all quite expensive and none of them worked very well.

---

* Trade credit is not that hard to get in the street drugs business either. It's not at all unusual for dealers to be able to buy large consignments on thirty- or even ninety-day terms, allowing them time to move the drugs on to dealers or consumers. Things do have a habit of getting messy though; the process by which drug cartels manage their 'accounts receivable' ledgers has been the subject of dozens of straight-to-DVD films.

The escrow system was therefore a pain in the neck for the drug dealers, and so they used their market power to get round it. Large dealers, with a reputation for reliability, would ask to be paid via 'finalise early' (or 'fast execution', in either case usually abbreviated to FE), a feature of the system which allowed the customer to forgo the protection of the escrow system. If you wanted to get the best quality and the most competitive prices, you paid via FE, effectively allowing the market to determine an implicit price that the customers were willing to pay to be certain that they were protected against long firms.

It turned out that this implicit price was quite low. There was significant honour among thieves, and the Silk Road marketplace had an elaborate feedback system (not unlike that of eBay) which allowed consumers to carry out their own credit analysis. As in the normal economy, vendors were able to build up a trading name, and to establish that they were good credit risks, encouraging buyers to deal with them without using escrow. So although the technology was there to do without it, the dark market ended up reinventing most of the apparatus of conventional trade credit.

A key difference between the online drugs trade and the normal economy, though, is that not all that many people are interested in building a career in online drug dealing and passing the firm down to their children. People grow up, leave college, or have the kind of short interaction with the legal system which suggests to them that a lifestyle change is in order. Businesses often tended to close down.

And having built up valuable goodwill on a dark market, it seems like a shame to just throw it all away as you disappear. The 'ethical' thing to do would be to simply decline to take new orders, but when people are literally emailing you untraceable money, this would require quite a bit of moral fibre. And so the 'exit scam' began to become a feature of Silk Road. A large vendor would start taking lots of FE payments (perhaps suggesting that this had been made necessary because he was being attacked by rival dealers using the escrow scam described above). There might even be a big 'sale' to attract the maximum possible volume of orders. And then ... disappear with the money. The bitcoins that had been sent to the defaulting vendor could not be reclaimed – that's not the way the system works. The disappointed customers tended not to have any details or address for the vendor, just an online screen name that wasn't being used any more. The exit scammer would even be free to set up a brand-new business, building up goodwill from the ground floor, and there would be no easy way of finding out that this was being done.*

By the time Silk Road was shut down by the law authorities and its market share taken by a number of smaller competitors, exit scams had become enough of a problem to materially affect the economics of the online marketplace, and

---

*As far as I can tell, mainly from copious poring through Reddit pages dedicated to dark markets, this didn't appear to be the case though – presumably the cost and effort of rebuilding a franchise wasn't worth the one-off gain for people who wanted to stay in the drugs business. Most exit scams seem to have been 'genuine', and occasionally the scammers would still hang around the same online forums, apologising to their former friends and explaining that they wanted to get out of the criminal lifestyle. In a few cases, it almost looked like the exit scam was a conscious attempt to burn down the storefront, by someone who was dealing with their own substance problems and who wanted to avoid the risk of being tempted back into drug dealing again.

to be a subject of lurid warnings to newcomers to the darknet economy. However, the suggested remedy of paying the price premium and only dealing via escrow turned out to have its own problems. The customers of 9THWONDER might have avoided this exit scam by using the Evolution escrow service, but this would not have protected them against the fact that Evolution turned out to be run by scammers itself. One day, it disappeared, taking roughly $12m of bitcoin which had been deposited in its escrow accounts.

This was a somewhat extreme example of darknet fraud, and in principle there is a technological solution to it – an extension to the bitcoin protocol to allow 'multi-signature escrow', so that bitcoins can't be spent by someone who is only holding them on behalf of another. Darknet researchers, however,* seem to more or less despair of this technology ever catching on – it's too inconvenient for users, most of whom can't even be convinced to pass up the price discounts you get for dealing via FE.

The conclusion once more must be that fraud is, as we said earlier, an equilibrium phenomenon. Precautions are expensive, or inconvenient, or both, and trust is free. This means that people will substitute trust for precautions up until the point at which the 'shadow cost of trust' – the expected fraud loss – begins to exceed the direct cost of precautions. Since this trade-off is likely to involve a mixture of both, there will always be trust and therefore there will always be

---

* Oh yes, they exist, albeit pseudonymously. Bloggers, mainly, but performing the recognisable functions of banking consultants and money brokers, writing research either for payment via bitcoin, or to promote their own markets and escrow services.

scams. When the same features of a system keep appearing without anyone designing them, you can usually be pretty sure that the cause is economic.

Exit scams are one solution to the core problem faced by a long firm fraudster – the problem of persuading anyone to give you enough credit to carry out a fraud worth doing. In an exit scam, there is no need to spend time and effort in creating an appearance of legitimacy; there is already an existing legitimate (or in the case of Silk Road, quasi-legitimate) business. The 'exit fraud' phenomenon, though, is comparatively rare in the world for this reason, because the combination of circumstances which come together to create it are uncommon. People who are successfully running a legitimate business don't usually suddenly turn crooked overnight. And even when they do, their criminality doesn't tend to lead them in the direction of a course of action which will destroy the goodwill and the value of the franchise they have built up.* The peculiar features of online drug dealing which motivated people to give up on thriving businesses are not found in many other areas. So for the most part, when a legitimate company is turned into a long firm, there are a few other things going on, and therefore a few more chances for the victims. In the next two sections, we will compare and contrast two cases in which a business which began as a (more or less) legitimate operation was gradually and inexorably

---

* The only other references I can find to cases where a successful business decided to commit 'exit fraud' was to a furniture dealership whose success had largely been driven by a profitable franchise in 'fencing' the proceeds of other people's long firm scams. The owner wanted to retire, and made good use of his knowledge, experience and contacts in the long firm world.

steered by its crooked owners into an outright – and massive
– fraud.

The Salad Oil King

'Bicycle racing developed me physically. I possess exceptional strength in my hands and legs,' Anthony 'Tino' De
Angelis used to say, crushing your knuckles in a bully's shake.
He was a short man, but huge; at the height of his powers, he
stood five feet five inches tall and weighed over 240 pounds,
with a face like Robert de Niro on a very bad day. He used to
sponsor cycle races and make charitable donations of bikes to
underprivileged kids in the name of his company, American
Crude Vegetable Oil, which had taken on the big players to
dominate the soybean market. He spent thousands of dollars
a month on flowers for funerals, because 'people keep on
dying'. They called him 'The King of Salad Oil'.

Tino had a shady past. In his youth, he had been known
as one of the fastest butchers in the Bronx, and he had set up
his own pork processing company in his early twenties. A
reserved occupation in butchering hogs kept him out of the
Second World War, during which there were strong rumours
that he had been a black marketeer. What is indisputable is that
in the 1950s, his company was convicted for shortchanging
the US government on school meals. Tino himself was also
charged with false accounting and perjury, but these charges
never stuck, because a key witness developed amnesia at the
last moment. It's a back story out of Mario Puzo, albeit with
somewhat more grease and offal.

For an Italian-American with this sort of track record,
there are always bound to be rumours and insinuations. Plenty

of people believed that Tino himself was responsible for the rumours, spreading them in order to make lenders believe that he had hidden illicit sources of money to pay them back. But despite going through several criminal trials, no reliable evidence ever turned up that Tino had any meaningful Mob connections. He just handed out largesse like a Godfather because, if you were a self-made multimillionaire son of a pizza chef, that was what you did. The few dozen loyal employees of American Crude were paid multiples of the going rate for their job, and this bought loyalty. Tino's core group of workers were the kind of people who would crawl over broken glass for the honour of buying him a drink.

American Crude Vegetable Oil was based in Bayonne, New Jersey. Bayonne is just across the Hudson River from Wall Street; you can see the major banks from the row of wharves, warehouses and storage tanks which make up its seafront. You used to be able to take a ferry from Bayonne to Manhattan, although you might be advised not to do so if your briefcase was anything like that of Tino De Angelis. Taking fraudulent securities across state lines is, it pays to remember, a federal crime. This became important in the eventual trial.

Although the commodity which will always be linked with Tino and his crimes is salad oil – as much as anything because of Norman Miller's Pulitzer Prize-winning journalism which is collected in his book *The Great Salad Oil Swindle* – American Crude's interests ran the gamut of whatever could be processed from the soya bean. Food was blander then, and 'salad oil' referred, in the USA, to the highest grade of soya oil. (Over in Italy and Spain, of course, other crooks were ensuring that European salads made their own contribution to the history of financial fraud. Since it is a heavily subsidised commodity with several grades of different values, olive oil has long been popular with fraudsters; the history of crime includes everything from mislabelled 'extra virgin' to entirely fictitious olive groves.)

The characteristic of soya oil which made it attractive to Tino was that the USA had massive surpluses of it, and that for this reason, the Department of Agriculture had a special program (Food For Peace) which subsidised exporters to get rid of it, mainly to Europe. Soya oil is hugely versatile, having applications from frying to fuel to plastics manufacture, so there was a strong export market for it, even from countries which were able to dress their own salads. But it was a highly political and opaque trade, which only a few international players were able to master. (For some reason, the trade with Spain was overseen by Opus Dei, the Catholic sect.) Being thoroughly crooked, as it often is when dealing with the governments of poor countries, was a big advantage. It should also be remembered that soybean oil used to be much more valuable than it is today. A tonne of soybean oil cost about $200 in the late 1960s, at a time when the average new home sold for less than $20,000. Tino did deals in the thousands of tonnes.

In any case, driven by Tino's dealmaking ability and uncanny sense for the right price, American Crude Vegetable Oil gained more and more market share, until it dominated the export trade, making itself an essential middleman and cutting out the Midwestern 'crushers' who produced the oil. In order to reach that position, however, it needed to invest. And that meant that the company needed to borrow money.

But who would lend money to a guy like Tino De Angelis?

As always, the answer is something along the lines of – greedy
people, desperate people and people who didn't know what
they were doing. In this case, the newly established business
lending division of American Express was unfortunate
enough to have all three characteristics.

It was the beginning of the 1960s, a period whose business
culture has been satirised on many occasions. Four-martini
lunches, casual sexual harassment and vintage two-piece suits
were very much the order of the day. So, unfortunately, were
the kind of bosses who said things like 'I don't care, just get
it done!', then went away without checking on anything.
American Express at the time had a policy that every division
needed to make at least half a million dollars of profit, and
they didn't give the impression of caring how it was made. In
retrospect, they were comically vulnerable to the next white-
collar criminal to walk through the door. It happened to be
Tino.

The way in which American Crude Vegetable Oil got
around the large and obvious character issues associated
with its owner was to borrow money based on collateral.
The practice was known as 'warehouse lending'; as a means
of financing traders' inventories it is practically as old as
banking itself, and it still goes on today. What happens is,
you take some of your inventory down to a secure warehouse
owned by a reputable bank, and they give you a 'warehouse
receipt' after checking and storing it. You can take this receipt
to any bank on Wall Street, and they will advance you money
against it. The bank which lends you the money does so based
on a guarantee from the bank which owns the warehouse,
and the bank which owns the warehouse is prepared to give
this guarantee because it has control over your goods. So

the borrower gets his money, and the banks don't need to worry too much about the solvency or honesty of the owner. In principle. It's all very convenient because you can shop around for the cheapest lending bank without having to shift the physical goods from warehouse to warehouse – the key piece of paper is the receipt which does it all for you.

The trouble with warehouse lending is that it doesn't work very well for commodities like vegetable oil which needs specialist storage. So, in a quest to grow their business and make their targets, the debonair risk-takers at American Express decided to innovate the concept of a 'field warehouse'. This was their name for an extension of the warehouse lending concept to a case where the borrower kept the collateral in their own storage facility, but the guarantor bank took over the employment of the staff and sent some inspectors around every now and then.

In the case of American Crude Vegetable Oil, this storage facility was the 'tank farm' in Bayonne, New Jersey.

The tank farm which Tino had built was an unpromising place. The winters in Bayonne are cold enough to solidify vegetable oil, and the tanks themselves were mostly reconditioned from the petroleum industry. The staff which ran the tank farm were all local boys, all part of Tino's 'family', and this did not change a bit when they nominally became employees of American Express Warehousing Inc. Part of the way that field warehousing worked was that Amex passed on the payroll costs back to the borrower, so nobody at American Express had any particular reason to check on the Bayonne staff, or to ask why they were being paid two or three times the going rate for warehousemen.

The reason why, of course, was that De Angelis regularly

needed them to do him little favours. It all had to do with the
fact that oil and water do not mix. Specifically, oil floats on
water. This made it very difficult (particularly in winter when
things freeze) for an Amex inspector to distinguish between a
tank full of salad oil, and a tank largely full of sea water with
a few gallons of oil floating on top. The warehousemen also
arranged 'trick' tanks, where a deep dip sample could be taken
which went into a length of metal tubing welded inside the
tank and filled with salad oil. They even rigged up elaborate
plumbing systems which allowed the same oil to reappear in
different tanks.

Oil came in on ships and trucks. It went out to customers
on ships and trucks. And inspectors from American Express
went back on the ferry to Manhattan, blowing on their hands
and signing off receipts which confirmed that the same oil
was still there in Bayonne. American Crude Vegetable Oil
took those receipts and borrowed money. Amex Warehouse
Leasing got a big customer who paid top-dollar fees –
they actually sold most of their non-Tino-related field
warehousing business in order to concentrate on their most
profitable niche. A few dozen Italian-American warehouse
staff got lifestyles wildly beyond their childhood aspirations.
And Tino got fatter (literally) and bigger (metaphorically),
to become the King of Salad Oil.

Then came the fateful day when an anonymous tipster
called 'Taylor' rang up the American Express offices, claiming
to have information that Tino De Angelis was a fraudster and
that the Bayonne tank farm was a fake. The caller demanded
$5,000 for more detailed information, and the Amex Field
Warehousing CEO, Donald Miller, sprang into action. On
the first day of the audit, the inspectors sampled five tanks

and found water in all five of them. Then they went home for the weekend.

On the second, and subsequent days of the audit, all the tanks sampled were full of oil. The water in the first five samples was declared to be statistically insignificant, and probably due to a faulty steam pipe. With the sort of judgement and acumen that one would expect from that dapper, bourbon-guzzling era of business, Miller had sent them to American Crude Vegetable Oil's own chief chemist for analysis rather than to an independent lab. He later admitted this was probably a mistake, but justified it by saying that 'they ought to know what was in their own tanks'.

As 1962 rolled into 1963, the need for loans became acute. Firstly, De Angelis was extracting money from the company. Half a million dollars showed up later in a Swiss bank account and got Tino an extra jail sentence, but accountants reckon that the total sum embezzled was probably closer to three million. Second, Tino was a man with dreams. His dreams tended to be somewhat incoherent, and to involve the dishonest extraction of money from other people, but give him this – he dreamed big. And third, American Crude got involved in a dispute over a payment made by the US government under the Food For Peace scheme which was either a conspiracy to undermine Tino by his enemies in Opus Dei (Tino De Angelis's version of events) or a fraudulent accounting scheme (everyone else's).

The solution which Tino De Angelis came up with to solve his problems was born, once more, from his genuine, non-fraudulent and deep understanding of the global vegetable oil market. As 1963 wore on, it became apparent that the Russian sunflower oil crop had failed. If Russia needed to replace its sunflower oil production with imported soya oil, and if the USA was willing to lift its trade embargo, there would be a huge new source of demand. And as the biggest international trader in soybeans, American Crude would be well placed to exploit this. Tino started buying more and more oil from the Midwestern crushers, and borrowing more and more money against it. He also – and this turned out to be a false move – started speculating in the futures market.

It is not wholly clear what the purpose of the speculation was. For a soybean trader who was claiming to have inventories of soybean oil which were getting on for a full year of US production, it was not obviously a good idea to be entering into lots more contracts for future purchase of soybean oil. At times, it looked as if Tino was attempting to make sure that he would have enough oil (rather than sea water) to fulfil the Russian contract when it arrived. At others, it looked like he might just be attempting to manipulate the futures market and make a killing by forcing it to a peak and then selling high.* In any case, being Tino, he went about his futures buying in the least honest and most manipulative way available: by placing orders with dozens of different brokers, to give the impression of genuine and widespread public demand. We can imagine that the Chicago and New York commodities brokers got the same crushing handshakes, bear-like backslaps, flowers and promises of Cadillacs which were familiar to all of Tino's business partners. They certainly got very good commissions, which seem to have blinded them to what was going on.

---

*If he was, this would have been a 'market corner', a type of market crime in our terminology. See p.255 on the 'Piggly Wiggly Corner' for a description of the mechanics of a corner and why they're not allowed.

Borrowing money should have got more difficult than it did a lot earlier than it did. As well as being a greater amount than total US production, by this point the warehouse receipts written on the Bayonne tank farm indicated a quantity of soybean oil about 30 per cent larger than the capacity of the farm itself. American Crude responded to these challenges with a two-pronged strategy.

First, a new tank farm was opened up, around the corner from the first one. This was sublet from the Harbor Tank Company, and it was widely acknowledged to be an even worse example of the genre than the first. The location was equally cold, bleak and depressing, and the vegetable oil tanks were little short of a joke. Some of the tanks were Tino specials with welded pipework inside them. Some were still leased to petroleum companies who were storing fuel oil in them. And some, as far as the eventual bankruptcy examiners could tell, never existed at all. The Harbor Tank Company salad oil farm was operated by Joe Lomuscio, a long-time friend of Tino's.

The second limb of the strategy was simpler. While on a visit to American Express's offices, Tino stole a book of blank warehouse receipts and started writing them himself.

It is probably fair to say that by this point, things were out of control.

Brokers talk; it's the nature of the job. As cocktails are poured in New York and Chicago, the men of the exchanges always meet up, to talk business and swap rumours. If Tino had stuck to the physical oil market rather than trading on a futures exchange, it might have taken much longer for the truth to come out. But as the summer turned to fall, the gossip mill was beginning to do its job. Over tables and shoeshines, on commuter trains and in country clubs, the financial community was beginning to realise that all the different companies pushing soybean orders through all the different brokerages were coming back to the same ultimate client. There was no broad-based public demand for soybean futures; it was all Tino.

In the futures market, where prices can be volatile and adverse movements can trigger a request for immediate settlement in cash, it can be dangerous for people to know when you are out on a limb. When brokers get nervous, they tend to ask the customer to either reduce the size of their trades, or to put up more cash as a surety that they will be able to meet losses. Tino couldn't do the first of these – it was only his attempts to corner the market which were holding the price up. And he certainly couldn't do the second.

Then it all happened. Talks in Congress collapsed on a wheat-export contract with Russia, and the market took the view that if the wheat deal wasn't happening, there would certainly be no soybean deal. No Russian buyer meant that there was probably no demand from anyone else, because Tino's speculation had pushed the price so high. The soybean futures market cracked and the futures losses meant that American Crude Vegetable Oils had no option but to declare bankruptcy. This in turn caused chaos on the soybean futures market, causing one of the brokers to require a bailout organised by the exchange. And as soon as the bankruptcy examiners arrived in Bayonne, they found a hundred tanks full of seawater and no more of Tino's loyal band to pull the wool over anyone's eyes. American Express realised that they were going to have to make good on $150m of guarantees, back in the days when that was a lot of money (it's the equivalent of about $1bn today). It would have made more headlines, except that the Salad Oil Swindle hit the news on exactly the same weekend that President Kennedy was assassinated.

De Angelis is still alive. He was sentenced to twenty years and served seven of them. While in prison, he designed an exercise regime for himself and dropped his weight to 170 pounds; when he came out, he gave *Life* magazine an interview in which he said that 'Prison saved my life', and that the Lewisburg federal penitentiary was 'a country club'. Several of his cellmates gave testimonials that they had found him an inspirational character who had encouraged them to succeed in other fields and give up on crime. Tino himself was sentenced to another sixteen years in 1980, for a brand-new investment scheme fraud unrelated to salad oil.

The Salad Oil scam was one of the biggest white-collar scandals of the Mad Men era. It was a shot of long firm fraud, with a chaser of counterfeit warehouse receipts.* From the lender's side, it was a perfect storm of the right conditions to get ripped off. Field warehousing was a new financial technology, which had not been thought through. The Amex subsidiary in charge of it had been given tough 'stretch' targets and so needed to land big customers. The Bayonne facility was staffed by people who were comparatively cheap to corrupt. And oil floats on water.

Once more, fraud shows up as an equilibrium quantity. Why did American Express lose money? Because they lent it against fake salad oil. Why did they lend money against fictitious collateral? Because they delegated the task of

---

*If you're being pedantic, genuine warehouse receipts for counterfeit oil. Apart from the ones that Tino forged.

checking it to a party which turned out not to be trustworthy. Why did they let Tino's men look after the field warehouse? Because it was cheaper that way. Why was it cheaper that way? Because rigorous fraud controls are expensive relative to the amount of profit that you're making on the deal. And now we arrive at the final 'why'?

Why is there always an incentive to economise on checks, audits and fraud prevention?

Because fraud is an unusual condition; it's a 'tail risk'. In an advanced, high-trust economy, a business can trade for years without ever seeing a big systematic fraud like Tino De Angelis. And normal businesspeople are, like all human beings, usually quite bad at judging the significance of small probabilities and rare events. It's all too easy a heuristic to deal with the small risk of a catastrophic fraud loss by assuming that because it's close to zero, it's reasonable to act as if it was actually zero. And that means – since pricing in a competitive industry tends to be set by the lowest bidder, not the smartest bidder – that there will always be pressure to get a short-term cost advantage by economising on the kinds of bureaucratic, not directly productive checks and balances that pick up frauds.

From the fraudster's side, it is clear that there was a genuine business there. Tino was a crook and his objectives were selfish and destructive, but he wasn't a fake – he really was the Salad Oil King. He traded more soya oil than anyone else, dominated shipping under the Food For Peace program and brought innovative business practices to the industry – he claimed to have been the first person ever to convert tanker ships to store food oil. American Crude Vegetable Oil could have been a strong legitimate business if it were not for

Tino's dreams of crushing the crushers, cornering the futures market and owning the entire industry. It was this plan, along with his desire to extract cash from the business illegally while continuing to grow it, which necessitated his shift into the world of sea-water floats, rigged tanks and forged receipts. If the price of soya oil had kept going up (impossibly), he might even have got away with it.

Tino's methodical shift from sharp business practice into fraud is an example of one way that a long firm can make use of a legitimate trading reputation. It contrasts with another possible scenario – the episode of OPM Leasing, a fraudulent business where nothing ever seemed to be planned.

Other People's Money

Bizarrely, this was what the acronym actually stood for – in 1970, Mordecai Weissman had originally planned to call the business he was setting up 'Leasing Services Division', but felt that the acronym 'LSD' would sound disreputable. So he decided to name the company after its business model; it is presumably a coincidence that at the same time the criminologist Donald Cressey was starting work on his 1972 classic work on occupational fraud, also titled *Other People's Money*. The founders of OPM were keen on acronyms – at the height of their success, the other partner tried to bid for the Madison Square Garden entertainment complex seemingly for no other reason than that its initials were the same as his – Myron S. Goodman.

Weissman and Goodman were a hell of a team; part Marx Brothers, part Gordon Gekko. They were brothers-in-law, highly regarded in the Orthodox Jewish community as philanthropists and for their devoutly religious and scholarly manner. Goodman would begin meetings by quoting Bible verses, while Weissman took time out from the business in 1973 to fight in the war against Egypt. They commuted by helicopter from their homes in Long Island to Manhattan until the neighbours objected to the noise. Mordy was the great salesman and passer-out of kickbacks, while Myron was the obsessively secretive office manager who casually threatened to have employees castrated. One might describe them as both *machers* and *mensches* if not for the fact that they had somehow missed out on any concept of business ethics or common sense.

The business model of OPM was indeed that it used other people's money – it was in the business of computer leasing. These were the days, remember, when computers were big pieces of capital investment. The first IBM PC did not come out until 1981, by which time OPM was well into its death throes. In the heyday of Mordy and Myron, a 'computer' was a large metal box which needed its own air-conditioned room with strengthened floors, and which could cost a few million dollars. Companies had special divisions of their planning teams who did nothing but keep up with technological progress, and the 'Head of Computer Strategy' was one of the most exciting roles in 1970s corporate America.

Computers were expensive and went obsolete quickly, and there were considerable tax incentives available to encourage their purchase. All of these were excellent reasons to lease them rather than buy them.* What OPM did was to

---

*Why do tax breaks mean that leasing is attractive? Basically, tech companies often make losses, and you can't reduce a tax bill below zero. So

send Mordy in to meet the client and find out his technical requirements. Then Myron would arrange a short-term 'bridging' loan from a bank to buy the computer, and Mordy would find out the client's non-technical requirements (usually a bribe or a donation to a favourite charity). Then the lease would be signed.

At this point, Other People's Money had to be brought in. With the help of an investment banker (initially, Goldman Sachs; then, when Goldman Sachs got scared off by OPM's chaotic ambitions, Lehman Brothers), Mordy and Myron would find a pension fund, insurance company or other investor who wanted a long-term stream of lease payments. The lease agreement would then be 'sold' to the investor, generating enough cash for OPM to pay back the bridging loan. This kept OPM's credit looking good with the banks, and allowed Mordy to go out fishing for new clients.

So far, so simple. However, Myron Goodman's need to keep control meant that the client company would not be allowed to just make its payments directly to the investor – everything had to go through OPM. This black hole of information turned out to be vital to the later fraud, as it meant that people on both sides of the deal were making and receiving payments entirely on Myron's say-so. These are occasionally referred to as 'mirrored' transactions in the jargon, but in this case the mirror in question was like the

---

the tax break is wasted unless the asset is owned by a company that makes a profit. So it can make sense to structure things so that the owner of the computer, for tax purposes, is something like an insurance company with big and reliable profits. The taxman is usually quite relaxed about this because the leasing companies tend to pass at least some of the benefits back to the tech firms they were intended for.

one in the film *Duck Soup*, where Groucho Marx stands in an empty frame and mimics his brother's movements.

Another crucial feature was the fact that at the end of the lease, the computer would still exist, and the investor who owned the lease agreement had no interest in the second-hand computer business. The 'residual value' was OPM's responsibility. Since computer leasing was a competitive market, firms would typically price the leasing payments well below the cost of the computer, looking to make the money back on the residual value. It can immediately be seen that a) it was pretty vital to get this residual value right, and b) that leasing companies which systematically overestimated residual values (and so set their bids aggressively for the lease payments) would probably gain a lot of market share in the short term, while storing up massive problems for the long term. Mordy and Myron were incredibly aggressive and growth-oriented, not very scrupulous and congenitally incapable of proper record-keeping (Goodman once yelled at his auditors that 'I went into business to make money, not to produce financial statements!'). It is hard to think of a worse business for two guys like this.

On any sensible accounting basis, rather than the one they actually used, OPM Leasing lost money every year it did business. The signature Mordy deal was one that did whatever it took to win the client business, without much attention to economic viability. They developed a particularly close relationship with Rockwell Inc., the aerospace manufacturer, where the Head of Computer Strategy, Sidney Hasin, was overawed by their ability to beat the competition's terms by miles. In retrospect, Rockwell later admitted, they would have done well to have been more sceptical.

The film *Dirty Harry* came out in 1971, introducing 'Dirty' Harry Callahan to the world. Myron Goodman followed his lead. He broke rules, but he got results. The key problem that Myron had was that Mordy had brought him such awful leases that when they were sold to investors, they didn't bring in enough cash to pay back the bridging loans. Or alternatively, they brought in enough cash to pay back the bridging loans, but not enough to also fund the very large 'advances' which OPM tended to make to its founders and top management.

The solution which OPM found to this problem was pretty unique, and wholly in keeping with the element of slapstick comedy which pervaded their way of doing business. The reception area of OPM Leasing Inc. had a glass coffee table. Mordy would lie underneath it shining a flashlight, while Myron would lean over it, tracing the signature of a lease client to adjust the value of the computer asset and increase the size of the bridging loan. When loans absolutely had to be paid back, the OPM team were not above pledging the same asset to two or three different lenders, just like Leslie Payne. Crazily enough, official accounts of the OPM Leasing scandal tend to describe this as the relatively honest period; in so far as anyone can tell from the chaotic and infrequently filed accounts, they were only, albeit illegally, hustling creditors to maintain cashflow at this stage rather than actually stealing money.

They might even have legitimately believed that they would eventually be proved right on resale values one day, and that OPM would find itself on a profitable footing. Since they had a tame accountant who allowed them to get away with their ridiculous assumptions, the company actually reported record profits. They even bought a bank of their own in Louisiana, although the thought of such a manifestly incompetent management team in charge of a regulated bank proved the last straw for Goldman Sachs.

Not only did Mordy overestimate residual values and underprice deals, he made one mistake which was absolutely lethal if one thinks for a minute about the computer industry in the 1970s – he offered generous early break terms.

Why is this lethal? It meant that he was at the mercy of the IBM product upgrade cycle just when microprocessor technology was beginning to show the exponential rate of improvement that became known as 'Moore's Law'. As new computers came out, the resale value of previous models would plummet. Clients who were signed into long leases would be stuck with the obsolete kit, but companies who could break their leases could upgrade their computers while sticking companies like OPM with all the residual risk on the equipment at the worst possible moment. Myron and Mordy, as well as underpricing their business, had bet everything on a strategy that could only fail to be disastrous if computer progress slowed down to a crawl.

It didn't slow down to a crawl. OPM had leased several million dollars worth of IBM 370 supercomputers to Rockwell Industries, all with early break clauses and minimal termination fees. What was their reaction to the announcement in March 1977 of the new 3033 Series? As Myron Goodman said, 'I nearly passed out.' The 370 mainframes which OPM had bought and leased to Rockwell were now yesterday's technology. They were in the position of claiming to their bankers that the market for second-hand 370s would hold up well, as IBM would be unable to deliver 3033s on time, or alternatively that their biggest client, Rockwell Industries, would be unwilling to accept the considerable physical disruption to their plant and operations that would result from taking out one mainframe and wheeling another one in. These were both pretty weak straws to clutch at – but they provided enough of a pretext for OPM to continue borrowing money and looking for new investors.

If they had a conscience, Weissman and Goodman could have shut down OPM and walked away from it, leaving behind nothing more serious than a lot of very bad feeling over some stupidly misstated residual values. They could even have sorted out the multiply pledged collateral, if they had been prepared to give up the money they had extracted by 'shareholder loans'.* But this was never on the cards. At various points, the two men discussed a strategy that might have allowed Mordy Weissman to escape with his reputation intact, as they unwound all the bad deals he had been a party to and left Myron Goodman to take the rap. Instead, they merrily danced across the line separating aggressive corporate strategy from outright theft, and started to take advantage of their unhealthy relationship with Sidney Hasin.

OPM's paperwork was notoriously bad, and Rockwell never checked up on it. Instead of doing anything themselves about the numerous inconsistencies and complaints from the investors who had bought their leases, they handed over a

---

* A sort of 'pink flag' rather than a red one. There are plenty of non-fraudulent reasons (mainly tax-related) you might want to take cash out of a company you own by making a loan to yourself rather than paying yourself a dividend or an executive salary. But it makes the accounts hard to read, particularly if the 'loan' is one that you never intend to pay back.

ream of official Rockwell letterhead to OPM and instructed them to sort everything out. The investors had no independent contact with the company who they were meant to be leasing to. And so there was nothing to stop Goodman from, for example, signing a lease for $20,000 of Tektronik computer equipment to Rockwell, but telling the Philadelphia Savings Fund that it was a lease for a $50,000 DEC tape storage unit. Obviously, Rockwell would only be making payments of less than half the amount the investor expected to receive, but the excess cash paid by the Philadelphians could be used to make up the difference for quite a while, and more contracts could be faked to generate more cash in the meantime.

Myron was not a good fraudster. His forged lease documents were covered with errors, and he was unable to keep his story consistent from one meeting to the next. He used the bank he had bought to write bad cheques, effectively taking an interest-free loan from the Federal Reserve. But this too fell apart quickly, and really contributed little to the fraud beyond making sure that the eventual charges were much more serious.* By the end of 1978, OPM was in collapse. Goodman's ability to raise new fraudulent loans was running out, and the company could no longer make the payments

---

* A brief note on American crime terminology. 'Mail fraud' is fraud using the US Postal Service, and 'wire fraud' is fraud using the telecoms system. Both are federal crimes in the USA, basically because they were declared to be so when the US Postal Service and the telegram systems were set up to avoid questions about state jurisdiction. Check-kiting, because it involves the Federal Reserve's payment system, is also a federal crime, as is anything which involves carrying fraudulent securities across state lines. It is difficult (although not impossible) to carry out a serious fraud in the USA without triggering federal jurisdiction.

on the old ones. The Philadelphia Savings Fund called up Rockwell to ask why they were delinquent on their payments, and Rockwell started to ask OPM why anyone should think that was the case. The reply was classic Myron & Mordy; they said that 'mistakes' had been made by other people and that they would send their father-in-law directly to Philadelphia to make the payment.

At this point, the story should have been close to its conclusion. Indeed, the main question people asked in 1981, when OPM finally gave up and went bankrupt, is why didn't it happen three years earlier? Like a *Looney Tunes* character, nothing seemed to stop it. New investors were brought in as the old ones gave up in disgust. One of the banks providing bridging loans found out about Myron Goodman's federal conviction for cheque fraud, but somehow this did not put off the rest of the industry. Lehman Brothers continued to help OPM find investors for their leases, despite the growing mound of 'administrative errors' every month. And the company's lawyers received a whistle-blower report and extracted a confession from Myron Goodman, but then unaccountably decided that, because the information related to past frauds rather than ongoing ones, it was covered by client–attorney privilege.

This is an important lesson: although professionals like lawyers and accountants usually function as the system's defence against bad actors, these defences can be overcome – usually by a fraudster who pays very well and who accounts for a large proportion of a professional services firm's total billings. Once a fraud has penetrated this layer of defence, there are few further constraints on its ability to grow and grow. People don't check up on things which they believe to have been 'signed off'. The threat is now inside the perimeter.

Myron and Mordy were not exactly honest businessmen tempted into bad behaviour. Although they were ostentatiously religious and prominent in philanthropic ventures (many of which were connected to clients' pet-charity projects), they were clearly strangers to business ethics from the moment they leased their first computer. But they had, pretty much despite themselves, built up a legitimate trading reputation as successful lessors in a complicated and competitive market, who had a track record of always paying their debts. Computer leasing was a new industry, and its profitability depended on questions of residual value which were very hard for an outsider to judge. This was how OPM built its franchise and credit, despite a business model that was bound to force Myron & Mordy into an ethical choice that they were comically ill-equipped to make. In the end, although Myron Goodman stood up in court and promised that 'the wrongs I have done are behind me', he was sentenced to twelve years, while Mordecai Weissman got ten.

This kind of 'slippery slope' effect is also seen in less dramatic cases, and in ones where the crooked nature of the principals is not so obvious. At the opposite end of the continuum from Weissman and Goodman, there is the businessman who drifts into long firm territory simply as a result of over-optimism in the context of a failing business. In terms of its prevalence, this kind of almost inadvertent long firm might be more dangerous to its suppliers, as the fraudster will look like (and may even sincerely believe himself to be) an otherwise good customer fallen on hard times and worthy of temporary support.

These, then, are some of the ways in which an existing legitimate business can get corrupted to provide the vital credit rating needed to establish a long firm. On the other hand, it is sometimes possible to take a faster way into other people's money, and to get your credibility and references by just making them up. You can have a sophisticated system of false references like Leslie Payne's alphabetical companies, or you can just put the pedal to the metal and rely on speed and high-octane dishonesty to carry you through. The second option was particularly attractive for the people who were dealing with one of the biggest and softest targets in the history of commercial fraud. There are only quite rare cases in which it is possible to carry out the fraudulent equivalent of a hit-and-run attack, but when they come along, they tend to be associated with victims who have few or no effective controls. That means they can be extremely lucrative.

Short firms and 1980s Medicare

Etymologically, a 'long firm' has little to do with either length or firms. It first appears in printed English in dictionaries of slang and thieves' cant, and both words are used in archaic senses. 'Long' had a meaning from the Anglo-Saxon 'gelang' meaning fraudulent and referring to fault or failure, while 'firm' (like the Italian *firma*) referred to a signature, and has only comparatively recently been used to refer to a kind of organisation. So a 'long firm' is a 'gelang firma', one Saxon word and one Latin, and refers to the crime of signing a fraudulent bill of goods. However, the pull of linguistic gravity has been strong over the years, and these days it is also common to talk about a 'short firm' in contrast to the long firm.

A short firm fraud is not really a different kind of operation though – it's just a half-arsed long firm. Nevertheless, the concept helps to outline some of the trade-offs that a long firm fraudster has to make, and some of the ways in which long-firm fraud attacks the normal mechanics of the economy.

Consider one of the most popular and lucrative forms of fraud there has ever been: Medicare fraud in the 1980s and 1990s. This was probably the single biggest fraud category on earth until the banking sector regained the title in the 2000s. Credible estimates* placed the proportion of fraudulent payments in the Medicare system as high as 25–30 per cent, which would correspond to hundreds of billions of dollars. The nature of the fraud was classic long firm stuff – you simply sent bills to your local Medicare insurer for expensive medical services that you hadn't provided.[†] But if you were going to carry out such a fraud, you had a big choice to make – should you bother with patients?

The advantages and disadvantages were pretty clear; if you just sent in fake bills for fictitious patients, you could set up quickly and start sending out fraudulent bills in the thousands. There were fewer overheads, no irritating ill

---

* Such as that made by Malcolm K. Sparrow in his book *License to Steal*, from which this example is taken.

† Or, in some ghastly cases, that you had provided but shouldn't have. One chain of blood analysis laboratories realised they could massively pad their bills by doing unnecessary tests. They got so greedy on this fraud that they quickly exhausted the normal pool of blood donation clinics and had to provide incentives to get more. A medical paper on 'Lab-Fraud Anaemia' ended up being published as hospitals in the New York area experienced a rash of emergency cases from homeless people who had been donating quarts of blood two or three times a week.

people to deal with and no possibility that someone would blow the whistle on you. On the other hand, if you're caught having sent in a load of crooked invoices for bogus medical procedures, it's a lot more difficult to argue that it was a genuine administrative error, a case of crossed wires* or a legitimate medical dispute if the patients don't even exist. You're trading off the ease of setting up the fraud against the likely consequences if it gets caught.

So which one is better? In fact, Medicare fraudsters did both. There were two viable business models given the way that fraud controls worked at the time. There were 'short firm' clinics with no patients, which had the objective of sending out as many crooked bills as possible (usually for standard treatments at standard rates for common ailments, to maximise the chance that the bill would be paid without much scrutiny), get as many of them paid as possible within a single billing cycle, then close down, disappear and start up somewhere else. At the time, the systems that Medicare used to check on billings were not able to identify sudden increases in the claims submitted by a single provider, so since the individual claims were unexceptional, these frauds would usually only be caught by pure chance.

There were also 'long firms' in Medicare, which persisted for many billing cycles, padding the claims of actually existing patients and stealing little but often. These frauds relied on another weakness of the system: the degree of trust

---

* Another aspect of Medicare fraud which will make you question your faith in humanity; because they were easily confused and did not make reliable witnesses as to what medical procedures they had or hadn't received, dementia patients were particularly prized by crooked clinics and doctors.

that society places in medical professionals was in general, and wrongly, extended to medical administrators. The claims-paying authorities were very reluctant to second-guess providers as to the necessity of treatments, and very quick to attribute obvious discrepancies to administrative errors rather than to fraud. The system was set up to challenge over-treatment and overuse of insured services, not fraudulent claims. So a provider which systematically added unnecessary blood tests, or billed for a more expensive procedure than it had carried out, or charged for an expensive customised wheelchair then delivered a cheap one, was likely to keep slipping through the net.

What Medicare teaches us is that there is a qualitative difference between a good company gone bad and an enterprise which has been wholly designed around a fraudulent purpose. The first is harder to detect given the usual checks, but the second is much easier to construct. In an environment like Medicare, where the systems and controls have been standardised and industrialised, this allows the fraudster to use a technique that the management professor and Medicare historian Malcolm Sparrow christened 'shotgun, then rifle'. You first create a panoply of fake transactions, claims or orders, and see which ones get rejected. Then, having used the 'shotgun' phase to gather information about the checking process, you move to the 'rifle', and fire off as many duplicates or slight variations as you can of the ones that worked. Versions of this tactic tend to crop up in situations where a large target is aiming to minimise its average cost of processing, and where it has not been sufficiently taken into account that fraud is a potential driver of the cost. The government is often a victim of this sort of tactic, because it has some unusual characteristics as a victim (it is large, and has problems turning customers away: see Chapter 10). Many defence procurement frauds work in a similar way. But large private sector entities are also vulnerable to shotgun/rifle approaches – something like this tactic is usually at the heart of organised insurance fraud, as well as some credit card and mortgage frauds.

More generally, the fact that a fictitious company requires very little investment to get started means that fraudsters can afford to experiment. The advantage of operating this way, rather than through an existing legitimate business, is clear. The disadvantage is that if you are caught, there is much more evidence of dishonesty and conspiracy. You steal the money and you take your choice.

Getting away with it

Having looked at some examples of ways of generating the kind of commercial confidence that one needs in order to carry out the first stage of a long firm fraud, we can turn to the second stage – escaping without being caught. The way one achieves this is either by attempting to make the fraud look like a normal business collapse, or by putting as many layers of obfuscation as possible between oneself and the long firm.

If there is enough confusion around, simply denying everything and throwing counter-accusations at your creditors can be a surprisingly successful tactic. Sir Gregor MacGregor took this approach; as the survivors trickled home, he started suing people for libel and publishing defamatory tracts of his own aimed at the merchants from Belize who had tried to rescue them – or in MacGregor's version of history, the robbers who had stolen goods and destroyed the settlement out of fear of competition from a thriving Poyais. These battles ended up inevitably with the Cazique being disgraced, but it created enough uncertainty in London to allow him to depart to Paris claiming that none of it was his fault and to restart selling Poyais bonds there. He was still trying to sell them, with admittedly dwindling success, by the time of his death in 1845.

In the modern day, the conviction rate for frauds brought to trial in England is between 60 and 80 per cent, depending on whether the Serious Fraud Office is having a good or bad year. The New York State courts seem to do better, with the Southern District of Manhattan regularly scoring over 90 per cent, although of course these figures are unlikely to be directly comparable because English courts have not recognised plea-bargains until recently, and because they do not take the same cases. This matters: the fraud cases which come to court are the tip of the iceberg. Prima facie, a failure to pay one's debts is regarded as a civil matter (a breach of contract) rather than a crime, and fairly or not, it is de facto the responsibility of the victim to show that there has been misrepresentation, dishonesty or conspiracy. Few other crimes give the criminal an explicit chance to 'cool out the mark',* but in general, if a bankrupt company can get three

---

* This useful phrase, brought to prominence by Erving Goffman, refers to the practice of con men of all kinds to assign some time and effort to the task of persuading the victim to frame things differently – to see himself not as the victim of a criminal act which requires justice, but as someone who has had a bit of bad luck, or engaged in a failed venture. Goffman contends that, sociologically, lots of non-criminal institutions in everyday and bureaucratic

quarters of its creditors to agree to a payment plan, it is highly
unlikely that the remaining quarter will be able to persuade
the law enforcement authorities to investigate further.

And although simply standing amid the wreckage with
an innocent expression is surprisingly effective, a second
line of defence can bring the risk down to very low levels
indeed. What you need is a person to take the blame for the
insolvency, and if the insolvency cannot be passed off as bad
luck, to take the criminal consequences. If the person chosen
for this role is part of the fraud, he is known as a 'front'; if
not, a 'patsy'.

Why might anyone act as a front for a long firm? It might
be because he has been bribed. It is by no means unknown for
long firm syndicates to pick up a street-dwelling alcoholic,
give him a haircut and a new suit and introduce him as the
chief executive of a new trading company. After a few weeks
of the high life, these characters ended up being dumped
back into the hostels they came from. If one thinks it a little
risky to have anything relying on the plausibility of a tramp,
there are career criminals who make a specialty of fronting
long firms;* given the conviction rates and typical sentences,
the risk/reward ratio is not necessarily so bad. But the other
common reason that someone might take the rap for a long
firm is that they are not aware that they are doing so. Such a
person is a patsy.

---

life can, once you have recognised the phenomenon, be seen as having
functions broadly similar to the cooling out of marks.
*It has been suggested that if you have access to an accountant who knows
how to keep his mouth shut and who is prepared to go to jail, then you are
either making money out of a long firm fraud or you aren't trying.

There is one more way to abuse the trading reputation of a legitimate firm, and it is significantly nastier than the methods discussed so far. What we are talking about is something like the classic 'bust-out', seen in the film *Goodfellas* and associated with organised crime. A moderately successful small business – a bar or restaurant, say – gets a new business partner for its owner. This can come about as the result of a brief period of financial distress and resort to a loan shark, or the bad guys can simply walk through the door with baseball bats. In any case, control has passed from a legitimate owner to a crook, and the new crooked owner can start abusing the trading record of the company to run up fraudulent credit.

A bust-out does not have to be carried out with violence or menace, though. Long firm fraudsters are often on the lookout for businesses up for sale at cheap prices, where the owners can be persuaded to accept payment in instalments. There are two benefits to the fraudster from paying to acquire a company on the never-never; as well as reducing the up-front cash outlay, it benefits the fraudster hugely to obfuscate the ownership of the firm. If the original owner still has an interest in the company's success, appears on the letterhead and so on, then credit bureaux and accounts receivable controllers will be less likely to notice that there has been a change of management, and therefore less likely to start checking the people placing the orders against their registers of known bad actors (either people who have served time for fraud, or those who have been associated with sufficiently many bankruptcies to carry the pall of suspicion).

There are even more audacious ways to take possession of another company's trading reputation. Even when fraudsters pay up front for a company, it can be surprisingly difficult for the selling owner to organise a final board meeting to formalise the transfer of title. The minutes of such meetings have a habit of getting lost, leaving the previous owner sitting around as the only remaining representative of a long firm, trying to convince the police that a bad boy did it and ran away.* *Never* sell a company for cash.

As well as taking care who you sell to, owners of businesses would be well advised to keep tight control of who is allowed to use their headed notepaper. Since companies don't have fingerprints or passport photographs, letterheads are often accepted as evidence of identity by credit controllers, and if they get into the wrong hands, they can cause serious mischief – fraudsters can write credit references for each other, and even place orders. One case from Michael Levi's classic book on long firms, *The Phantom Capitalists*, shows what you can get away with if you really have nerves of steel:

> Part of the fraudster's craft is the ability to tell a good story, and this is done both to banks and to trade victims. A good example of this craft is a long firm which was carried out in South Wales in the 1960s. A man with an American accent arrived at a Welsh coastal resort and announced that he represented an American syndicate (sic!) which wished to purchase a leisure and amusement arcade in the town. He offered a generous price, which was accepted gratefully by the owners. Unfortunately, however, there was a small snag preventing immediate

---

* The police are entirely correct to be suspicious of such people, by the way. The classic defence of a front – or even of the fraudster himself if he hasn't used a front man – is to pretend to be an unwilling patsy.

completion; the money was temporarily tied up. However, he asked the owners if, pending completion of the sale, they would allow him to order goods for the coming season. This request was acceded to, the owners even going so far as to give him their headed notepaper to use in ordering. He wrote off to a number of suppliers as if he already owned the arcades and obtained some £350,000 worth of fancy goods, toiletries and groceries on credit. One night all of these goods were covertly taken away and the man disappeared for good. His identity remains unknown to this day.

Finally, a short word about the 'fence' – the party who turns stolen goods into cash. Fencing the goods acquired in a long firm is easier than with the proceeds of a robbery, simply because the crime involves a time dimension. The moment a car is stolen, its owner will be on the lookout for it, and its sale will be difficult and risky. But if a dozen cars are stolen by an automotive dealership acting as a long firm, the victim of the crime will expect to see them on the forecourt, being sold for cash to the public. The crime only comes into existence once the payment is overdue and the debt is in default. Fences for long firm fraudsters always have the cast-iron excuse that the business did not look like a fraud when they were dealing with it, *because it did not*, and in general, they have to screw things up pretty badly to end up being convicted.

The time dimension doesn't make it easy for everyone involved in a fraud, however. Although it puts distance between the crime and its discovery, that distance comes at a cost. Business people expect to be paid for waiting – that's why they say things like 'time is money'. And the time value of money means that while a sum of undiscovered fraud exists, the size of the deception is often growing. This complicates the economics of the thing a lot.

3

THE SNOWBALL EFFECT

'Accumulate! Accumulate! That is Moses and the Prophets!'

Karl Marx, *Grundrisse*

Ponzi and his scheme

The signs, it is almost trite to observe, were there. Charles Ponzi arrived as an almost penniless Italian immigrant to Boston in 1903, having lost all his money to a card shark *en voyage* and owning only a ticket via New York to meet his relatives in Pittsburgh. He bumped through a series of clerical and menial jobs before fetching up in a Montreal jail, claiming that the banking fraud which had put him there was all a big misunderstanding, probably the fault of one of his love rivals, and that he would one day be avenged. After being encouraged to seek fortune outside the Dominions of Canada, he headed back to the USA in the company of a party of illegal immigrants, which resulted in another short jail sentence.

He promoted power and light investment schemes, pretended to be in a secret society in New Orleans, hung around with medical insurance fraudsters in Alabama, got married and ended up back in Boston in 1919. Here, he turned to a seemingly legitimate business, aiming to use his natural gifts for languages and for salesmanship to publish *The Trader's Guide*, a compendium of useful addresses, consulates, customs details and similar information. The idea was that he would distribute it for free to companies worldwide in the import and export trades and make a profit by selling advertising. Ahead of its time, Ponzi's international trade gazette was not a success. But while trying to promote it, he made a discovery that would change the course of his life. He received a request for a sample copy from a company based in Spain, accompanied by an International Reply Coupon (IRC) to cover postage.

While cashing in the IRC, Ponzi realised that while these coupons were convertible into a set amount of postage in each of the participating systems of the Universal Postal Union, they also sold for a set amount of local currency in each of the countries. The IRC system therefore defined a set of fixed exchange rates via its table of prices, and these exchange rates could differ significantly from the market rates. This was particularly true with respect to countries like Italy or Portugal which had devalued their currencies significantly in the aftermath of the First World War.

Ponzi even carried out a trial transaction, sending dollars to a relative in Italy to convert into lire, buy IRCs and mail them back to Boston. He then took these coupons to the post office in Milk Street, exchanging them for US stamps worth around double his initial investment. It looked like a free money machine, and all he needed was more capital. He took down the sign on his rented office for 'The Bostonian Advertising and Publishing Company' and put one up for the 'Securities Exchange Corporation'.* He was ready to start borrowing money.

---

* The US regulatory authorities had not formed the Securities Exchange

His first 'investor' was an office furniture salesman to whom Ponzi owed money; Ponzi successfully exchanged his commercial debt for a ninety-day note promising to pay 50 per cent interest. He had to explain the mechanics of the IRC scheme to convince his irate creditor that he was not just playing for time, but once that was clear the salesman was hooked. In general, Ponzi was never reluctant to give away the details of his scheme to potential investors. He claimed to be unafraid of having his idea stolen because nobody else had the contacts in Europe which were needed to buy the coupons in large amounts. This was true, but neither did Ponzi.

Postal inspectors regularly visited his offices accusing him of fraud; all of them left convinced by Ponzi's charm and intelligence that the scheme was legitimate. Seemingly none of them were sufficiently familiar with the rules of the Universal Postal Union, which had anticipated the problem of implied exchange rates and gave significant amount of protection against having money drawn out of the system by speculators. If Ponzi had ever tried to put his scheme into action, his overseas agents would have found it very difficult to buy coupons in bulk and he would not have been able to convert them into cash in the USA. There is, however, no real evidence that he ever made any serious effort to trade them – Ponzi claimed that unspecified administrative problems prevented the profitable coupon trading business

---

Commission by this point, so Ponzi was not attempting to pass himself off as something he was not. In general, however, the 'Tennessee Fried Chicken' effect is by no means uncommon in the world of commercial fraud; a company name similar to an established and trusted existing entity is often chosen.

from getting off the ground, but this was almost certainly a lie.

Other investors soon followed the furniture salesman. Ponzi offered them the same terms – 50 per cent interest payable in ninety days (he later shortened the term to sixty days). Word first spread through Boston's Italian-American community but soon went beyond it into the wider New England scene. He started to employ commission sales agents, giving them 10 per cent of the amount that they raised. The rented office was quickly outgrown (Ponzi had become a serious local traffic problem) and he moved into marble-clad premises on School Street, in the heart of the city's business district. Ponzi bought automobiles, smoked large cigars and made himself prominent about town.

His expansion plans seem to have proceeded as much by luck as by design.* A fellow former Montreal jailbird came to him looking for a job and threatening to expose his murky past. Ponzi sent him out into the Boston suburbs and New England towns to set up new branches. This new employee turned out to be a natural, and soon the branch network was generating as many new customers as the central Boston office. By 1920, Ponzi had over 30,000 individual customers, a float of millions of dollars of cash and absolutely no hope of redeeming all the promises he had made.

---

* According to him, that is. His autobiography, *The Rise of Mr Ponzi*, written while in jail after the collapse of the scheme, is a unique insight into the psychology of a man who always has a reason why nothing was his fault. Even when giving literally true descriptions of actions which were obviously crooked, he always claims he was acting honestly. For this reason if no other, none of the factual assertions in the book should be treated as necessarily true, and many of them, including this anecdote, do not appear in other histories.

Ponzi's scheme differed from most of its imitators in that, in the early stages at least, rather than discouraging withdrawals he actually welcomed them. The marketing proposition he gave to his investors was that interest was only paid at maturity – it was possible to get one's money back at any time before the ninety days were up, but without interest. Each early withdrawal, then, actually reduced the size of his underlying problem, at the expense of draining his sources of ready cash. Conversely, customers who rolled over their investments into new Ponzi notes at maturity would be increasing the size of his problem, but not draining cash. This was how the scheme managed to continue rather than collapsing at the first maturity date. Having bought time, Ponzi was as industrious as he was unscrupulous in using it. He set out to try to use his lies and fake assets to take control of some real wealth.

Those who live by the sword tend to die by it. Ponzi's scheme was fated to collapse in the equivalent of a bank run, but while he was operating it he was not averse to using threats of bank runs as a weapon of his own. At the height of his scheme, the Securities Exchange Corporation's cash balances (which were held on hand as short-term bank deposits, ostensibly to keep them ready to pay cash for postal coupons) were a significant percentage of the local money supply in Boston and its surrounding area. For a number of large and important banks, Ponzi's deposits were a greater sum than they could raise at short notice and were essential to their ability to maintain enough liquidity to sustain their operations. This gave him considerable leverage, and he used it.

After buying some small blocks of shares, he threatened

the Hanover Trust Company with an immediate demand for repayment of his deposits, unless the board of directors sold him enough of their own personal shareholdings to make him the majority owner. This left Charles Ponzi in control of a bank, spending about $2m to gain control over several times that much in potential lending resources. He used his new firepower to make bids for other banks and for real estate companies all over Boston, and to bid for the surplus ships of the US Navy. He even started trying to underwrite a bond issue for the Republic of Poland (and, in doing so, spread his sales network into another large ethnic community).

The crash when it came was triggered by Ponzi's first investor (who cannot really be called his first 'victim', as he had long since been paid out). The furniture salesman who accepted Ponzi's note at the beginning had taken notice of the apparently meteoric success which followed, and sued in court over a claim that the initial deal had involved Charles Ponzi selling him a 50 per cent interest in the Securities Exchange Corporation itself. The lawsuit itself was not so much the problem as the interest it stimulated in Ponzi's background, and particularly in the number of times he had been convicted of crimes of dishonesty. He did his best to fight back and defend his reputation, even submitting to public examination by a celebrated psychic to show that his mind contained no hint of turpitude. But the suspicions kept returning. A particular problem for him, of course, was the fact that he could not display records of successful transactions in IRCs because there were none; he had never put the scheme to work. Ponzi tried to bribe officials and used his and the Hanover Trust's deposits as a weapon against the bankers he believed were his enemies. He hired an attorney who was if anything a bigger crook than he was ('Dapper Dan' Coakley, a Boston-Irish political operator). He even attempted to intercept the telegram traffic between Boston and Montreal.

The denouement came just as Charles Ponzi was on the point of another ahead-of-his-time discovery in the world of fraud – he had begun to make loans from the Hanover Trust to his own corporation in order to cover cash demands, anticipating the 'control frauds' (see Chapter 6) of the Savings & Loan crisis by half a century. This, however, raised an alert with the remaining honest employees, and brought the state banking commission into the picture. As an audit report on the SEC came in (the valuation of which was pointlessly disputed by Ponzi), it finally became indisputable that there had never been anything like enough assets to pay the bonds back with 50 per cent interest, and Ponzi was taken away by a US marshal.

Ponzi is ill-served as a fraudster by his eponym. He was a considerably more sophisticated operator than the epigones and wannabes behind most modern 'Ponzi' schemes. He was aware from the earliest stages of his scheme that he was only buying time and was relying on his ability to find another idea, as brilliant as the postal scheme but not as impossible to execute. He was decades ahead of his time in understanding that 'assets controlled' is more important to a wholly dishonest actor than 'assets owned'. But Charles Ponzi is not like Laszlo Biro or Rudolf Diesel; he did not invent the investment scam, or even the idea of targeting affinity groups. In fact, not only was Charles Ponzi not the first Ponzi schemer, he was not even the first Ponzi schemer in the town of Boston. Sarah Howe and her Ladies' Deposit Company, discussed below on p.117, predated him by nearly fifty years. But women never get the credit.

Halfway through the life of his scam, Ponzi might even have been on the way to gaining enough real assets (particularly through the US Navy scheme, where it really looked as if the US government might be selling thousands of ships at a fraction of their true value) to close out at a profit. All he would have needed was for a large proportion of his investors to redeem before maturity and sacrifice their accrued interest. But of course, if they did so, this would increase the demand on his resources of ready cash. And any attempt to alleviate the cash drain by selling more bonds was just increasing the size of the underlying problem. The mathematics of compound interest, particularly at 50 per cent every ninety days, was too much for him. Despite his claims to the contrary, the possibility of escape never looks to have been better than theoretical. And this is the essence of the 'Ponzi scheme' – the single feature that unites all subsequent frauds bearing the name of Charles Ponzi is the attempt to defeat the runaway nature of fraud by raising new money faster than you pay out old.

Pyramid schemes

The modern 'pyramid scheme' is a rough pile of rocks compared to the Venetian palazzo of Ponzi's original template. There is little of the design, hardly any of the flair and a virtual certainty of collapse in the most predictable way possible, rather than Ponzi's elegant dance of risks and intrigue. The only real points of commonality are the tendency toward crass public consumption on the part of the promoters in the interim, and the attraction to affinity groups. Pyramid schemes are so rife among churches in America, for example, that guides to pastors have been published on how to spot one developing in your congregation. These come complete with lists of Biblical references to use in preaching sermons on the illusory nature of promised riches. (Ecclesiastes 4:5, 'Better is it that thou shouldest not vow, than that thou shouldest vow and not pay'.)

In the simplest form, the pyramid scheme operates without any goods changing hands and takes the form of the 'chain letters' which used to circulate through the post and nowadays replicate via email and on Facebook. The 'Infinity Game', for example, was marketed at self-help and New Age seminars in the 1980s. It used an analogy to an aeroplane to explain the financial transactions involved. You have a 'pilot', two 'co-pilots', four 'crew' and eight 'passengers'.* The passengers give $1,500 to the pilot, who then 'pilots-out'. In the next step, the group splits and the two co-pilots are promoted to pilots of the two new 'aeroplanes'. The crew are promoted to co-pilots and divided between the two new pilots, and the passengers are similarly split, promoted to 'crew' and given the job of recruiting passengers to fill out the two new aeroplanes. This keeps on repeating, so someone who joins as a passenger and successfully pilots-out will get a return of $12,000 on their initial $1,500 gift.

---

* Hokey names for the levels of the pyramids tend to be a feature. The 'Original Dinner Party' saw you move from 'salad' to 'dessert'. The 'World of Giving' had 'sowers, gardeners, reapers and harvesters'. In general, the levels ought to be called 'sucker, recruiter, extra degree of separation and fraudster'.

Where does the money come from? Well, it comes from the fact that sooner or later the pool of recruits will be fished out, and some large number of people will send their $1,500 gifts to someone, but have no possibility of recruiting enough 'passengers' to pilot-out themselves. In the Infinity Game, this fact was disguised by encouraging successful 'pilots' to rejoin newly formed planes at the passenger level, but the mathematics is the same – the scheme depends on finding new passengers to get funds in equal to the money taken out by the organisers.

The more people you recruit at every stage, and the more money you charge, the more lucrative the scheme is for the people at the top, but the quicker it will burn out. So you can fine-tune your larceny to try to maximise your profit while minimising the chance of the thing collapsing before you have had time to make an escape – this is a business decision, rather like the choice as to whether to run a 'long' or 'short' firm.

As you can see from the example, involvement in the scheme is inherently self-terminating, which is a good thing from the point of view of the criminal – if the pyramid continues for five or six more iterations after you have cashed out, it may have spread to an entirely different population and the authorities will have a difficult time tracing up through the levels to confirm that the original fraudster was you.

In this form it is an ugly, stupid scheme which attracts some of the least appetising characters in crime. That's because it doesn't work on anyone intelligent enough to think two or three moves into the future, or to understand that the world's population is not infinite. For this reason, pyramid schemes of this sort tend to disproportionately victimise vulnerable people – the Infinity Game was specifically marketed to people who were attending seminars because they felt something missing from their lives, and authorities in the southern states of the USA report that about half their complaints about pyramid schemes come from churches in poor communities.*

A sophistication of the pyramid scam involves bringing a tangible good into the picture. Rather than just making the payments, recruits are encouraged to buy inventory, sell to the public, recruit other salespeople and take 'commissions' on sales made by those they have recruited. This brings some significant advantages to the operation. First, it can obscure the essential nature of a pyramid; people who would immediately spot a 'gifting' pyramid are often less likely to notice the underlying economics if the scheme is dressed up to look like a normal business. There is less of a sense of 'something for nothing', which tends to raise the scepticism of potential recruits.

And second, depending on the product, it raises the possibility of the pyramid becoming a legitimate business. If the recruits are actually selling something valuable to

---

* Not to be too smug though here, reader. 'Women Empowering Women' ran like wildfire through early forms of social media in the 2000s, targeting professional women or those able to start off their pyramid scheme membership with a $5,000 donation. Although poor churchgoers and dementia patients are more frequent victims, no social class or affinity group seems to be immune. As an aside, someone originated Women Empowering Women, and by a quick calculation probably made about half a million dollars from doing so. A bitter congratulations to her; as well as being (most likely) one of a very small number of women among our villains, she is the only fraudster in this book to have escaped detection. Her creation ran away from her and has caused untold misery (and, to be fair, quite a few episodes of five-figure joy) across the developed world.

the general public, it is no longer the case that the scheme requires constant new recruits to keep making payments; in a steady state, it is not as lucrative to the upper levels, but the lower levels do not give their money away for nothing. There are actually some legitimate businesses which recruit their sales force on the basis of their being able to earn 'downline commission'. And this creates a very strange grey area. It can be quite possible for something to exist and operate and for nobody to be quite sure whether it is a pyramid scheme or not.

Of course, legal legitimacy is not everything; for every Tupperware in the world of multilevel sales, there is an Amway – a cleaning products company which has passed every formal investigation and been classed as not a pyramid, but which has still left huge numbers of people (many of whom seem to have started websites) feeling badly treated by the friends and relatives who brought them into the circle. This is one of the nastier properties of both pyramid schemes and legal multilevel marketing companies – because they tend to spread through affinity groups, they can develop an almost cult-like atmosphere, in which belief in the economic validity of the scheme becomes a condition of continued group membership, and unbelievers are 'frozen out'. There are some success stories of multilevel marketing, but in general it does not seem to be a field that attracts many quiet and saintly types.

Getting out of hand

The thing that makes pyramid schemes crash is a crucial feature of any fraud which persists longer than a short-term hit-and-run long firm – they snowball. It's intrinsic to capitalism – money goes into business, and comes out as more money. Then the increased sum is reinvested in business assets, and grows even more. Even a comparatively small positive return will tend to build up over time, like the interest in a bank account. But one key difference between fraudsters and legitimate businesses is that compound interest, the driver of growth and returns for the honest firm, is the enemy of the fraud.

The reason for this is that unlike a genuine business, a fraud does not generate enough real returns to support itself, particularly as money is extracted by the criminal. Because of this, at every date when repayment is expected, the fraudster has to make the choice whether to shut the fraud down and try to make an escape, or to increase its size; more and more money has to be defrauded in order to keep the scheme going as time progresses.

Consider a simple investment fraud, like Ponzi's or the one run by Bernard Madoff, simplifying away all the detail and concentrating on the mathematics of the investment returns. You take in a million dollars from your investors, promising them a return of 25 per cent on their money. Instead, you steal it. A year goes by, and you aim to keep the fraud going by raising new money from another set of mugs. You get a tame accountant to 'verify' that you have made a 25 per cent profit, and armed with these amazing performance figures, you go out on the road to raise … how much?

At the very least, you have to raise $1.25m. You need to pay back your investors not only their original stake, but the fictitious profits which you pretended to earn. And it gets worse. Even presuming you never steal any more, at the end of Year 2, the people who gave you the $1.25m are going to want $1,562,500 back. If you keep going for five years, then your original million-dollar theft will require you to commit just over $3m of new fraud. After a while, the amount of the roll-over will get too big to manage and the fraud will collapse.

Ponzi schemes show this feature of crime most clearly. But a similar problem tends to show up in any kind of fraud which necessitates keeping two sets of books. As soon as money is extracted, there is a gap between the 'real' set of accounts and the 'public' set. This gap needs to be filled by some sort of fakery – either an accounting fiddle or a simple lie that the cash is there when it isn't. And once the gap is there, it will tend to grow. The public books have to keep showing profits and valuable investments, to maintain people's confidence. Meanwhile, the real books are not going to show anything like the same growth, firstly because the true business is nothing like as successful as the fiction, and secondly because valuable cash and goods are being extracted by the fraudster. So the fraud has to get bigger and bigger, just by the passage of time.

If borrowed money is involved, compound interest is often even more important. Loans have monthly payments which need to be made, and you can't pay real debts with fake cash. What often happens is that the fraudster takes out a second loan to make payments on the first. Unfortunately, payments have to be made on the new loan as well as the old one, and although the fake assets are growing at a healthy clip, they're still not generating any real cash. Credit card frauds often spiral in this way – a small fraud against a single lender ends up as a much larger fraud with multiple banks involved. The need to keep up with snowballing loans seems to have been a big part of what drove the team at OPM Leasing further down the slope into criminality than they might necessarily have chosen to go.

This tends to catch out a lot of amateurs and first-time criminals. A shoplifter or robber can carry out one or two thefts and then take a break; avoiding capture for a blue-collar criminal is just a matter of trying not to be the person who is connected to the crime. An embezzler, though, or a rogue trader or a tax swindler, has to cover up the existence of the crime itself. That means that it's very difficult to be a one-time-only embezzler. The original crime creates an ongoing need to commit a series of further crimes, usually growing in magnitude. Small-time white-collar criminals often burst into tears of relief when they are finally captured. As Leslie Payne put it:

> Often these businesses, run by people of rare energy and intelligence, could have been very successful. There is nothing sadder in some ways than the managers of a fraudulent firm who then find they have a commercial success on their hands. They try desperately to repay their first plunderings, but the canker in the rose spreads inexorably and eats it all up.

One way to close the gap, by the way, is to take big risks with the money which hasn't been stolen yet. This is how 'rogue' traders like Nick Leeson tend to expand their concealed losses to levels that blow up banks. But it's by no means unknown for even a small-time embezzler to take the float of company cash to a racetrack or casino in a last desperate gamble for redemption.

But if compound growth is such a killer, how do frauds keep going for so long? The need to manage the snowball effect is one of the biggest problems facing a fraudster with ambitions to steal a lot or keep going for longer than a single billing cycle. If you want to steal a lot of money, you have to keep the fraud going. You also have to keep the fraud going if you haven't figured out your escape route yet, or if you just blundered into it and don't have a plan at all. But while the fraud is going, it has to be growing; the returns and repayments you owe to other people are growing at a compound rate of return, so you have to commit ever-increasing amounts of new fraud to stand still. This snowball property is the main challenge in managing an ongoing fraud.

The Pigeon King

Modern versions of Ponzi's scheme tend to follow him in trying to avoid dealing with even lightly regulated markets. One of Ponzi's highest priorities from the start of the scheme was to be sure that his dealings in postal reply coupons were not covered by the Commonwealth of Massachussetts' 'blue-sky laws', which had been enacted to regulate the activities of stock promoters who would 'sell shares in the blue sky' unless prevented from doing so. Later generations of crooks would follow Ponzi's example in working with assets not covered by financial regulation, for two good reasons. First, there is less constraint on one's marketing material, so one's sales patter can be utterly shameless. And second, one is not exposed to the quite draconian and arbitrary powers usually exercised by securities regulators to shut down investment schemes for any one of dozens of technical breaches or audit failures. If a fraud is operating outside the regulated sphere, it can only be dealt with by the authorities *as a fraud* (rather than merely as a lousy or Mittyish investment scheme), and unless the scheme is blatant, it is usually difficult to assemble this kind of proof until after it has collapsed.

A particularly intriguing species of modern Ponzi scheme involves investment in agriculture or livestock. Living creatures – particularly birds with relatively short breeding cycles – fit a number of uses for the aspiring Ponzi schemer, because while their sale, even for speculative purposes, is largely unregulated, their tendency to breed can form a putative basis for the kind of high double-digit percentage returns which get investors dreaming of yachts and sunny islands, and help people to turn off their critical faculties.

It is a fact, for example, that a breeding pair of racing pigeons will typically lay two eggs in a clutch, and that with reasonable luck and diligence in care, the owner might reasonably expect to get a further breeding pair within a year. This could be described as a 100 per cent return on the initial investment, presuming that one was able to sell the new racing pigeons for roughly the same price that one bought the original breeding pair.

Some people earn a living like this, although readers who follow the society pages will be aware that there are no racing pigeon billionaires and quite likely no racing pigeon millionaires either. So we can be pretty sure that nobody has ever started with a $30,000 investment in racing pigeons and earned a compound return of 100 per cent on it for fifteen years. The problem is that the global market for racing pigeons is modestly sized and barely grows from one year to another. But it is true that, for very small investments and without unlimited compounding, breeding pigeons can have a high percentage return.

It was this failure to understand that investment returns do not necessarily compound and that market size can be limited which was the undoing for the victims of Arlan Galbraith, the 'Pigeon King' of Canada. A former farmer who had gone bankrupt in the 1990s, he travelled the farming communities in Canada (and in the USA, until the Iowa State Attorney General started asking questions), extolling the virtues of his 'Strathclyde Genetics' breeding program and encouraging people to take out loans of $100,000 and more to buy breeding pigeons from him at around $165 a pair. This seemed like a low-risk proposition to the buyers, because Galbraith committed to buy all the offspring for the next ten years at the same price he sold the original birds for. People mortgaged their farms and gave up their second jobs.

And for years, it worked. In the early days, Arlan's 'Pigeon King International' corporation allowed people to believe that the number of breeders would be limited to a few dozen (as it would have to be, if they were being sold to the racing market*). This promise was soon dropped, however, and replaced with a lot of marketing material (there was a picture of noted pigeon-fancier Mike Tyson cuddling one of Arlan's birds on the website), and with the basic machinery of a Ponzi scheme: namely, an aggressive, highly motivated

---

* There was never any chance of this, by the way. The 'Strathclyde' genetic line was regarded as a joke in pigeon-racing circles. Galbraith's top salesman later turned against him and served as a prosecution witness, the trigger being a chance encounter with a group of racing-pigeon enthusiasts who had never heard of Pigeon King International.

sales force. The Pigeon King himself never let anyone in on the secret of where he was selling the pigeons, hinting at Middle Eastern syndicates and impressing on the breeders that his personal knowledge of the world pigeon market was the key to his success. In actual fact, the birds were being bought from the breeders and more or less immediately sold to new investors.

For several years, crazily, there was actually a waiting list to join the pigeon scam – the sales force was much more productive than the birds. But a breeding population of pigeons grows at an exponential rate, so there would always be a glut in the end. In about 2008, with sales down thanks to the US authorities and some bad publicity in *Better Farming* magazine, it all started to fall apart. Galbraith started failing to buy birds. His company made a 'pivot' to producing meat from the pigeons* and told the breeders that they were building a processing plant. And finally, under pressure from the bookkeepers, Pigeon King International sent out a letter informing everyone that it was bust – no further pigeons would be bought and the dream was over.

The Canadian Pigeon Scam is a good example of how the Ponzi schemer benefits from promising his victims that it will always be possible to redeem the investment for cash. Fewer people would have thought that it was a good idea to get into pigeon breeding as a business if they had not been reassured that Arlan Galbraith would handle the marketing for them, and during the initial stages, the steady cash flows back to the earlier investors reinforced public confidence in the Pigeon

---

* Also useless; having been bred (incompetently) for racing, they were too small.

King and supported the sales force in their task of recruiting the final tier who would take the total loss.

Some of the initial investors actually did as well as or better than Arlan Galbraith himself. By the time the scam collapsed, he had taken in around $42m from investors, but had paid $30m of it back out to breeders, leaving only $12m stolen. In order to do that, of course, he had to create much larger liabilities in the form of promises to buy future pigeons – the amount written off in bankruptcy was slightly more than $350m, giving a ratio of less than 5 per cent theft to more than 95 per cent hot air and pigeon shit. The sentencing was for the most part based on the higher figure, but the true loss to the victims is closer to the lower one.

And even from the lower figure, the Pigeon King did not take it all. Salespeople's commissions were between 10 per cent and 20 per cent of the gross, accounting for as much as $6m of the total amount stolen, and Pigeon King International was a substantial business with sheds, vans and employees whose only contribution to the fraud was the honest shovelling of guano. At the height of his success, Galbraith paid himself a salary of $400,000: good money for a former bankrupt farmer but hardly the dreams of avarice. The real benefit to him from this bizarre fraud was that he was able to be the Pigeon King for ten years, devoting himself to his eccentric theories about their breeding. Whatever Arlan Galbraith's faults, he did genuinely love pigeons. Which makes it something of a shame that as a direct result of his deception, as well as losing their houses and farms, the bankrupt investors ended up having to gas or strangle as many as 175,000 birds.

Pigeon King International had no control over 'redemptions' – it had to come up with the money at a pace determined by the fecundity of its pigeons. So it attempted to manage its snowball by very aggressive sales practices. This isn't the best way of doing things. In an investment scam, history has shown us that you are better off doing what you can to manage the outflows directly. If people hardly ever take the money out of your scam, you're home free. For a while, anyway. Which brings us to:

Hedge fund fraud

The name synonymous with hedge fund fraud in the twenty-first century is Bernard Madoff. Bernie played a very long game, typically promising returns of only 8–12 per cent to his investors rather than the spectacular numbers usually associated with a Ponzi scheme. But it was this careful management which motivated his investors to keep their money with him, rather than withdrawing it; his fund never had the volatile ups and downs which drive redemptions. Ironically, though, because of the way compound interest works, the fact that the scheme went on so long meant that the fiction ended up being truly immense. In order to misappropriate a sum which could not have been more than a few hundred million dollars, Madoff ended up taking in $20bn of cash and inflating it to $65bn of fictitious assets, meaning that the ratio of nonsense to theft was well above 99 per cent.

Or at least it was if we assume that the only money stolen was that stolen by Madoff himself, and that all the investors in his fund – even the 'net winners' who invested early, withdrew late and therefore took out 'profits' several multiples of their initial investment – were victims rather than conspirators. There is no particular reason to suspect otherwise, we should emphasise, but many of the repayments made by Madoff in the last year of his operation (which total $13bn, a large sum relative to the cash invested), might be regarded by the courts as 'fraudulent conveyances',* and are currently the subject of litigation as to whether they need to be handed back to the bankruptcy trustee.

Madoff, however, was not the first big hedge fund collapse of the financial crisis era, and he was not the most interesting one, so we're going to focus on someone else. One of the reasons why Madoff's redemptions loomed so large in the financial crisis was that investors had suddenly become scared of secretive funds with unusually consistent returns and small or obscure firms of accountants as their auditors. This fear arose in the aftermath of the collapse of Bayou Capital in 2005. Bayou anticipated almost all the problems of Madoff – and provides a clear insight into the central issue of redemption management and the unique characteristics of a hedge fund Ponzi scheme. It also reads as if a Hollywood studio had commissioned a script for 'The Bernard Madoff Story', then handed it to Quentin Tarantino with instructions to punch it up a bit.

Bayou Capital

Sam Israel had always been a devout believer in the possibility of easy money. As a stock trader specialising in short-term

---

* This legal term generated predictable outrage among the people being sued, but it does not carry any implication that the lucky Madoff investors were in on the fraud. The word 'fraudulent' refers to Madoff himself – the payments out of the fund were 'conveyances' made by the fraudster, to keep his fraud going. Nonetheless, bankruptcy law often allows for the clock to be turned back on this kind of payment in the interest of overall fairness.

and opportunistic speculative ideas, he had been apprenticed to some of the most legendary names on Wall Street and had learned exactly the wrong lessons from all of them. As he started out with his own new hedge fund, Sam planned to make profits from two main sources. First, a computer program of his own devising called 'Forward Propagation', which aimed to forecast share prices using patterns from historic price charts. And second, a diligent search for corporate insiders to bribe for inside information.

Despite this ostensibly attractive value proposition (and despite his own family background from New Orleans commodity trading royalty), Sam found it extremely difficult to raise money. When Bayou Capital launched, it only had $600,000 under management, charging a small fixed management fee and a royalty of 20 per cent on trading gains. This was not enough money to pay the rent on a fancy office (or indeed any office at all), and it was difficult to impress potential investors while trading out of Sam's basement.

In order to attract more money to manage, Bayou needed to show trading profits. In the first year of its existence, it achieved this by dodgy if not wholly illegal means – the returns were increased because Sam agreed to rebate all the trading commissions which the hedge fund had paid to a brokerage which he also owned. Persuading the fund's auditors (at the time, Grant Thornton) to agree to this aggressive accounting treatment took time and money; investors were not impressed that the audited returns were filed two months late and Sam Israel was not impressed with the fact that he was charged $50,000 for the privilege. For the second year, he was determined to find an audit firm that was both cheaper and easier to push around.

And so it was that Bayou Capital came to be audited by 'Richmond-Fairfield'. This was a smaller audit partnership. In fact, it was not so much 'smaller' as 'completely fictitious'. There was no such firm; it was purely a creation of Dan Marino,* the down-on-his-luck accountant who Sam had hired to be the fund's chief operating officer. This obviously cut down on expenses, but it also allowed Sam and Dan to improve their results in the second and subsequent years of trading by the simple expedient of lying about them.

In order to create fake returns in an audited set of hedge fund accounts, though, you need to be able to answer the question 'Where's the money then?'. Dan Marino's solution to this problem represents his major intellectual contribution to the history of crime. It comes in two parts; the second is considerably more impressive than the first.

The first part of the Bayou fraud was an unsophisticated and risky lie. In order to make the books balance – to create an asset which corresponded to the fake element of the returns – Marino started to include an item titled 'Due from Brokers' in the balance sheet. Normally, this ought to be only a small amount, reflecting trades which happened to be halfway through the settlement† process on the day on which

---

* In this age of ubiquitous and permanent internet records, it may come to be a massive asset to a fraudster to have the same name as someone so much more famous than you that it's almost impossible to check you out. This Dan Marino is no relation to the iconic Miami Dolphins quarterback.

† 'Settlement'. The process of checking the trade's paperwork, updating the shareholders' registers and sending the payments from the buyer's bank account to the seller's. The sort of thing which people, even very experienced traders and investors, don't tend to think about. People outside the market would presume that this happens instantaneously and

the books were closed. In Bayou's accounts it spiralled into the hundreds of millions.

This was a very risky lie to tell, not only because the 'Due from Brokers' balance would immediately set off red flags to anyone who looked over the accounts with anything other than a cursory glance, but because it obviously implied the existence of a similar-sized item 'Due to Bayou Capital' in the accounts of the brokers. And the accounts had to be sent to Bayou's main broker, SLK Securities, among other parties. Marino dealt with the problem by sending the accounts late on a Friday, on the assumption that by Monday morning they would be buried under a pile of stuff that arrived over the weekend and would never get any real scrutiny. This shows a pretty good understanding of the brokerage business.*

The second of Marino's insights, however, was a work of genius. A fraudulent hedge fund, unlike traditional Ponzi schemes, could go on indefinitely. The mechanics of a Ponzi scheme work by using new inflows to cover investor withdrawals, and since the returns promised to investors compound over time, the fraud needs to keep finding new

---

auto-magically over big sophisticated computers and tend to be surprised and appalled when they find out the extent to which it doesn't. Actually, things have got a lot better since 2008, but that only means that if you wanted to carry out this sort of fraud today, you'd have to do it in emerging markets or in credit derivatives or some other market with less efficient settlement systems than the New York Stock Exchange. Things tend to improve in settlement systems one megafraud at a time.

* You might have thought the broker would have more of an obligation to check up on things. Maybe they do, maybe they don't. Rather than take the matter to court, SLK paid $26m in an arbitration agreement.

victims at an ever increasing rate. But what if there aren't any withdrawals? A hedge fund with good (reported) performance won't get many requests from investors for their money back – they want to keep it in the fund if it's doing well. Ponzi's scheme fell apart because of the redemption dates for his 'notes' and the Pigeon King scheme fell apart when cash ran out to buy birds as they hatched. But a hedge fund investment account has no set maturity date.

Sam Israel also knew enough about the high-net-worth investing game to select the right kinds of investors – mainly overworked institutional investors operating with other peoples' money and a defined series of checks, all of which were based off analysis of the 'audited' accounts. As far as possible he avoided taking money from wealthy individuals, because they tended to have sons and daughters with too much time on their hands who might make site visits or ask questions around Wall Street.

Bayou Capital continued to grow. It survived 9/11, although Dan Marino begged Sam to simply use the World Trade Center attacks and the associated market dislocation as an excuse to declare huge losses and close the fund. It survived a detailed inquiry after the SEC demanded comprehensive trading records. (They were looking for evidence of overcharging clients for trading commissions, and never checked to see if the trades in question added up to the reported cumulative performance.) The gap between the actual trading returns and those reported to the investors grew and grew. In the end, what killed it was Sam Israel's own obsession with the easy buck.

In the hope of closing the gap, he attempted to buy an illegal copy of a CIA computer program that was said to monitor all bank transactions everywhere in the world and would allow Bayou Capital to stay one step ahead of the Federal Reserve. There is, of course, no such computer program. This set off the second phase of the collapse of Bayou Capital, in which things took a turn that is less directly relevant to the economic analysis of crime, but bizarre and (grimly) amusing enough to be worth summarising. (It's worth remembering, to temper the rising sense of incredulity, that during the episodes that followed, Sam Israel was taking an awful lot of drugs.)

The man from whom Sam Israel wanted to buy the computer program was Robert Booth Nichols, who represented himself as a top-level CIA assassin familiar with the secret government of the world, but who others have suggested is a serial con man and Walter Mitty figure. (A quick review of the history of US intelligence organisations will confirm that there is no necessary contradiction between these two descriptions.) Over a series of meetings with Nichols, all of which were heavily accompanied by spy-thriller staging and theatrics, Sam was convinced that the secret computer program was small beer, and that Nichols could make real money by introducing Bayou Capital to the lucrative market for 'prime bank securities'. What's that, you say? I'm so glad you asked.

The market for 'prime bank securities' (also known as 'prime bank guarantees', 'prime bank high yield instruments', etc.) is a global fraud category based on, and symbiotically related to, the conspiracy theory that the Federal Reserve is bankrupt, that government-backed money has been intrinsically worthless since the collapse of the Gold Standard, and that as a result the Fed is beholden to and controlled by a small number of wealthy families.* This relatively commonplace conspiracy theory is extended to a belief that the way central banks manipulate the money supply is by selling bonds to 'prime banks', in denominations of billions of dollars at a fraction of their true worth, creating an opportunity to make huge returns for anyone lucky enough to be admitted to this incredibly lucrative private market.

Analytically, this is hardly even a commercial fraud – it's a simple con game, based on looking for a very rich and greedy person, charging them a huge commission or finder's fee to get them 'access' to the secret market, then putting them off with excuses for a while until you can arrange a pretext to disappear.† What makes it interesting is that there is, as far as experts can tell, a global community of prime bank fraudsters, many of whom appear to genuinely believe in the market and who seem to spend most of their time taking commissions from, and making excuses to, each other while believing that one day they will be let into the inner sanctum of the *real* 'dark market'. Robert Nichols appears to have spent a lot

---

*Families like the Rothschilds, Goldmans, etc., usually with a few Anglo-Saxon and Chinese names thrown in to try and make the whole thing look less obviously anti-Semitic. The number of families is typically thirteen, with variance about five in either direction. Optional bolt-on conspiracy theories regarding descent from lizards, construction of the Pyramids, responsibility for the Second World War and so on, but these are usually left out by people hoping to make money directly (rather than through book sales or podcast subscriptions) out of the conspiracy.

† Having a mysterious and scary backstory to do with secret organisations helps with this. Sam Israel believes himself to have shot an attempted assassin who attacked him when he fell out with Nichols, although no body has ever been found, no police record indicates anything of the sort and his biographer definitely believes the event was staged.

of his commission from Sam Israel on investments in prime bank securities and related projects,* and he passed Bayou on to a number of other corrupt individuals making similar promises. So what we have here is a fraud investing in a fraud, which then took their money and invested it in a fraud.

Sam Israel's story ended in a faked suicide, a short period as a fugitive and a long prison sentence, which he is currently serving. Bayou Capital's story, however, ends in a way which is certainly ironic and possibly even a little optimistic. Robert Nichols and the prime bank fraud community had a piece of bad luck in that they introduced Sam Israel – and a number of other wealthy individuals – to an honest brokerage in London, in the belief that they would be able to take it over and corrupt it. This turned out not to be the case; the settlement staff at ODL Securities were meticulous in checking securities identification numbers and the chief executive was adamant under pressure in refusing to make bank transfers when the transactions could not be confirmed.†

---

* 'Related projects' in this case being treasure-hunting expeditions for an alleged cache of US Treasury bonds originally sent to finance Chiang Kai-shek and lost somewhere in Southeast Asia. Frauds based on the existence of this cache and of 'Yamashita's gold' have considerable overlap with the prime bank community, and indeed they played a cameo role in the swan-dive phase of Bayou Capital, but now we are several digressions deep and really need to get back to the important points. A few references are in the bibliography but please, don't bother – the further you go down this rabbit hole the more confusing and annoying it becomes, plus there is always the danger of convincing yourself there's something to it, which would be an expensive error to make. Even the books are overpriced.

† No good deed goes unpunished; ODL had reason to regret ever meeting these clients, as a ream of their headed notepaper took a holiday, and spent the next few years showing up in other people's frauds.

The money that Sam transferred to his prime bank scheme actually spent most of 2004–5 sitting in a blocked account in London, while the staff of Bayou Capital effectively did nothing and Sam Israel got increasingly angry. Finally, ODL ran out of reasons to refuse Sam Israel access to his fund's money, and transferred it on his instruction to an account controlled by a fraudster who was promising to sell Bayou a gold mine worth $152bn in Arizona. In a farcical final coincidence, however, this transaction alerted the Arizona State Attorney General's office, one of the employees of which had a hobby as the US law enforcement community's most notable expert on prime bank investment scams. By pure luck, $100m of the $450m that investors had subscribed to Bayou Capital was saved (although this may not have been much comfort to them given that they believed they had $7.1bn based on Dan Marino's faked accounting statements).

So ended the farce of Bayou Capital, just in time for the beginning of the Bernard Madoff saga, which was similar in its broad analytical structure, bigger in size but much duller in its plot details. Madoff also had a sidekick; his Dan Marino figure was Frank DiPascali, a wizard at forging trading reports. Before we move on, it's worth taking a moment to understand why these Sancho Panzas are as vital to the big ticket fraud as the Don Quixote.

Circles of trust

The value of a crooked auditor is that he can sign off on a crooked set of accounts. All accountants (like Dan Marino in the Bayou Capital scandal) can also provide useful technical advice on how to hide your theft by creating difficult-to-check receivables balances to disguise the withdrawals. But an experienced fraudster is usually capable of working out that sort of thing for himself. What you can't do for yourself is create a valid set of audited accounts to present to investors, creditors and the general public.

The professional qualifications and memberships of lawyers, accountants and actuaries give them a special status in the business world. Certain kinds of documents are only valid with an accountant's seal of approval, and once they have gained this seal of validity, they are taken as 'audited accounts' which are much less likely to be subjected to additional verification or checking. Similarly, a document drafted by a qualified lawyer and stamped by a notary is more likely to be presumed valid than one drafted by a layman, even on matters where technical legal expertise is less relevant than simple checking of facts (like, for example, whether the person selling a piece of land is actually the owner).

What is going on here, of course, is that these professions are considered to be circles of trust. The idea is partly that the long training and apprenticeship processes of the professions ought to develop values of trust and honesty, and weed out candidates who do not possess them. And it is partly that professional status is a valuable asset for the person who possesses it, which can be taken away with a stroke of the pen by a disciplinary tribunal. So the sum of money needed to corrupt a professional is significantly larger than that needed to corrupt a layman; as well as compensating for the risk of being caught and paying the normal penalty, a professional needs to be compensated for the risk of losing his or her professional status, and the lifetime stream of earnings which would otherwise derive from it. If we presume that the premium earned by someone with a professional qualification over the same person without that status is in the order of tens of thousands, and that the duration of a professional career is around twenty-five years, it is not difficult to see that the majority of lawyers and accountants, even if they have no moral sense at all and are looking for opportunities for corruption, are not necessarily going to find it worth their while to get involved in a fraud in which their share of the proceeds is less than about a million dollars.

In the Bayou Capital case, not only was the information available to check up on Sam Israel, it was actually put into the hands of people who had both the ability and the incentive to do so. Dan Marino gave the entire record of Bayou's trades to the SEC to go through to look for commission overcharging. This record of trades, if someone had gone through it adding up the individual profits and losses, would have shown that the aggregate results were obviously being falsified. Even more simply, the clearing brokers at SLK were given a set of accounts which showed a large number for 'Balance Due from Brokers', which was obviously hundreds of millions larger than any amount they could have owed. If anyone had checked, they would have seen.

But why would you check, if you had the audited accounts? This would be a weird thing to do. Marino maximised his chances with SLK by sending them the faked accounts late on a Friday, in the (correct) belief that they would go to the bottom of an in-tray and be swamped with new mail on Monday morning. It was a risk. But this was a high-percentage strategy, simply because these 'obvious' checks are the sort of thing that you would only do if you already had a strong reason for suspicion. It would be utterly unfeasible to exercise that level of scrutiny on every single hedge fund; you would be employing a tower block full of accountants, the majority of whom would spend every working day finding out that accounts had been filed correctly and filing null returns. If you wanted to catch Sam Israel, you would have done better to keep an ear out for gossip about his drug and alcohol problems, which might have given you a short* list of people who should be subjected to extra scrutiny.

Another way into the circle of trust, of course, is through an affinity group, as we saw with pyramid schemes. In principle, the economics of this ought to work; the more socially connected you are to a person, the more interests and ties you share, and the more costly it would be for that person to rip you off. This is how the Greek side of the 'Canadian Paradox' works; as well as doing deals with handshakes over brandy, Greek shipowners know each other well, see each other every day and marry into one another's families. If one of them were to treat another one sufficiently badly, he would lose his business career and social life all at a stroke. The danger arises because people can identify with affinity groups even when the actual commonality of interest is pretty weak. There was no real reason for Boston's Italians to trust Charles Ponzi just because of his second name. And although the widows and spinsters of Boston might have identified with Sarah Howe, they really had nothing in common with her but their marital status and gender. That certainly wasn't enough to protect them from her. But it might have given her a useful insight into them.

---

* Not necessarily that short, to be honest. The threshold of seriousness for a coke habit would have to be pretty high to cut down the list of potentially problematic hedge fund traders.

The Boston Ladies' Deposit Company

'Unprotected females' had quite a difficult time of it in 1878. By owning property in their own right rather than through their husbands, they were unusual and vulnerable, particularly if they had been brought up to be 'provided for' rather than to work for a living. It was possible to live off an inheritance or a capital sum, but usually not to live well, and if you used the interest on your savings to live on, you would have a fixed income in a period of modest but meaningful inflation. This meant that a woman in this position would tend to find it difficult to maintain her social standing if she stuck to safe investments, and any unforeseen expenses might see her having to 'dip into capital', and sacrifice permanently a proportion of her future income.*

For this reason, widows and spinsters tended to be surprisingly willing to make risky investments in search of a higher dividend. The shares of a newly floated railway company† might rise or fall, but the 'prudent' investments recommended by lawyers and bankers would deliver the eventual certainty of having to work as a governess. In the reams of Victorian melodramas of evil deceit on the Stock

---

* The thrift of Bostonians was the subject of a bawdy joke of the late nineteenth century in which Maud meets Sally walking through an ill-reputed area of town, the punchline of which is 'My dear, it was this or dip into capital!'.

† Or something even more romantic. In the early chapters of *Moby-Dick* it is noted that the ownership structure of the *Pequod* includes 'a crowd of old annuitants; widows, fatherless children and chancery wards, each owning about the value of a timber head, or a foot of plank or a nail or two'. German ladies of the same class might aspire to own 'a little factory' as a dowry or to provide pin money.

Exchange, the villain's perfidy is generally underlined by the high proportion of helpless women in his investor base; the ladies might not have been quite as financially innocent as it suited the authors to paint them, but they were real and they were not always risk averse.

But who would resist an offer for a safe investment that paid 8 per cent per month, promising an annual income of $96 for every $100 deposited? How about if it gave you the first three months' interest payment in advance? When Sarah Howe opened the Ladies' Deposit Company in 1878, she created a stir pretty quickly.

Ms Howe allowed it to be suggested, without necessarily saying so herself, that her bank was in fact backed by a Quaker charity, dedicated to the promotion of thrift and the protection of virtue, and that for this reason it had to place certain restrictions. The depositors had to be unmarried women, and they had to agree only to withdraw the interest proportion of their savings.* The Ladies' Deposit quickly grew by referrals (for which Ms Howe paid $5 each to her customers), and quickly attracted an investor base which included women of all classes, with maids and shopkeepers lining up to deposit their few dollars alongside rich widows investing their whole capital sum.

Because there was no cover story about postal coupons or anything similar, it was not difficult to work out that this

---

*In other words, there was to be no 'dipping into capital'. Bostonians really had a thing about that. But of course, at that rate of interest, the 'capital' proportion of any given account would be modest relative to the accrued interest after even a couple of years, so this was less of a protection against a run on the bank than one might think.

was a scam. A letter to the *Boston Daily Advertiser* entitled 'Ladies' Deposit Banking – How it is Supposed To Work' explained what Sarah Howe was doing, complete with diagrams and a (correct) prediction that the potential investor base would be mined out and the scheme would collapse in approximately three years. Spurred by its readers, the *Daily Advertiser* investigated Sarah Howe's background, and began to ask questions about why what would have to be one of the biggest charities in the USA would have appointed a fortune teller and stage psychic to be the manager of their financial scheme.

Faced with the bad publicity, Sarah announced that, to prove the doubters wrong, she would change the rules and allow anyone who felt dissatisfied to withdraw their entire capital sum as well as accrued interest. This ended up being a bad miscalculation; she had nowhere near enough ready cash and the Ladies' Deposit Company declared bankruptcy. Inevitably, Sarah Howe went to prison; somewhat more unaccountably she came back and executed the exact same scam again (the Boston Women's Bank, 1884). One cannot say she had learned nothing though; when the *Daily Advertiser* in 1887 exposed the fact that the Women's Bank was being managed not by Mrs J. C. Ewell but by Sarah Howe, she had the sense to skip town rather than waiting for the collapse. She reached Chicago with $50,000 of investors' money and might have got away with it if she had not attempted to open the Ladies' Provident Aid Society there. When she got out of jail in 1889, she went back to the fortune telling.

4
COUNTERFEITS

'The habit does not make the monk.'

François Rabelais

The Portuguese Banknote Affair

When one thinks of counterfeiting, the first commodity that comes to mind is banknotes, with designer jeans possibly a distant second. What exactly is the nature of the deceit when counterfeit money is created and passed? The important thing is not the simulation of a physical object;* it's the claim that it is an 'authentic' product. An exact copy of a Van Gogh painting would still be a fake if you claimed that it was by Van Gogh, and a pair of Lacoste jeans are still deemed to be 'counterfeit' even if they have been run off from the same cloth and patterns and by the same workers in a subcontractor's factory.

Similarly, even a perfect forgery of a banknote produced on the monetary authority's own presses would still be a forgery, if it hadn't been produced with the permission of the central bank in question. This has actually happened on a few occasions, most notably in one of the most macroeconomically

---

* Unlike in a case of software piracy or patent infringement, where the crime is the copying itself.

and politically significant frauds ever. This was the Portuguese Banknote Affair of 1925, the culmination of the short but insanely ambitious career of Artur Virgílio Alves dos Reis.

Both Alves Reis and the country of Portugal were in tough economic straits at the beginning of the Roaring Twenties. Portugal had resorted to printing money to finance its government deficit after the Great War, and had changed the constitution of the Bank of Portugal to make this possible. The Bank of Portugal, for its part, had not been able to keep up with investment in modern anti-counterfeiting technology (like serial numbers) and had outsourced its production to the English firm of Waterlow & Sons.* Artur, on the other hand, had been forced to seek his fortune in Angola after his family's fortune had been lost.

He decided to take a Portuguese university diploma, copy it, attribute it to the 'Oxford University Polytechnic School of Engineering' and give himself qualifications in engineering, geology, geometry, physics, metallurgy, mathematics, palaeography, chemistry, mechanics and civil design. As well as teaching him that Portuguese notaries would stamp anything, this helped him get a job as chief engineer of Angola's railway system. Despite the fact that his degree was a fake, Alves Reis managed to teach himself enough engineering on the job to avoid disaster, and returned to his homeland in 1923 with a little money of his own and a good reputation.

Neither lasted long. He had ambitions to enter the world

---

* Banknote printing was, and still is, a competitive game. Waterlow & Sons had been around since 1810, but had missed out on the contract to print Bank of Poyais notes, which went to Perkins, Bacon & Co.

of high finance, but the way he went about a hostile takeover of a company called Ambaca led instead to the world of jail. While inside, he concentrated on reading improving books – not the Bible or Shakespeare, but the statutes relating to the Bank of Portugal.

A number of features of the 1920s Portuguese monetary system came together to create the conditions for what happened next. First, the Bank of Portugal, despite having the monopoly on printing escudo banknotes, was a private company with shareholders (this was not unusual; so was the Bank of England until it was nationalised in 1945, and the Federal Reserve still nominally is*). Second, the currency used in Angola was the Angolan escudo, worth one-tenth of a Portuguese escudo. But the Angolan escudo banknotes were simply escudo notes, with the word 'ANGOLA' overstamped on them. Fourth, there was no systematic checking of the serial numbers of escudo notes in circulation. And finally, the Portuguese government and the Bank of Portugal were in the habit of occasionally authorising 'secret' issues of banknotes for purposes they felt would be politically unpopular.

When combined with the fact that Artur already knew – that Portuguese notaries of the day would stamp nearly anything – these facts could be put together to form a plan. He forged a contract, on a reasonable simulacrum of government letterhead, and had it notarised four or five

---

* Nominally! The regional feds are owned by the banks in their area, and sometimes pay dividends out of the interest income they earn on various deposits required by the payment system. The shareholders have no rights of control any more, though. Do not think on this subject too hard – a morbid interest in the technical workings of the Fed is often an early symptom of being a victim of prime bank guarantee fraud.

times. This contract said, in summary, that the Governor of
the Bank of Portugal had deputised Artur Alves dos Reis
to put together a syndicate of investors to make a loan to
Angola, with the investors to be compensated by being given
the right to print the equivalent of $5m in Angolan escudos.
He took his fake contract to the Portuguese minister to the
Netherlands, explaining that the Angola loan was a secret,
that the governor didn't want his shareholders to know about
it, and that for this reason, Artur needed some friends with
money and official Portuguese letterhead who could help him
get the notes printed. By luck or design, the minister was a
crook anyway, so whether he was convinced by the story or
by the promised commissions, he assembled a consortium.

This consortium approached Sir William Waterlow, whose
suspicions were immediately raised. For such a transaction,
he would obviously need the personal authorisation of the
Governor of the Bank of Portugal. Unaccountably, though,
rather than contacting the Bank of Portugal himself, Waterlow
asked the consortium to provide him with a personal letter.
Back it came – another Alves Reis forgery.* Finally, there was
the issue of serial numbers.

Artur had persuaded his backers to make him a large cash
advance, so that he could go through dozens of 500-escudo
notes and reverse-engineer the format of Portuguese bank
note serial numbers. He did a pretty good job, but was
unlucky in not having a copy of the master list of serial
numbers which was kept by Waterlow & Sons. Some of the

---

* Central bank governors' signatures are not all that difficult to forge,
because there tends to be a good-quality example on every banknote in
circulation. Arturo used a pantograph to make it a bit bigger.

numbers he requested would already be in use. But he thought quickly; since these notes would only circulate in Angola, this was not a problem! Waterlow accepted this excuse and got on with printing. Of course, Alves Reis had no intention at all of stamping his notes and decimating their value; he relied on the lack of systematic checking to ensure that duplicates would not be detected.

As the notes were sent back to Lisbon and spent (introducing them to the system via a small army of back-street money changers, known as 'zangoes', or 'drones'), all hell broke loose. The sum of counterfeit money totalled slightly less than 1 per cent of Portuguese GDP. There was a mini-boom. The members of Alves Reis' syndicate never seemed to ask why the loan to Angola didn't happen, but they were happy enough when the banknotes were split four ways. And Alves Reis went on to even greater ideas.

Recall that the Bank of Portugal was the only entity that would be in a position to check up on fake banknotes. And that it was a private company with shareholders. And Artur Alves dos Reis was now a man with his own bank (the Bank of Angola and Metropole, founded with fake money) and sudden unbelievable riches. It was almost the logical thing to do – try to take over control of the Bank of Portugal's shares and become its governor, thus ensuring that the fraud could never be detected.

Obviously this sort of thing leads to gossip. The Bank of Portugal was doing its best to quell rumours of its own – the sudden explosion of activity among the drones had immediately caused people to think the country was being flooded with forged notes, possibly as an act of foreign aggression. The Bank of Portugal, though, wanted to maintain confidence in the currency, and so kept testing for suspect notes, naturally finding that all of the notes in circulation in Lisbon were genuine stock, printed in England by Waterlow & Sons.

It was pure coincidence that the scam was found out. Hostile rumours were spread in the newspapers about the Bank of Angola and Metropole by people who feared its bid for the central bank. Media pressure then forced the authorities to inspect the notes in Artur's vaults. While confirming them to be genuine, the inspector happened to find two notes with the same serial numbers – a genuine one had been stacked next to its twin. Once he knew what to look for, it was not too difficult to find more pairs. Alves Reis was off to prison, where this time he did start reading the Bible.

Inflation took off as confidence in the currency slumped. The Bank of Portugal ended up having to recall all 500-escudo notes and swap them for 1,000-escudo notes. The army staged a coup, and brought in the 'Estado Novo' dictatorship which ruled Portugal until 1974. For most of this time, the country was ruled by an economics professor, Antonio Salazar, who must have occasionally pondered the series of events that brought him to power.

The Portuguese Bank Note Affair remains one of the most tragic cases in which the weak link in a high-trust society (in this case, notaries) ended up pulling down the whole structure of trust itself. In 1955, Alves dos Reis got an obituary in *The Economist* saying that his scheme had been good for Portugal on Keynesian principles, which probably ranks as one of the stupidest things that newspaper has ever printed.

A banknote, of course, is an unusual thing because it certifies nothing but itself. For this reason, banknote counterfeiting is something of a closed loop; once the paper is created the crime is complete. It's more typical for a fraud of this kind to involve the exploitation of a wider system of trust, one in which pieces of paper or similar delegated authorities are used to certify something else, like the value of a gold deposit in the ground.

Mining fraud and Bre-X

There's something about the mining industry, particularly in precious metals, that attracts crooks. On the one hand, the lure of a literal gold mine is often enough to make investors switch off their critical faculties. On the other side of the equation, even a basically honest miner is quite capable of deceiving himself that the mother lode is only a few more metres' drilling away, and this can often shade into the telling of white lies to backers to raise the money for a few more holes. A popular joke on the Vancouver Stock Exchange* used to define a mine as 'a hole in the ground with a liar at the top of it'.

And mining is a sector of the economy in which standards of honesty are variable but the requirement for capital is large, and you can keep raising money for a long time before you have to show results. Unsurprisingly, it's a magnet for people who, whether or not they started honest but deluded,

---

*The Vancouver Stock Exchange no longer exists, to the distinct relief of other Canadian stock exchanges, to which it was giving a bad name, as the ratio of fraudulent mining promotions to genuine companies grew excessive. In its heyday it was known to financial journalists as 'The Scam Capital of the World'.

end up as thieves. Digging a gold mine is much more difficult than pretending to have one and mining for gold in investors' pockets.

In the old days, what you used to do was to get a shotgun cartridge and remove all the shot. You then filled the cartridge with gold dust, took it down to the site of your mine, loaded it into a shotgun, pointed it at some rocks and pulled the trigger. Then you picked up the rocks you had shot at, and sent them off to be crushed and assayed. Lo and behold, the results would come back from the laboratory saying that the rock samples from your mine were shot through with flecks of metallic gold. You then took this assay report (signed by a reputable mining chemist at a well-regarded lab) and went to investors to start the real process of getting rich. It was known as 'salting' a mine.

In the modern era, however … well, the process is really not all that much more sophisticated than it was in the Gold Rush of 1849. Now as then, the key input to the process of carrying out a mining fraud is the manipulation of assay reports and geologists' studies, and the way that you do it is still to introduce gold from somewhere else into a sample taken from under the ground. Since a few micrograms in a sample will give you an assay report of five grams per tonne, which is eminently commercially exploitable, it can be as simple as taking a file to a wedding ring.

There have been some improvements to the process since the nineteenth century. There are standard procedures for taking samples, and for logging the time and place at which they are sealed and placed into (hopefully) tamper-proof bags. It is considered good practice to 'split' a drill core down its length, allowing a second set of tests to be carried out at a later date. And geologists and assay labs have become professionalised and regulated. But it still remains the case that if you can find a crooked geologist, and if your fake mine is remote enough to make inspections unfeasible, you can get away with a lot. As recently as 1997, a more or less valueless hole in the ground in Indonesia was valued by Canadian investors at $12bn, on the basis of reports which seemed to suggest that it was the largest gold discovery in the history of the world.

The Busang mine in Kalimantan, Borneo, and Bre-X, the company which claimed to have discovered it, was the largest mining fraud recorded to date, and it offers a classic case study in how this form of counterfeiting works. Miguel de Guzman, an ambitious geologist down on his luck, was hired by David Walsh, a nearly penniless stock promoter working out of the basement of his foreclosed house. Somehow, they managed to raise enough money to hire equipment and drill holes deep in the Borneo jungle. Under Guzman's strict personal supervision, the drill cores were logged and sealed (but, controversially, not split) and then sent off for assay.

There was gold in the ground – everybody agrees about that. The local villagers sometimes supplemented their income by panning for gold in the rivers. But every other mining firm to have staked a claim in Kalimantan ended up concluding that there was not enough gold in the rock to make a commercially viable mine and that the really valuable mineral rights were elsewhere. That's why, of course, the rights to the Busang region were selling cheaply enough to have been picked up by a nearly bankrupt Canadian promoter.

Miguel de Guzman had his own theories, though; among mining geologists he was known as an expert in 'diatremes' –

quartz formations like inverted funnels which can go very deep into the ground and contain rich veins of gold. At some point shortly after his being hired by Walsh, he developed a strong belief that the Busang claim was exactly such a diatreme. He wrote academic-sounding papers on it and gave presentations at mining conferences. (This is normal behaviour, by the way, for the geological staff of small mining companies. It is part of the capital-raising process and by no means evidence of dishonesty in and of itself. Like the pool hall next to a saloon, however, geological presentations at investor conferences are often places where trouble starts.)

The market for Bre-X stock* really heated up, however, when the assay data came back from de Guzman's drill cores. They showed very high percentages of gold in the rock, once it was crushed and heated. The Bre-X investor presentations started to use a couple of new slides – microscope photographs taken of the crushed rock, clearly showing the smooth metallic gold micro-nuggets.

Readers with a background in geology might note at this stage that when you find gold in rock, it doesn't come in smooth nuggets. You find smooth gold nuggets if it

---

* Bre-X was originally quoted on the Alberta Stock Exchange, then later moved to the Toronto Stock Exchange in Canada when it became a big deal and wanted to sell more stock. Its eventual collapse prompted a commission of inquiry into why the previous round of shareholder-protection measures against mining-stock fraud (the ones which closed down the Vancouver Stock Exchange) hadn't worked. Readers with a taste for regulatory trivia might be interested to know that although securities law in Canada operates on a province-by-province basis, financial fraud is investigated by the Royal Canadian Mounted Police. I am told that they don't wear the hats if they come to arrest you for insider dealing.

has been acted on and eroded by running water ('alluvial' gold). For example, you might find smooth nuggets if you had bought your gold dust from the villagers panning for it downstream from the Busang claim, and added it to the drill cores manually.

This was, however, pretty much the only slip-up that Bre-X made in what was otherwise a textbook mining scam. The key to any kind of certification fraud is to exploit the weakest link in the chain; in this case, the initial logging and sealing of the drill cores, which took place at a remote mining camp high up in the Indonesian jungle, where the only people present were either labourers, or very junior geologists hired by de Guzman personally and intimidated by him. Once the core samples had been tampered with, there was no further opportunity for the fraud to be detected, and the process leading to an objective, reputable third-party certification of utterly fraudulent gold reserves was as certain and inexorable as the path from the rock crusher to the forge itself. Analysts and investors back in Canada believed that the Bre-X data had been analysed by three separate independent consultants, without realising that none of the three had access to anything but the fraudulent data prepared by Bre-X.

The weak link is nearly always there, unfortunately. The purpose of a certification system is to economise on time and effort spent in checking. This implies that the checking process itself is laborious and difficult. Ideally, you would want to have as few stages in the process as possible, and you would prefer to have all the checking carried out by the same person, or at least the same organisation. Sadly, this is often not possible. It would be unreasonably expensive for an assay company to send someone all the way out to the mining camp to supervise the drill cores from the moment that they came out of the ground. (Although, given the size of the Bre-X fraud, some might say that it would have been worth it.)

And errors are easy to make. The question of why it took so long to notice that Bre-X was reporting alluvial gold in rock-drill cores is one that a lot of Canadian mining analysts prefer not to discuss. Later, after it had all fallen apart, people who had been on a trip to the Busang mining camp realised that it ought to have raised suspicions that the drilling samples were very carefully laid out in a specific pattern. If you're just bagging the samples as they come out of the ground, you can do it any old how. But if you're salting them, you need to take huge care to construct a consistent 'model' of the ore structure in the ground – it wouldn't do to have huge concentrations of gold in one drill hole and nothing at all in one two metres away.

Even in the process of handing out certifications which are meant to economise on trust, some trust is necessary in the process itself. It's often a very good idea to make sure that one is absolutely clear about what a certification process is actually capable of certifying – the assay was able to establish that the core samples contained gold, but was not in a position to certify that this meant the rock in the ground did.

Gaps like this – between the facts that a certification authority can actually make sure of, and those which it is generally assumed it can – are the making of a counterfeit fraud. Having got one set of facts certified, the crook immediately promotes his operation as if the whole thing had a seal of approval. And this is exactly what Bre-X did, with spectacular success; while they never made specific claims about 'reserves', which would be a specific technical claim that someone would want to audit, de Guzman and his boss John Felderhof were keen on making public 'estimates' of the size of the Busang deposit which, if true, would have implied it was the biggest gold mine in the world. For a while, it was the ultimate penny stock fairy story, as the share price* climbed from pennies to over $264 on a split-adjusted basis, and hundreds of Canadian stockbrokers and investors got rich.

However, in the end, discovery was inevitable. The Indonesian government demanded that Bre-X develop the mine, rather than just drilling assay holes and issuing stock market press releases. They were totally incapable of this, and so were forced into a joint venture with an established mining company. This company (Freeport-McMoRan) wanted to drill its own holes to be sure of the ore body. On his way to a meeting called at Busang to discuss the fact that Freeport's drill cores had come up gold-free, Michael de Guzman fell out of a helicopter, in circumstances which have never been satisfactorily explained. He later had to be identified by dental records; wild pigs discovered the body before investigators did. Bre-X stock certificates can still be bought in novelty

---

*I am oversimplifying mightily once more. Bre-X had multiple classes of stock, and its relationship to the Busang project was definitely not one of simple ownership – lots of other companies claimed bits and pieces of ownership of the rights, there was a joint venture and the Indonesian government did its best to profit from ambiguity. This sort of confusion is often helpful to the fraudster in two ways. First, as we keep mentioning, the layers of complexity are likely to bore and baffle the jury in the eventual trial and make an acquittal more likely. And second, faced with a mound of confusing garbage, capital markets tend to simplify things down to a single overarching narrative. In this case, the narrative was Bre-X = Busang = Biggest Gold Mine in the World.

shops in Toronto as souvenirs, having largely got there from middle-class Canadian households who got caught up in the mania and lost a proportion of their savings.

The Bre-X fiasco was grim enough in itself, but certification frauds get worse. It is one of the areas where fraud can turn into a crime of violence. The certification system is not only used to certify value and authenticity. There are also circles of trust based on the certification of safety and purity. When those start getting faked, people die.

Certification and medical fraud

Even in cases of straightforward banknote forgery, the deep structure of the crime is an attack on the certification system – the presentation of something as having had a particular provenance and origin when it was actually produced in some other, cheaper or less honest way. One of the parts of the economy which has taken the most time and trouble over issues of certification, monitoring and verification of claims of authenticity is the pharmaceutical and medical industry. And because we know that fraud is an equilibrium phenomenon, we can guess that one reason why so much trouble has been taken to build a robust system of certification is that the industry has a lot of potential fraud. This turns out to be true. In fact, one could say that there are two main kinds of medical fraud: frauds carried out against the medical industry, and frauds carried out *by* the medical industry. It is not obvious which is the more serious problem.

Both sides of the pharmaceutical fraud problem, however, are facilitated by the fact that certification is supposed to be a one-time process. As with a notary or other professional, one of the roles of a professional is to provide assurance and trust to other parties, so that checking effort does not need to be duplicated. For this reason, strong social norms exist against questioning or second-guessing the judgement or opinions of professionals. When these social norms get intermingled with all the emotional and cultural baggage which is inevitably attached to the concepts of sickness and disease, the end result is a very powerful collective mental block.

One of the reasons why fraud controls were not properly built into the Medicare system, for example, is exactly this issue – nobody wants to say or imply that they don't trust doctors. The Medicare program had some tough political ground to tread, and inserting its cost-control bureaucrats into the doctor–patient relationship would certainly have made things worse. The relatively low social status of claims administrators compared to doctors made sure that it was difficult to get the paperwork submitted on a timely and orderly basis even from honest professionals. This, in turn, fed into a culture in which all anomalies tended to be deemed 'administrative errors' or 'mistakes' and the paperwork was sent back to the submitting care provider for rectification. In short it was a disastrous policy, as it facilitated the 'shotgun/ rifle' methodology described on p.76 and turned the claims administration process into a training program for fraudsters.

The culture of deference would have been bad enough, but in practice, the special consideration and trust in doctors got extended to any and all providers to the system. While medical professionals make good gatekeepers – they have a long training program, a strong ethical code and a lot to lose if caught in a dishonest act – there is no Hippocratic code binding the proprietors of medical device firms, wheelchair dealers or the managers of assisted living facilities for the elderly. And this kind of company (where it was entirely possible for a convicted felon to set up a new company and register it as an approved provider to the Medicare program with only a few cursory checks) ended up being given the same gatekeeper status as a hospital or GP practice; anything which originated from them was already past the front line of defence. This is how Medicare ended up losing as much as a third of its program spending in fraud. And then things got really bad.

Drugs counterfeiting

When the pop legend Prince died, one of the things found near him was a bottle of generic Vicodin painkiller tablets. These tablets were counterfeits; they contained fentanyl, a synthetic opioid many times stronger than morphine. At its worst the counterfeiting of pharmaceutical products is a crime of violence, in which vulnerable patients are deceived into putting substances into their body without informed consent about what they are doing.

The incentive to commit the crime comes from the fact that all the value in the medicine industry is tied up in the certification system. The manufacturing of pharmaceutical products is difficult and competitive, and as a result profitability is always under pressure. The bit of the system where the money is made is right at the end of the journey from molecule to patient, where a large mark-up over the cost of manufacture can be made, either because there is a strong brand or patent protection. As a result there is always a temptation for someone who can manufacture pills, and has no brands or patents of their own, to fake someone else's.

We can note once more that the crime of drug counterfeiting is essentially an attack on the certification system; even if the counterfeit is chemically identical to the 'real' drug, there is still a diversion of profits from what was intended by the patent system, and the fake drug is still fake. The thing is, the certification system for pharmaceuticals is also a safety system. A counterfeit manufacturer cannot be subject to the same audit requirements and checks on manufacturing processes and purity of ingredients, because all the authorities which might be able to certify these elements of the manufacture are also part of the system which underpins the patent. And once the step into criminality has been made, you tend to be dealing with the kind of person who might introduce fentanyl into a pill that was only meant to contain codeine simply because they don't care and are a bastard.

The battle against counterfeit drugs is also a case study of the problems in trying to create a zero-fraud system. The pharmaceutical industry has expended more effort than practically any other in building mechanisms to track products from the start of the process to the end, often at significant inconvenience to itself. Medical wholesalers, for example, used to manage their inventories of drugs by trading with each other on the 'grey market'. This was quite important to the business model, particularly since drugs are perishable products which cannot be kept forever. But the grey market was such a conduit for fake drugs (particularly since, in states like Florida, a criminal record for fraud or even narcotics addiction was no barrier to being licensed as a wholesaler) that it ended up being regulated down to a fraction of its former size.

And yet fraud creeps back in. The 'track and trace' systems which have been mandated in more and more markets over the last decade have ensured that randomised serial numbers are applied to every packet of pills, and each link in the supply chain keeps an audit record when an item changes hands. In principle, this ought to make it impossible for fake drugs to enter the market.

In practice, what happened is what we might have expected from the original insight that fraud is an equilibrium quantity; as the audited chain has become more inconvenient, it has become less relevant. The majority of counterfeit pharmaceuticals bought in the developed world are now sold through unlicensed internet pharmacies. It's quite possible for people to become the victims of a darknet exit fraud while trying to commit a counterfeit drugs fraud. As the Ghanaian proverb has it, 'When a thief thieves a thief, God laughs.'

And the track-and-trace system cannot protect against counterfeiting when it is carried out by people within the circle of trust. Ranbaxy Laboratories, for example, pleaded guilty in 2013 to seven criminal charges relating to the generic drugs it manufactured for sale in the USA and worldwide. The company was in the habit of using substandard ingredients and manufacturing processes, and then faking test results by buying boxes of its competitors' branded product to submit to the lab.

Vioxx

Ranbaxy's frauds were an extreme case (although apparently not so extreme as to throw it out of the circle of trust entirely;

under new management it still exists and produces drugs today). However, pharmaceutical fraud is not restricted to minor or marginal players; it has been seen at the highest levels and from people and companies whose reputations were previously spotless. The Merck corporation's drug Vioxx (the brand name chosen for the compound known to pharmacologists as rofecoxib*) had already been through the US Food and Drug Administration (FDA) process and had been approved for prescription as a painkiller when the trouble started.

It was initially approved in May 1999 for the treatment of osteoarthritis and of severe menstrual pain, but its manufacturers had ongoing research programs aiming to demonstrate wider benefits. One of them was a test of whether it could help sufferers from Alzheimer's disease; another was a very large study aiming to show that it had fewer gastrointestinal side effects than a competing drug for rheumatoid arthritis (naproxen). The Vioxx Gastrointestinal Outcomes Research study (VIGOR) had 8,000 patients in total, half taking Vioxx and half taking the other drug.

Early on in the study, there were two stock-taking meetings between the researchers on the project, and two key findings. First, the Vioxx patients were indeed suffering fewer ulcers

---

*Decoding pharmaceutical names, and indeed distinguishing them from excerpts of Ella Fitzgerald scat solos, is something of a puzzle. In this case, 'coxib' at the end identifies Vioxx as a 'cyclo-oxygenase-2 inhibitor', part of a whole class of drugs. At the time, many of the world's most respected researchers believed that cox-2 inhibitors were potentially wonder drugs which could be used for all manner of inflammatory conditions. A lot of the problem with Vioxx seems to have been that people fell in love with this theory and stopped doing their job of looking at the evidence as it piled up.

and less bleeding. But second, they were suffering serious (including deadly) heart problems at twice the rate. This clearly posed a scientific and ethical problem, but not one with an obvious solution – it could have been that the alternative drug naproxen was lowering the risk of heart attacks, or the data could have been a fluke. It was decided to carry on with the trial, but to add a data analysis of heart symptoms. For reasons best known to themselves, the researchers decided that they would analyse data on heart attacks if they happened before the end of February, but gastrointestinal symptoms up to the end of the study, a month later. This meant that the eventual paper they published in the *New England Journal of Medicine* overstated the benefits of Vioxx and understated the risks.

This practice had become standard at Merck. Vioxx was aggressively marketed as a 'super-aspirin' bringing new life to sufferers from arthritis. Merck's sales force was highly trained in rebuttals to concerns about cardiac side effects (the sales training team even produced a science fiction cartoon series featuring 'V-Man', a superhero who battled Vioxx doubters in outer space). Toward the end of the year, the FDA rebuked Merck for portraying their theories about the VIGOR study as if they were fact, and in general for their aggressive sales tactics with respect to cardiac risk.

Nevertheless, as the worrying evidence mounted, the drug stayed on the market. External statisticians analysed data from a collection of Vioxx research and kept finding the same cardiac side effects. They also found three heart attacks in the VIGOR data which hadn't been included in the *NEJM* paper. Their study was criticised by Merck as inadequate in its analysis, and their recommendation for the company to carry out specific research into cardiac risks was ignored.

Merck continued to carry out studies to extend the range of conditions for which Vioxx could be prescribed though, and so it almost incidentally continued to pile up evidence that it caused heart attacks. The Merck sales force received new and slicker rebuttal sheets, and were instructed not to bring up the growing controversies in discussions with doctors. The FDA required a change to the labelling on Vioxx to refer to the results of the VIGOR study, and point out that it had found an unknown level of risk – the sales force were instructed to emphasise the word 'unknown'. An 'obstacle response' document was provided, to support 'Project Offense', the sales drive to gain market share for Vioxx by concentrating on the intestinal benefits while minimising the cardiological risks.

Finally, in 2004, the data from studies into whether Vioxx could be used to treat colon polyps and Alzheimer's disease was the final straw. The control system at Merck had not broken down entirely, and the management of the Vioxx issue switched from trying to keep the drug on the market to minimising the legal costs of the damage already caused. Vioxx was withdrawn from sale, and the litigation began. A later study estimated that, because Vioxx was such a successful drug in sales terms, in the five years that it was on sale it probably caused around 80,000 patients to have heart attacks, some 40,000 of whom most likely died.

Partly as a result of this, many practices have been tightened since 2004, particularly with regard to the disclosure of conflicts of interest by medical researchers who also work as consultants to pharmaceutical manufacturers. But the broad shape of the Vioxx scandal is by no means a thing of the past. We can note here that there is no real 'smoking gun' in terms of a specific act of counterfeiting, even though the company eventually settled and admitted criminal wrongdoing in its marketing practices. The lesson of Vioxx is that the concept of a crime against the certification system – a counterfeit in the most generalised sense – is a breach of an overall system of trust, not an isolated attack on a single victim like a long firm.

The trust in question in the pharmaceutical industry is that prescription drugs are the output of a process which is managed and regulated on a clinical and scientific basis rather than a commercial one. The patients who took Vioxx were entitled to assume that the company would behave in such a way as to take an objective, rather than optimistic, view of the clinical risks, and that it would communicate with prescribing doctors in a similar manner. Different histories of the Vioxx affair disagree on the extent to which the senior scientists at Merck understood the risks, or to which they were distracted by dreams of scientific glory from discovering a new wonder drug. But what is clear from the admitted facts in successive court settlements is that the system of checks and balances broke down and scientifically unsupportable claims were made.

There is a tension here, given that the economy is organised on the basis that pharmaceuticals are produced by commercial companies, but that tension is exactly what the system is meant to manage. So the 'counterfeit' item in the Vioxx case was not a drug, or a warning label, or even really a scientific paper. It was a counterfeited image of how business is carried out.

5

COOKED BOOKS

'Well thank you for that ... we appreciate it ... asshole.'

Jeff Skilling, CEO of Enron, on being asked why his company
could not produce a balance sheet

There are many reasons one might want a crooked set of books – to present an image of financial soundness to the victim of a long firm, for example, or to pretend that a sum of money has been spent honestly rather than embezzled. But the most common one is that you want to show your crooked accounts to investors so that they give you money. For this reason, any discussion of accounting fraud needs to be put in the context of stock market fraud, because one is usually the point of the other. With that in mind, here's how one steals money by lying to the stock market.

A public financial market provides the same service to liars that it provides to honest businesses – it converts stories into cash. If you own a profitable enterprise in an economy with functioning stock markets, you hold a form of 'Supermoney', as the fund manager and author George Goodman noted in a book of that name. Super how? Not only does the business provide a steady stream of income; the stock market offers a way to acquire and spend years of future profits before you make them.

The first step is simply to sell a share in the company. A quick envelope calculation shows how it works. Pretend you own a sandwich business, which makes $1m a year of profit. You want to buy a yacht which costs $5m, but you don't want to save up and you don't want to go into debt. So you have a meeting with an investment banker, who tells you that, at present, stock market investors are prepared to buy and sell shares in sandwich businesses at a price equivalent to 15 times their annual earnings. Since you currently own all the shares in your business, you can consider yourself to own an asset worth $15m. If you sell a third of your shares,* you can buy the yacht. This will, of course, reduce your annual share of the profits to $660,000, but if you can't live on that much you shouldn't have been buying the yacht.

In the very simple example, this looks almost offensively prosaic; it is hardly different from an even simpler case where you owned a building producing $1m in rent and used it as collateral for a loan. And the extension to more exciting cases – for example, ones where your company has no earnings currently, but is assigned a stock market valuation based on a small percentage chance that it will one day dominate the online retail market – is not really much of an intellectual challenge either. The important abstract concept here is that the stock market *capitalises* expectations of future profits – literally, it is the place where claims on these expected future profits are exchanged for a capital sum. The story is turned into cash.

Which means, of course, that stock markets can also be the place where a lie gets turned into a fraud. If companies are trading at a multiple of fifteen times earnings, then every

---

* Actually, slightly more than a third. The investment banker is going to want his commission.

dollar of accounting overstatement is potentially directly convertible into fifteen dollars of cash.

In fact, this one-for-fifteen ratio of lies to profit would be the theoretical maximum. It would be hard, though not impossible, to sell all the shares in a fraudulent enterprise in a short enough period of time* to keep the fraud alive. Your ability to convert accounting misstatement into profit is limited by how many shares you can sell to the public. But on the other hand, fake accounts are cheap to produce – a mark-up of only three dollars of cash to one dollar of fakery is still a fantastic return.

In principle, it is the institution of buying and selling shares in companies which converts the story into cash, rather than the stock market per se. You could carry out the example transaction with the sandwich shop by selling a stake in the business to a single investor, and it's just as possible to tell lies to the private equity industry† as it is to the stock market. At the time of writing, if you want to convert a ludicrously false story about the internet into enough money to buy a yacht, private venture capital is probably the way to do it. But public markets have some advantages too.

---

* And even if you did, you'd get the sum net of the bankers' commission.
† 'The private equity industry' – people, and pools of savings that they manage, who do deals buying stakes in companies but not on the normal stock market. Two main kinds – management buy-out merchants who do what the name implies, and 'venture capitalists' who invest in companies that don't have enough profits of their own to raise money from the public. The former kind tend to get defrauded by accounting misstatements, the latter to be victims of companies which are simply frauds from top to bottom. Neither of them are keen on admitting they've been taken for a ride, as they need to portray themselves to their own clients as well-connected geniuses.

The first is that the process of checking up on you is distributed across the market rather than being assigned as the responsibility of any one individual. And better than that, it's distributed across a lot of individuals, most of whom only have a small stake in your story. Like a lot of other areas where counterfeiting frauds work, stock markets tend to operate on a certification basis; there is meant to be a lot of checking up ('due diligence') at the first occasion on which you enter the market, but once you're in, you're in. Compared to the size of the potential opportunity for fraud, there is surprisingly little ongoing monitoring of companies that are already quoted on a stock market. The numbers that a company posts are, for the most part, treated as facts and it is very difficult to gainsay them from the outside.

This feature of public stock markets introduces the vital element of time into an investment fraud. If you are able to corrupt the initial due diligence process and float a fake company, it is quite possible that it will survive, and continue to publish deceitful statements, for quite a while before it goes bust. And when the cash finally runs out and the company collapses, it will be significantly less likely for the initial fraud to be connected back to you. This was the version of securities fraud which marked the career of Jordan Belfort.

The founder of Stratton Oakmont called his autobiography *The Wolf of Wall Street*, presumably because 'Tales of a Parasite' would not have been as good for sales. It is a memorably emetic book, full of simpering, sniggering self-aggrandisment and insincere contrition, and it starts with four consecutive chapters about a time he passed out on his front lawn from taking drugs. But it does contain one paragraph which partly redeems the rest of the book and which summarises the business model of 'boiler room' stockbroking:

> And what secret formula had Stratton discovered that allowed all these obscenely young kids to make such obscene amounts of money? For the most part it was based on two simple truths; first, that a majority of the richest one per cent of Americans* are closet degenerate gamblers, who can't withstand the temptation to keep rolling the dice again and again, even if they know the dice are loaded against them; and second, that contrary to previous assumptions, young men and women who possess the collective social graces of a herd of sex-crazed water buffalo and have an intelligence quotient in the range of Forrest Gump on three hits of acid, can be taught to sound like Wall Street wizards, as long as you write every last word down for them and then keep drilling it into their heads again and again – every day, twice a day – for a year straight.

The stereotypical Stratton Oakmont stock would be a flotation of a new company, in a fashionable industry like defence or high-tech, which had either seriously-overstated and fraudulent accounts, or no earnings at all but a 'story' about a new product that was just about to launch. (Biotechnology companies were popular as they could be pitched to doctors,

---

* Even in this almost-redeeming paragraph, he is still lying in an amazingly self-serving way. Lots of the victims of his securities frauds were ordinary middle-class Americans; the repeated claims in his book that he was a Robin Hood figure who only stole from the rich are just not true.

who turned out to be highly credulous about miracle cancer cures.) Stratton Oakmont would contract to sell shares in the company to the public, taking a significant proportion for themselves as payment for doing so. The shares owned by Stratton would usually have their ownership concealed to avoid the stock exchange regulations on disclosing the owners of large stakes, with the front people used as nominal owners charmingly referred to as 'ratholes'.

Once the company had been floated and had a stock market quote, the second stage of the fraud would begin. Specialists in market manipulation would send the new issue sky high, attracting interest from outside investors and allowing Stratton to sell the shares they had hidden in the ratholes. While the 'pump' phase of the operation was going on, Belfort's teenage brokers would persuade their victims to buy even more of the shares as their price soared. Finally, the company and its investors would be abandoned by its high-flying crooked brokers, leaving them to find out, at a later date, that the accounts were fake and the business was worthless.*

The stock manipulations formed the basis of the majority of the charges which sent Belfort to jail, but these were 'market

---

* With one exception. The shoe designer Steve Madden was a boyhood friend of one of the Oakmont partners, and they took his womenswear company public. Although the initial flotation of Steve Madden Shoes was as crooked as anything, and Madden himself was prosecuted for acting as a rathole, it turned out that the actual business was so wildly successful that the good news outweighed the bad. Purely by accident, Stratton Oakmont managed to float a profitable company (and in doing so, caused huge amounts of pain for the small cottage industry of hedge funds who had come to regard short-selling any Stratton Oakmont IPO as an easy way to make money).

crimes' – breaches of that part of the stock exchange's own rules which have, over time, become sufficiently important to the operation of the overall economy to be regarded as a matter for the state and the criminal authorities. But the real fraud committed by Stratton Oakmont was in facilitating so many companies to go public in the first place – taking money from investors on the basis of false accounts. At base, it was another example of counterfeiting: a certification fraud against anyone who believed that a seemingly reputable brokerage would not get involved with fake companies.

One final thing worth knowing about the way that stock markets capitalise future earnings – they don't always do it very efficiently. In principle, everyone ought to focus purely on cash, and do so with a very long-term forecast horizon. But that's extremely difficult, so people who actually have to trade shares will often look for shortcuts. One such shortcut is to look only at short-term earnings and assume they're a reasonable proxy for long-term cash flows. This means that manipulating a single year's earnings, even at the expense of future years, can often create enough of a bump in the share price to extract some fraudulent cash. And another important shortcut is that for fast-growing companies, people often look at revenues (or sales) rather than earnings, presuming that these are a better guide to the long term than a profit number which might be weighed down by start-up costs. This can be useful to an accounting fraudster: revenues are often easier to manipulate than earnings. Assets can also be manipulated, and sometimes (as with Bre-X) you can manipulate a stock market by talking about gold reserve numbers that aren't even in the accounts. But in order to get a feel for how accounting fraud works, it's necessary to get a bit technical.

Techniques of accounting fraud

There are two species of false accounting. It is tempting to call them 'accounting fraud' versus 'accounting manipulation', but really they are both forms of fraud. Just think of them as 'things you have to lie to the auditors about' and 'things that the auditors will help you with'.

The second of the two categories, by the way, is not meant as a joke and is only to a slight degree a calumny on the auditing profession. Since the dawn of capital markets, audit firms, including the most prestigious, have helped dishonest managers to present utterly misleading sets of accounts. On many occasions they have stretched things so far that it is not credible to claim that the auditors believed they were within the letter of the accounting rules (which are themselves bad enough). This happens despite the fact that auditing is a profession, and performs a crucial gatekeeping role. We'll look into the reasons why this keeps happening later in the chapter, but for the time being, remember that as well as lying to the auditors, it's possible to fake a set of accounts with the help of those same auditors. A full list of accounting shenanigans would fill a book of its own, but here are seven techniques which show up regularly and give you a flavour of what can go on. We'll mainly be taking examples from the most recent Golden Age of accounts fiddling, the dot com and telecoms bubble of the late 1990s/early 2000s.

Completely fake sales

As in sales which never happened, but which you record in a ledger as if they did, and present the fictitious ledger to the auditor. Usually best to make these fake sales overseas, perhaps in an emerging market, but in any case somewhere where there's a substantial time zone gap or an equally substantial language issue and where company registration is opaque. That way, you can set things up so that if the auditor checks at all, he gets through to one of your conspirators, confirming that the fictitious order exists. When the cash doesn't show up, say it's been banked locally and hope that the auditor is on too tight a deadline to question your faked statements. The computer software company Lernout & Hauspie recorded millions of dollars of sales to South Korea out of their offices in Belgium in a fraud of this kind.

Completely fake sales were also generated by Gowex (also known as Let's Gowex), a Madrid-based company which claimed to be in the business of providing roughly nine times as many free municipal WiFi setups across Europe and the Americas as it actually had. This was in some ways a more audacious fraud than Lernout & Hauspie because the completely fake sales would have required fake capital equipment to be bought and installed, which should be easier to check up on than software licences. If nothing else, the auditors could have walked down the street in one of the cities where Gowex claimed to be providing free WiFi and established that they hadn't. In fact, Gowex's auditor was a small local practice and was prosecuted alongside the directors, but Lernout & Hauspie were audited by KPMG, showing that these things can happen in the best ordered of families.

Fake sales by economically meaningless transactions

Let's pretend I am a US long-distance telecoms company (say, Qwest Communications in 2001). And pretend that you are also a US telecoms company (say, Global Crossing, also in 2001). We both own lots of telephone cables and charge other companies for their use. What happens if we make a 'capacity swap' and let each other use our cables free of charge, up to a reasonable limit? It feels like both of us should record some kind of revenue, and an equal amount of cost – the swap is kind of like a pair of mutually offsetting sales. Usually the way to establish that number is to guess what the market price of selling that much telecoms capacity would be, and add it to both the revenue line and the cost line of the accounts. But if we happen to know that the stock market is paying attention to our revenues rather than our earnings, we might choose to use a much higher number, and tell the auditors it was a 'strategic' deal, or some other pretext for why open market pricing was not relevant.

This tactic was massively overused during the dot com boom of the 1990s, as websites swapped ad inventory with one another and acted as if they had sold it. No cash changed hands, and so not only were two companies both able to pretend that they had sold more ad space than they really had, there was no constraint on their ability to pretend that the market price of their adverts was higher than it really was. This feature of swap-sales can be highly useful in other contexts, because it allows a 'market' price to be set which then becomes the basis for valuing assets. Two property developers, for example, might sell small parts of their developments to each other at an inflated valuation in order to create a 'recent transaction' which would allow them to value their whole business higher, and persuade their banks to keep lending against what they believed to be valuable collateral.

A further extension and generalisation of the fake sales

gambit is one which no longer involves two offsetting transactions, and looks for all the world like an open market sale for cash. You find another company which the auditors don't know is controlled by you, either by directly being owned by a connected party, or by being an actually independent company which has agreed to take the role of a 'front' for this transaction. Then you lend this company a sum of money (either as an ordinary loan, or by buying newly issued shares in it), on condition that it uses the money you lend it to buy goods from you. In this way, you can effectively buy from yourself, recycling money raised from investors and making it look like profits. Another popular dot com scandal, this was one of the many restatements made by telecoms giant Worldcom shortly before its CEO and CFO did the perp walk.

Up-front recognition of revenues

Myron and Mordy from OPM Leasing used to call their version of this accounting fiddle the 'Kutz Method', after the accountant who managed to persuade their auditors to agree to it. In a long-term contract, like a lease, the usual method of accounting is to report the payments made by the customer as revenue, spread out over the life of the lease.* The 'Kutz

---

*Matching the time period in which you report revenues and costs to the time period in which the services or goods are provided is known as the 'accruals principle' and accountants fight the most unbelievable holy wars over how it should be done properly. The example they use in accounting textbooks is usually an annual newspaper subscription, which might be paid for up front in cash terms, but which is accounted for as if it were a sale of one newspaper per day for a year.

Method' was to record all the payments as revenue on the day the contract was signed. This obviously made the accounts look a lot better in the short term, and equally obviously it created accounting disasters when clients took advantage of the early break clauses that Mordy Weissman negotiated; not only was there no new revenue coming in, but a large proportion of revenue reported in the past under the Kutz Method had to be 'un-accrued'.

This was also a favourite of 2000s-vintage telecom companies, and is particularly associated with the internet ventures of Jeff Skilling's Enron. Skilling's version of the Kutz Method was even more extreme; rather than restricting itself to contractual revenues, Enron would account up front for revenues that it merely hoped to earn. In one memorable episode in 2000, they signed a joint venture contract with Blockbuster Video to deliver films on demand over their internet cables, and reported all the profits they expected to earn in the next twenty years as revenue. The following year, Blockbuster decided not to go ahead with their part of the joint venture – meaning that Enron reported *another* lump of revenue, reflecting their new assumption that they would no longer have to share the profits from their internet film idea with Blockbuster! In the end, almost no revenue was ever actually generated and the internet video idea joined the rest of the footnotes to the mammoth accounting restatement which marked Enron's slump into bankruptcy.

Delayed recognition of costs

The obvious counterpart of recognising a load of up-front revenue is the practice of spreading costs out into the future.

This was how Worldcom managed to over-report $3.8bn of profits, and the nature of the scam had a sort of symmetry with Enron's practice of accounting for revenue as soon as they had a bright idea. Worldcom used to pay line-rental fees to regional telecom companies in order to connect up their long-distance cables with the customers' actual telephones. This was a cost, and obviously needed to be accounted for as such – there was no long-term contract, and telecoms capacity cannot be stored. But … what if you persuaded yourself that your decision to pay a lot of line fees to a local telecom operator in, say, Wisconsin, was a brilliant strategic move, incurring some short-term expenses in order to build market share and get to a much more profitable position in ten years' time? Wouldn't that mean it made more sense to spread out the cost of the line fees you were paying, so that they were reported over the ten-year period of your strategic plan rather than all in the year that the cash was paid?

Well no, it would make no sense at all, but Scott Sullivan (the Chief Financial Officer of Worldcom at the time) convinced both himself and Arthur Andersen LLC that it did, for a short time. Since failing to report a cost does not make it go away, however, Worldcom ended up being considerably less cash-rich than it reported to its investors, a factor in its eventual bankruptcy.

Completely fake assets

Although it is more usual for the accounting faker to take an existing asset and overvalue it, it is by no means unknown to create a complete fiction. Gowex's network of European municipal WiFi hot spots would be one example, although the biggest fake asset frauds tend to involve offshore bank accounts. There are legitimate reasons* why a company might want to have a lot of cash sitting in an offshore account – it might be the proceeds of a large asset sale which need to be reinvested, or be money raised through a loan or bond issue from an offshore bank. But offshore accounts by their nature tend not to be very transparent, and it occasionally happens that the account gets emptied by an embezzler, or that the ownership of the account turns out to belong to a corporate entity other than the one that is reporting it in its accounts. It's even possible to just pay the money into your own bank account and fake some paperwork. The Italian milk company Parmalat was briefly (between Enron and Worldcom) the holder of the world record for the largest fraud-driven bankruptcy scandal, largely due to the auditors' sudden discovery that a bank account with $4.9bn in it, which made the difference between solvency and insolvency, did not exist.

Unreported debt

You don't want to show too much debt on the balance sheet. But you do want to borrow too much – borrowing money in a corporate vehicle you control is a basic step in getting cash out of a fraud. So what do you do? Get a separate company to borrow the money, telling the bank that you guarantee the debt, then (because the separate company is controlled by

---

* People with a moralistic view of tax-driven structuring may question the use here of the word 'legitimate'; all we mean to convey is 'not intrinsically fraudulent'.

you) use the loan for your own corporate purposes. The accounting rules are meant to protect against this – the concept of 'consolidation' in a set of accounts means that the balance sheet ought to show *all* of the assets and liabilities controlled by your company, and for which it is responsible, whatever company name is on the loan paperwork. But what does the word 'controlled' mean? What does it *really* mean? What's the exact definition of a 'guarantee'? People who loved semantic debates over beer and pot in college will find that there are thick books full of rules relating to these seemingly simple concepts, and that it's possible to argue literally without end about when debts taken out by one company should also appear as liabilities of another. There is massive scope for browbeating your auditors here, although this is not always necessary – in a lot of cases, you can just tell the auditor, 'I don't want this debt to appear on the balance sheet', and off he will go, hitting the books and looking for loopholes, before coming back to you with a funny-looking diagram covered in boxes and arrows which, for a while, gives you the result you wanted.

This was why Enron decided that it was going to create lots of 'off-balance sheet vehicles' – effectively, brass plate companies with offshore registrations, which had no business activities of their own, except to borrow money from global capital markets and then buy large assets which Enron wanted to operate. Of course, the only reason that these shells of companies were able to borrow money in the first place was that they were guaranteed by Enron, and so, with the benefit of hindsight, it was quite obvious that their debts should have been reported by Enron as if they were the company's own. Or at least, that's what the eventual bankruptcy examiner thought – if there is a convincing argument to the contrary, it's probably lost in a shredder somewhere in the Houston offices of Arthur Andersen.

Auditors, analysts and other disappointments

All of these frauds should have been prevented by the auditors, whose job it specifically is to review every set of accounts as a neutral outside party and certify that they are a true and fair view of the business. But they didn't. Why not? The answer is simple; some auditors are crooks, and some are easily fooled by crooks. And whatever reforms are made to the accounting standards and to the rules governing the profession, the same problems have cropped up again and again. As always, when something keeps happening in different times and places, it's likely to be an equilibrium phenomenon linked to the deep underlying economic structure.

First, there is the problem that the vast majority of auditors are both honest and competent. This is a good thing, of course, but the bad thing about it is that it means that most people have never met a crooked or incompetent auditor and therefore have no real understanding that such people exist. In order to find a really bad guy at a Big Four* accountancy

---

* Formerly Big Five, Big Six and numbers up to Big Eight, as the accounting profession consolidated and Arthur Andersen collapsed in the wake of the Enron scandal. Presumably to become Big Three and Big Two before the regulators get involved to prevent Big One. People complain bitterly about the lack of choice, but it probably doesn't have many bad consequences other than to slightly reduce competition in the market for audit fees. And in all honesty, the extreme unprofitability of audit compared to all the other consulting and advisory work done by the same firms is a lot of the problem here.

firm, you have to be quite unlucky (or quite lucky if that was what you were looking for). But as a crooked manager of a company, churning around your auditors until you find a bad 'un is exactly what you do, and when you find one, you hang on to them. This means that the bad auditors are gravitationally drawn into auditing the bad companies, while the majority of the profession has an unrepresentative view of how likely that could be.

Second, there is the problem that even if an auditor is both honest and competent, he has to have a spine or he might as well not be. Fraudsters can be both persistent and overbearing and not all the people who went into accountancy firms out of university (and then ended up doing audit rather than a more glamorous specialty) did so because they were commanding alpha-type personalities. Added to this, fraudsters are really keen on going over auditors' heads and complaining to their bosses at the accounting firm, claiming that the auditor is being unhelpful and bureaucratic, not allowing the CEO to use his legitimate judgement in presenting the results of his own business. Partly because auditors *are* often awful stick-in-the-muds and ass-coverers, and partly because audit is a surprisingly competitive and unprofitable business which is typically used as a loss-leader to sell more remunerative consulting and IT work, you can't at all assume that the auditor's boss will support his employee, even though the employee is the one who is placing his signature (and the reputation of the whole practice) on the set of accounts. As with several other patterns of behaviour that tend to generate frauds, the dynamic by which a difficult audit partner gets overruled or removed happens so often and reproduces itself so exactly that it's got to reflect a fairly deep and ubiquitous incentive problem which will be very difficult to remove.

Analysts

By way of a second line of defence, investors and broking firms employ their own 'analysts' to critically read sets of published accounts. The analyst is meant to be an industry expert, with enough financial training to read company accounts and to carry out valuations of companies and other assets. Although their primary job is to identify profitable opportunities in securities trading – shares or bonds which are either very undervalued or very overvalued – it would surely seem to be the case that part of this job would involve the identification of companies which are very overvalued because they are frauds.

Well, sometimes it works. A set of fraudulent accounts will often generate 'tells' – in particular, fraudsters in a hurry, or with limited ability to browbeat the auditors, will not be able to fake the balance sheet to match the way they have faked the profits. So inflated sales may show up as having been carried out without need for inventories, and without any trace of the cash they should have generated.* Analysts are also often good at spotting practices like 'channel stuffing', when a company (usually one with a highly motivated and target-oriented sales force) sells a lot of product to wholesalers and intermediaries towards the end of the quarter, booking sales

---

*Fraudsters are also highly reluctant to dig into their own pockets to pay tax on fake accounting profits with no corresponding cash, so an anomalously low average tax rate is also often a red flag.

and moving inventory off its books. This makes growth look good in the short term, at the expense of future sales (and of refunds on any sale-or-return arrangements, and of the general brand damage of having a lot of product in the shops which has been sitting around in wholesalers' inventories going stale).

Often, an honest auditor who has buckled under pressure will put a cryptic-looking passage of legalese, buried in the notes to the accounts, explaining what accounting treatment has been used, and hoping that someone will read it and understand that the significance of this note is that all of the headline numbers are fake. Nearly all of the fraudulent accounting policies adopted by Enron could have been deduced from its public filings if you knew where to look. There are analysts who make a career out of this kind of close analysis, but it is a niche and not a particularly profitable one; because most companies are honest, most 'red flags' turn out to be red herrings.

More common is the situation which prevailed in the period immediately preceding the Global Financial Crisis.* Analysts occasionally noticed that some things didn't add up and said so, and one or two of them wrote reports which, if taken seriously, could have been seen as prescient warnings. But for the most part, when things were going up they wrote reports saying things were going well, and when things were going down they wrote reports saying things were

---

*I should mention at this point that 'securities analyst' was my own profession up until 2014, and my track record was pretty mediocre in the way described; I had a few inklings of what was going on, but never really understood how prevalent crime actually was.

going badly. The same thing happened during the dot com bubble, and in every bubble going back to the South Sea. The independent, market-driven watchdogs suffer exactly the same flaws as those with statutory status and backing.

The problem is that spotting frauds is difficult, and for the majority of investors not worth expending the effort on. That means it is not worth it for most analysts too. Frauds are rare. Frauds which can be spotted by careful analysis are even more rare. And frauds which meet both the preceding criteria and are also large enough to offer serious rewards for betting against them come along roughly once every business cycle, in waves.

Analysts are also subject to very similar pressures to those which cause auditors to compromise their principles. Anyone accusing a company publicly of being a fraud is taking a big risk and can expect significant retaliation. It is well to remember that frauds generally look like very successful companies and there are sound accounting reasons for this. It is not just that once you have decided to fiddle the accounts, you might as well make them look great rather than mediocre. The snowball property of growing companies means that if you are extracting cash fraudulently, you usually need to be growing the fake earnings at a higher rate. So people who are correctly identifying frauds can often look like they are jealously attacking success. Frauds also tend to carry out lots of financial transactions and pay large commissions to investment banks, all the while making investors believe that they are rich. The psychological barriers against questioning a successful CEO are not quite as powerful as those against questioning the honesty of a doctor or lawyer, but they are substantial.

And finally, most analysts' opinions are not read. A fraudster does not have to fool everyone; he just needs to fool enough people to get his money. The *Quarterly Review* in 1822 published, under the guise of a book review of Thomas Strangeways' *Sketch of the Mosquito Shore*, an absolutely forensic dissection of the Poyais fraud. The anonymous author of the review noticed that the majority of the book was plagiarised from gazetteers of the West Indies. They set out the real facts relating to the Spanish territorial claims to Honduras, and the extreme unlikelihood of a local tribal chief having ceded sovereignty to a British entrepreneur. They cast derision on Gregor MacGregor's war record and noted his past exploits as a con man. They even suggested that his title 'KGC' stood for 'Knight of the Gull-Catchers' rather than of the Green Cross of Portgual. And yet, for all the good it did in terms of slowing down the progress of investors' capital onto the *Kennersley Castle* and *Honduras Packet*, they might as well not have bothered.

6

CONTROL FRAUD

'Larry Holmes said that he makes more money with Don King stealing from him than getting 100 per cent from other promoters'

Don King at a press conference, 2001

What Leslie Payne's electrical goods warehouses were to the long firm, the Brazilian straddle is to the control fraud. It's the very simplest form of the crime, where the key elements are all exposed. It's interesting because it's the first case we've come across where all the individual components are legitimate and the deceit is in the overarching structure.

The name is a joke: financial options contracts often have nicknames to help traders remember their specific contract rules, awarded based on the exchanges where they were first invented. There are 'European', 'American', 'Asian' and 'Bermudan' options, for example. And a 'Brazilian straddle' is named after a particular trading strategy in options markets, which is equivalent to selling insurance to the market against large price movements in either direction. If a stock index is trading at, say, 15,000, you can give one person (who wants to buy it) the right to lock in a price of 15,500, and another person (who wants to sell it) the right to lock in a price of 14,500. If the market doesn't move by the agreed settlement date, you keep both of the up-front payments. If a crash happens, though, the guy who paid you a small premium now has the right to sell to you at 14,500 when the index is trading at 12,000. (By now, we can identify structures where you get cash up front in return for a risk in the future as being somewhat fraud-susceptible.)

What we have described in the last paragraph would be a normal 'straddle' – a position consisting of writing one option to buy at 15,500 and one option to sell at 14,500. A 'Brazilian' straddle consists of as many options as you can write at 14,500, and a plane ticket to Brazil. It's a position best entered into late in the afternoon, on the day before the options settle. That way, you can wake up next morning and make your decision; if the index has gone up, you go to the exchange and collect your profits, but if it has gone down, you drive to the airport and fly off to somewhere that doesn't have an extradition treaty.

This kind of fraud has been around for a long time. If you consider a version where you write insurance on ships rather than share price movements, it's as old as the Lloyd's market itself. It has an interesting characteristic that it is a *subjunctive* crime, where the size of the fraud can only be measured in retrospect; if everything goes well, the victim never knows that he or she would have been conned.

Something like the Brazilian straddle is the basic engine of a control fraud, much as trade credit is the engine of the long firm. The victim is usually someone who understands that risk is intrinsic to some part of his or her economic life, but hopes to manage it by delegation to a trusted outsider.

Nick Leeson

Nick Leeson was luckier than many convicted fraudsters in that he got Ewan McGregor to play him (and Anna Friel to play his wife) in the film of his story. In real life he had neither Hollywood dentistry nor a film-star physique; by the time he was captured, he had stress-eaten so many tubes of Fruit Pastilles that they had destroyed the enamel on his teeth. He had a lot to be stressed about, as he was the proprietor of an 'error account' in which around $600m of losses were concealed – more than enough to cause the bankruptcy of his employer, the 200-year-old investment bank Baring Brothers.

Leeson's career in Baring Futures Singapore was such a perfect anti-template for how to run a financial institution that it provided years of work for regulators in drafting new rules to forbid the managerial pathologies that had allowed him to do what he did. One might have hoped that these new rules would have prevented the strikingly similar cases of Jérôme Kerviel (€1bn) and Kweku Adoboli (SFr2bn) fifteen years later, but that's finance.

The Barings scandal was a classic control fraud at the branch-manager level, where an employee takes advantage of a position of responsibility to run someone else's business for his own benefit. And the way that Leeson and other rogue traders benefit is through the bonus system of an investment bank – in particular, the feature whereby successful ones share in the upside of the profits they generate but aren't affected by losses if things go wrong. This means they have a huge incentive to take risks as large as possible. In fact, a good deal of the art of managing them is to keep this tendency under control. The root of the Leeson scandal was that a man who was brilliant at paperwork got promoted into a position where he was responsible for checking up on himself.

Nick first caught the eye of his superiors through sorting out a gnarly administrative problem for them. He had taken what was at the time a fairly common route into the City from Watford – he had joined the 'back office' of Barings, taking on the task of matching up payment instructions and records of securities transactions, and helping to sort out the inevitable (and frighteningly frequent) mistakes.* He did well enough at this to be handpicked for a special project, in the new markets of Asia. Barings had opened an office in Jakarta to trade Indonesian stocks and bonds, and had done very well at it and made a lot of money. Or at least, in principle.

Indonesian securities markets at the time were not electronic; they relied on physical movement of stock and bond certificates. Barings' Jakarta office had got into a mess with its filing, so it was unable to present certificates to the people it had done trades with, and so its reported profits were proving difficult to turn into cash. (Normally, goodwill

---

* A friend who once had to listen for litigation purposes to hours of recorded phone conversations between securities traders described them as 'fifteen minutes of sport chat, five minutes of mildly racist banter, ten minutes of insults and then half a sentence each which constituted the only definitive record of a million-dollar transaction'. After putting the phone down, these charmers would scribble 'tickets' and pass them to a runner, whose job it was to take them down to the equivalent of young Nick Leeson, who would then get on the phone to his counterpart to make sure both sides' understanding of the trade matched up. One gulps, but actually, from our point of view this is a sign of strength in the culture of financial markets – you could only ever afford to do this in the ultimate of high-trust societies. Try to do it somewhere like Indonesia in the 1990s and people will take it as an invitation to screw you in roughly the way that they did to Barings.

and a general sense that a broker's word is his or her bond
will take you through these teething problems as people pay
up and sort out the certificates later. This kind of goodwill
tends to suddenly be absent in low-trust societies when a
foreign newcomer shows up and starts winning the game at
the expense of locals.) Nick Leeson arrived, spent six months
sorting through certificates in an office, a further few months
hiring lawyers, and managed to turn several million pounds
from 'in principle' to 'money in the bank'. No wonder he was
earmarked for promotion. It came with a new challenge: to
set up a futures brokerage for Barings in Singapore. In order
to cut costs, a fateful decision was taken. Although Leeson
was being given a 'front office' role, trading and managing
the new brokerage, he would keep a lot of his paperwork
responsibilities and take charge of the 'back office' record-
keeping too. It is no coincidence that this combination of
responsibilities is now banned in most financial centres.

One of Nick Leeson's employees, inevitably, made a
small(ish) mistake, losing the equivalent of £20,000 in a few
minutes by selling a contract when an external client wanted
to buy. In order to make the client good, money needed to
be taken from the overall trading account of Barings Futures
Singapore, and to keep track of this sort of thing, a new
'errors and omissions' account was created.* To give it a bit

---

*Or was it? This version of events is given by Leeson himself in his memoir,
Rogue Trader, claiming that it was an act of kindness to one of his traders
who would otherwise have been fired. However, it's a very self-serving book
(it also claims that at one point he had managed to bring the 88888 account
back to a zero balance, which isn't really true either; it got to a zero-cash
position but had huge unrealised losses). None of the histories of Barings
written by people who weren't convicted fraudsters, including the official

of luck, the account was numbered 88888, the number eight being regarded as lucky.

In and of itself, creating the 88888 account was not a false move; it's a fairly normal thing to do. What made it disastrous was the fact that Nick Leeson, master of the paperwork, was responsible both for administering and reconciling it (in his role as chief of the 'back office'), making trades that could generate errors that would be put into it (in his role as a trader) and making decisions about what items would be moved into it (in his role as general manager). This meant that if he ever made any disastrous mistakes himself, he would be perfectly placed to cover them up.

The final piece of the trap was the inadequacy of the controls in London, and the sheer remoteness of Singapore from the time zone in which major decisions were taken. Nobody in head office was really very clear in their own minds whether 88888 was an account owned by the company itself (it was) or whether it was a client account for a big unnamed customer (it wasn't, although Leeson later repeatedly claimed it was). Nobody in senior management had a particularly good feel for the numbers which would have allowed them to realise what was or wasn't a reasonable amount of money to be appearing in the 88888 account, or how much financing the Barings Futures Singapore subsidiary ought to need. With the combination of responsibilities in Singapore and the lack of oversight from London, a control system had been set in

---

Bank of England enquiry report, mention this; they all find that he started screwing things up and hiding them pretty much immediately on arriving in Singapore.

place which had a massive hole in it. This system then set out to sea on the oceans of commerce.

The way it all started was with one of those pieces of slightly sharp practice which are technically against the rules but which everybody does. And in Leeson's case, it genuinely was, seemingly, a more or less honest piece of rule-pushing that set him on the slope. Barings Futures Singapore needed to grow, and to do that, it needed to attract clients. But futures trading is very much an economies-of-scale business; if you have a strong existing flow of buy and sell orders, you are more likely to be able to match them off against a new order coming in from a client.

If you don't have a strong existing order flow, what you do is fake it until you make it. You pretend to have the order flow and offer better prices than your competition. You therefore report trading losses to head office, reflecting the difference between the price you offered the client, and the price at which you were actually able to make the transaction. It's a strategic decision, not a million miles away from a supermarket's decision to use 'loss-leader' pricing on loaves of bread. The decision is taken jointly between the trader on the ground, and the management team back in head office.

But what if that trader had a secret error account that he could credit all the trading losses to? That trader would be able to offer the keenest pricing without ever having to have the difficult conversation about subsidy with head office. He would look like the golden boy genius who was able to attract client business simply by being a hell of a drinker and diner, and then execute it at better prices just by being sharp and market savvy. That's what Leeson did. He bought business by undercutting his rivals' pricing, put the cost of doing so into the 88888 account and exploited London's ignorance as to whether 88888 was a client account or Barings' own money.

From this first act of dishonesty, many consequences followed. A losing futures position has to be funded – cash needed to be wired from London to Singapore in order to settle up with the Singapore exchange every evening. In order to stop London from asking too many questions about why such large amounts of funding was needed, the impression had to be created of a profitable and growing business. So Leeson began to expand his trading into 'index arbitrage', the practice of trading the small differences between the pricing of the same futures contracts in Japan versus Singapore. He would usually sell the Nikkei index in Osaka, then buy it on the SIMEX (Singapore Mercantile Exchange), where it tended to be slightly cheaper.

When everything goes well, this is a reliable money-maker, with low risk because you are exploiting small pricing differences rather than taking positions. It was the reason why Peter Baring was prepared to say, at a shareholders' meeting in 1993, that 'we have found that it is not terribly difficult to make money in the securities industry', a remark which came back to haunt him. The trouble is that although the pricing differentials between the same contract traded on different exchanges are often quite reliable, they are small. So in order to make money out of exploiting them, you need to trade lots and lots of futures contracts. And the problem with that is that if there's an error or unforeseen blip, it gets multiplied up by the large number of futures you are trading. Big operations find it difficult to make small mistakes. This is why most other banks had given up on the Osaka/SIMEX arbitrage. But Leeson was able to report his good trades and hide his losers.

Of course, the books have to balance, and Barings management did send auditors out to check that everything was in order. Leeson, however, was the master of paperwork, and had an inexperienced locally recruited staff who felt considerable personal loyalty to him. So he was able to fool the auditors by creating fictitious records of client money owed to Barings. But you can't pay real cash calls out of fake profits, and he remained dependent on continued transfers from London. And the initial fraud in the 88888 account required further frauds to be carried out in order to finance it.

Here is another textbook example of the tendency of crimes to snowball. All of the stratagems that he used to try and minimise the appearance of losses generated larger losses at later dates. He would take in up-front payments at the start of a quarter, by effectively selling insurance to his clients against the market moving too far.* Then when the market did move, he would have to settle up at the end of the quarter, then write even more contracts to cover up the new losses, and even more than that in order to continue the impression of smoothly increasing profitability. He also exploited his unique knowledge of the back-office processes to claim that his client business required much more cash to be posted with the exchange than it really did.

It was around this point that the stress-eating began. Then the Kobe earthquake happened. The Nikkei index fell by 200 points overnight.

---

* The strategy was an 'options straddle', as we discussed earlier. Leeson didn't carry out the full 'Brazilian' version of the strategy, but he did make use of the fact that it generates cash up front in return for a risk somewhere down the line.

Leeson was now such a large player on the Osaka and Singapore exchanges that people were beginning to ask questions. Some large players had taken advantage of his favourable pricing, and he started to suggest that there was a mysterious 'Client X' who was behind his trades.* He thought that if he kept buying futures he would hold the market up, which would reduce his liability under the options contracts.

He had, in short, lost his mind. As the old New Zealand road safety slogan has it, 'The faster the speed, the bigger the mess'. The only thing this desperate last strategy ensured was that the eventual losses would be even bigger. He lasted only a couple of weeks before the writing was on the wall, at which point he and his wife tried to escape. A short manhunt ended on the airport tarmac in Frankfurt.

Nick Leeson was something of a sad sack compared to lots of major fraudsters. Even if his fraud had worked, all he would have got out of it would have been a bankers' bonus in six figures of pounds sterling, roughly a hundredth of what he lost for Barings. What seems to have motivated him is an initial desire for validation in a competitive world. Rogue traders almost always come from underprivileged backgrounds and have a sense of themselves as outsiders and battlers. But, of

---

* The person widely assumed at the time to be 'Client X' was Philippe Bonnefoy, a French hedge fund manager working in the Bahamas who had indeed done a lot of business with Nick Leeson. The eventual inquiries made it clear that he had not been involved in any of the fraud, however, and certainly hadn't taken the massive risks that Leeson implied for 'Client X'. In the immediate aftermath of the Barings crash, a few people in its management exacerbated the damage to their own reputations by pretending there might have been a conspiracy between Leeson and 'Client X'.

course, so do lots of the very best legitimate traders.* The key psychological element is the inability to accept that one has made a mistake; it is not much exaggeration to say that Nick Leeson destroyed a 200-year-old banking dynasty because he didn't want to say sorry.

Leeson did not have an easy life after his fraud. He spent seven years in the Singapore prison system, and was very lucky not to have died from stomach cancer while in there. Although he did get to see Ewan McGregor play him in the film, most of the money went on legal bills, and he has not written another successful book since his autobiography. Today he makes a living consulting companies on fraud risk (although one gets the sense from his website that he's brought in more for light relief and entertainment than for serious advice). At the date of writing, he has not committed any more crimes that we know of, and on 9 October 2017 the Nikkei index finally crawled back to a break-even level for his trade.

The key to Leeson's fraud, and similar rogue traders, was the ability to control information about the size of the position, and to keep funding the losses by having a sufficient position of trust to persuade the bank to keep making payments. It is not so big a step from the rogue trader to consider what might happen if an entire bank came under the control of fraudsters and if the rogue was at the very top.

---

* Of course, the dividing line between 'rogue' and 'non-rogue' traders tends to be drawn ex post. There are few cases of anyone being sacked for making an unauthorised trading profit.

The Savings and Loan scandals

The Savings and Loan (S&L) crisis of the 1980s set the tone for many of the financial scandals to come. It was the first really major banking crisis of the post-Bretton Woods era and marked the transition from the inflationary 1970s to the hard-money era in the USA and into the Great Moderation. It also gave the first foreshadowings of the fact that financial deregulation tends to lead to crises; the interaction between the economic conditions of the time and the two major deregulation bills was particularly destructive. And related to this, the S&L crisis happened at the start of the Reagan era, as the power of government was being rolled back and that of corporations was waxing fat, leading to a sea change in the nature of the relationship between powerful bankers and the officials meant to supervise them. But most of all, for our purposes, it was with respect to the S&L industry that the term 'control fraud' really came of age.

It is probably fair to note at this point that the economic history of the S&L crisis is contested territory from an intellectual point of view, with both market-oriented and pro-government economists having written studies of the crisis which blamed the other side. Broadly speaking, if you did your economics degree in Chicago and call yourself a libertarian or small-government conservative, you tend to view the S&L crisis as the result of broad macroeconomic factors which destroyed the underlying business model of the industry and couldn't be stopped. If you did your economics degree at Yale and vote Democrat, you tend to view it as the natural consequence of the deregulation of the sector removing constraints on the banks while keeping their implicit state guarantee, creating an inevitable incentive toward wrongdoing. Either point of view is defensible, because the S&L crisis was, in reality, at least two crises, and the policy measures which, partly successfully, aimed to solve the first arguably helped to bring about the second.

The crisis had its roots in the 1970s and the attempt to tame inflation by raising interest rates. Savings and Loans (also known as 'thrifts') were a kind of small bank which had grown up in the pioneer era, taking deposits and making loans in a small local area. The legacy of bank runs and instability in the early days of the USA had, before the 1980s, left a legacy of mistrust of large or multi-branch operations, but the S&Ls had strict limits on what they could do and tended to operate in uncompetitive local markets. For this reason, it was felt that they didn't need much scrutiny from bank examiners. The joke about their style of banking was always that they followed the 3-6-3 rule: pay 3 per cent on deposits, charge 6 per cent for loans and make sure you are on the golf course by 3 p.m.

This was all very well. But it was a business model with an obvious failure mode. The loans that the S&Ls made were thirty-year mortgages paying a fixed rate of interest, while the deposits were short-term or variable-rate ones. As interest rates went up, the rate paid on deposits went up with them while the interest on the mortgages stayed the same. The 3-6-3 rule became a 12-6-12 rule: if you're paying 12 per cent on deposits but still only getting 6 per cent on loans, you'll be bankrupt within twelve months.

Because it was the early 1980s and the Reagan Revolution was beginning to find its form, the solution to the S&Ls' problems had to involve deregulation. The idea that the main problem of finance is excessive red tape and that all problems can be solved by leaving things to the market has been a constant since the Victorian Railway Mania. And so, successive rounds of deregulation took place.

The first one removed size limits on S&Ls, in the hope that they would be able to 'grow out of trouble'. Immediately, a wave of mergers began. This had the short-term effect of improving things. Because of an accounting quirk – not itself dishonest, but open to abuse – merging an insolvent S&L with a borderline-solvent one tended to make the accounts look better.* To finance this growth, they were allowed to borrow from sources other than small depositors, including the junk bond market. In cash terms, however, growth tended to make bankrupt S&Ls bigger but still bankrupt; they needed to be able to earn a return on their assets that exceeded the cost of their liabilities. So the regulations which kept them out of business loans, commercial property loans and – crucially – direct ownership of speculative property developments were also relaxed, on the basis that higher risk meant higher return, and that was what was needed.

Before long, the S&L industry had moved on from

---

* 'Goodwill' is the key here. If you have a bunch (say $100m) of mortgages paying 5 per cent interest, and the going rate is 10 per cent, then your mortgages are actually only worth about $50m. If you write them down to that value, you're bust. But if someone takes you over for $100m, they can say that the mortgages are clearly only worth $50m, but your unique franchise, reputation, etc. is worth another $50m. It sounds crazy, but even honest auditors will usually go along with it – as the acquirer is paying $100m and he is presumed to know his business. If interest rates subsequently fall to 8 per cent, the acquirer can sell your mortgages for $80m, locking in a real loss of $20m but declaring an accounting profit of $30m. The way in which goodwill is accounted for has changed since the 1980s, but it's still a big problem area.

its history of small local banks, and was increasingly characterised by quite large organisations, often owned or controlled by property developers, and several of which were connected to the junk bond financier (and later convicted securities fraudster) Michael Milken. It was at this point that the second phase of the S&L crisis can be said to have begun.

Nobody better epitomises the S&L scandal than Charles Keating, an amazing fraud, crook and hypocrite. He was the owner of American Continental Corporation (ACC), a real estate company with its headquarters in Phoenix, Arizona. One of ACC's subsidiary companies was Lincoln Savings & Loan, which was licensed in the considerably more deregulated state of California.

The financial structure which Keating brought to the game was a clever means of cash extraction. Lincoln, in order to satisfy regulators, had to declare strong profits, and it did. ACC, on the other hand, did not carry out much profitable business other than borrowing money to finance half-built housing developments and acting as a place for Michael Milken to park junk bond deals. The two companies therefore entered into a 'tax-sharing agreement' which allowed ACC's losses to offset Lincoln's profits for corporation tax purposes, and incidentally allowed Keating to mingle the cash flows of the regulated bank he controlled with the less-regulated company that he owned.

Keating himself was a memorable character. He was a tall, good-looking former champion swimmer. He liked the finer things in life – private jets, luxury hotels and politicians – and spent lots of money buying all of them. He also had an extreme horror of pornography and was a major financial backer of moral crusades at the time, including one attempt to discourage high school girls from wearing shorts in case they distracted motorists. As well as founding 'Citizens for Decent Literature' and commissioning the documentary film *Perversion for Profit*, he had served on a Presidential Commission on Obscenity. He even managed to combine his hobby of sexual prudery with his job of undermining financial regulators at one point; he tried to convince a judge that the Federal Home Loan Bank of San Francisco was staffed by a conspiratorial network of gay fraud examiners who had a vendetta against Keating for being such a virulent and outspoken homophobe.

Keating's modus operandi was growth. Banking is a business in which time is one of the crucial commodity inputs; interest payments are accrued as revenue from day one of a new loan, and bad loans only show up as problems at some point in the future. Because of this, a fast-growing bank will generally look better than a slow-growing or shrinking one – it has a greater proportion of new loans and new loans have not had a chance to go bad. Keating pushed this fundamental truth about banking to extremes, and as a result appeared to be one of the most successful and profitable bankers in America. The problem was, if you use fast growth to create the illusion of success, eventually the new loans get old and the problems catch up with you. But Keating had a solution to that too. He lied.

Keating's Lincoln Savings & Loan had taken full advantage of the deregulation of the industry. Previously restricted to mortgage lending, S&Ls were now allowed to invest in loans to real estate developers. Since property developers as a group tend to have an almost insatiable appetite for borrowing money, it was possible to grow much more rapidly by making million-dollar loans to developers than by making five-figure mortgage loans to retail customers. This was the pattern followed by all of the group of 'superstar' S&Ls who dominated the scene in the early 1980s and were held up as examples to the rest of the sleepy, half-bankrupt industry. Every one of them turned out to be frauds. This wasn't a coincidence. The same process that made them disasters in real life had the side effect of making them look like stars under the accounting standard.

The property development loans still had to be collateralised, however. An S&L could only make the loan if it could be shown that the value of the real estate was greater than the value of the loan. So if growth was the key to S&L fraud, the key to growth was 'appraisal fraud' – the art of convincing the auditors that a half-built shopping centre in California's Inland Empire was worth a lot more than it really was.

The first building block of appraisal fraud is to corrupt or intimidate the appraiser. Real estate assets are valued by professional surveyors and estate agents, and it is a competitive business. A bank always has a choice of dozens of appraisers to choose from when it needs to get a third-party valuation in order to complete its mortgage documentation, or to show to its auditors or to fraud examiners. And so a crook like Charles Keating will ensure that his employees both 'shop around' by sending more business to appraisers with a more optimistic view of the world, and make it known to the pessimists that they will lose a major client if they don't start looking on the sunny side. This sort of pressure tends to start out soft and difficult to detect, but to quickly become very blunt and blatant – steak dinners, jet rides and even new Porsche sports cars for the co-operative appraisers, threats and angry phone calls to the recalcitrant ones. By 1986, Lincoln Savings had a small community of valuers who were thoroughly bent to their will.

However, although appraisal fraud starts with a corrupt appraiser, it usually cannot end there. Bank examiners would have an easy time if all that was backing up a crooked bank's books was a set of subjective opinions of nominally independent 'professionals'. To make the most obvious point, an appraiser only has a certain amount of leeway in his or her valuation to make assumptions which depart from the price paid in relevantly similar recent open market transactions. If you want to systematically fiddle the valuations, you need to fiddle the market too.

It is at this stage that the 'control' element of a control fraud starts to become the key to the operation. The more things you control, the greater your ability to create fake evidence to justify the fake valuations which underpin the fake profits earned from your fake assets. Control of the top of the organisation allows you to undermine *all* the controls and *completely* corrupt the infrastructure of trust and checking which is meant to protect the system against external attackers. So a Charles Keating figure has a surprisingly wide menu of options to choose from in creating fake 'open market' transactions. Bill Black, the lawyer who was Keating's nemesis at the Federal Home Loan Bank Board (and later the FHLB of San Francisco), used to give the different methods little nicknames, as follow:

My dead horse for your dead cow. One corrupt S&L owns one half-built development. Another owns a similar one a few miles down the highway. They sell them to each other at an inflated valuation, creating two new market data points for the value of that kind of property in that kind of location.

Cash for trash. A borrower is desperate for a $10m loan against a property which is probably worth $8m. You refuse to lend it to him. Instead, you tell him that you will lend him $30m, as long as he uses $20m of it to buy another exactly similar property from one of Charles Keating's real estate companies. This is a wonderful scheme for Keating; he has extracted $20m in cash in exchange for a $8m property – a profit of $12m. And it looks good for the S&L too; the supplicant borrower's property can now be revalued based on this 'open market' transaction, so instead of a $10m loan against an $8m building, you now have a $30m loan secured against a $40m real estate portfolio.

The horse-for-cow trick has the best name, but the cash-for-trash deal really gives the flavour of the control fraud: the combination of facilitating growth at much faster rates than would economically be possible, plus extracting cash for the controlling party, plus faking the accounts to make the loan book look much safer than it is. The problem is that, as can also be seen, the raw material of this scam is other scams; to keep growing you need borrowers. And the only kind of borrower who will participate in transactions like this is a deadbeat real estate developer, desperate for money and building a questionable asset. So the growth plan of the S&L control fraud depended on being able to find and proliferate this kind of borrower.

It also depended on keeping people like Bill Black out of your bank. Keating always had a problem with people who were capable of seeing the wood for the trees. All of the appraisal scams, cow-for-horse tricks and the like, would work on a complaisant auditor as long as they were presented one by one and against a checklist of tests to verify that a professional appraiser had given an opinion and justified it against market transactions. Where they fell apart was when people started to look at the portfolio as a whole, seeing a string of massively overbuilt projects along a dusty stretch of highway, all of which were financed by the same small group of lenders and none of which were remotely capable of generating the cash to repay even a fraction of their owners' debts.

For this reason, Keating used all the political capital he had built up in his porn-campaigning days, and bought a lot more with Lincoln and ACC's money. He had nearly – but not quite – enough political influence to get a lawyer on his payroll onto the Federal Home Loan Bank Board, and lobbied the board to have supervision of Lincoln removed from the San Francisco office and passed on to less experienced supervisors in Seattle. At one point he had made significant enough campaign contributions to get no fewer than five serving US senators to intervene on his behalf with the federal authorities; the 'Keating Five' were later investigated and censured for their involvement.

In the end, though, the manner in which Charles Keating was brought down has to be considered a qualified success for the forces of regulation. Although he was able to bring huge amounts of political influence to bear, his attempts to get bank supervisors fired never really bore fruit. He found out that his detractors were simply better at bureaucratic infighting than his supporters. It did not help matters that ACC, his holding company, went ever more extravagantly bust as it got further and further involved with Michael Milken's junk bond empire, and that he was financing ACC by selling bonds to widows and orphans in a way that was bound to attract the attention of other regulators, and burn the goodwill and political influence built up by his corrupt S&L. Lincoln Savings & Loan was seized by regulators in April 1989 and at $3.4bn was the most expensive of all the S&L failures. Keating made a long, incomprehensible and rambling speech to his employees towards the end, attempting to tie his own business failings in to a more general picture of American decline caused by communism, immorality and pornography.

The S&L scandal illustrates the 'control' element of a control fraud, but it also suggests that we need to be somewhat more subtle in our understanding of the relationship between control fraud and risk. The loans that people like Charles Keating made were often described in the reports of inquiry commissions as 'high risk', and in a sense, that's what they were. But when several multiples of the capital of a small savings bank had been invested in shopping centre developments being built into a glut, and fraudulently refinanced at multiples of their true value to connected parties, then it somehow stops making sense to talk about eventual insolvency as a 'risk' rather than a certainty. Sure, you might strike oil in the foundations of one of them, or the local government might suddenly need to buy the land to build a road,* but realistically, even if a broke S&L did

---

* Or, maybe *slightly* less fancifully, the original fraudster might find a new and incredibly rich mug to defraud, and sell the control fraud's assets at a premium to the fraudulent valuation, making the original victims whole at

suddenly turn up a miraculous source of profits, they would just be reinvested into bigger frauds. Like playing chicken by running back and forth across the train tracks, each individual project might be considered 'high risk' but the eventual outcome is certain. The difference between good and bad borrowers in this context isn't one of probability – it's one of quality.

Distributed control fraud

The S&L crisis was an example of the classic control fraud. A crook took control of an economic entity and used it to create fake profits, which could then be extracted by 'legitimate' means (in the sense that large fake profits justified large salaries, bonuses and dividends, which are all normal ways to distribute earnings, as opposed to theft). It's intellectually interesting because of the change in the method of theft, but it's still a case where a single controlling mind took a decision to steal money.

The control fraud also, however, permits of an even higher degree of abstraction. In the run-up to the 2000s financial crisis, we saw the development of what might be called a 'distributed' or 'self-organising' control fraud. As we move into discussion of this, a pre-emptive apology might be needed in case the language gets annoyingly elliptical, allusive

---

the expense of the new victim. The 'rich buyer', usually from one of the Arab states (or these days sometimes Russia) is a stock character in the stories fraudsters spin in the later stages of being found out. Maybe one in a zillion times he shows up, but usually he is a fiction, like the powerfully connected political power broker who is always about to make a transaction in the prime bank securities market.

and over-inclined to use the passive voice. If this happens, the reason will be that most of these people are still alive, and hardly any of them have been convicted of a criminal offence, and they might be unhappy to see the word 'fraud' chucked around when the context is them. Sorry about that.

The reason that many of the perpetrators of the 2000s control frauds are still walking around and enjoying their profits is that one can actually develop the technology of a control fraud to a significantly more sophisticated level than the rather crude versions used by the original S&L crooks. One important aspect of a control fraud is that the method of extracting cash is usually not intrinsically criminal. You set up an organisation such that it will legitimately pay out a percentage of its value to you through dividends, bonuses and commercial transactions with other controlled entities, then you blow up the size of that entity to an absurd level by taking on a load of debt, and let the normal and legitimate mechanisms of the corporation transfer the fraudulent value into your pocket.

Now, consider this – what would happen if, rather than organising the fraudulent inflation of the corporation yourself, you simply set up a system of incentives and (non-) checks and balances, such that other people were likely to inflate it for you? In other words, rather than committing crimes yourself to inflate the value, you just created a massively criminogenic* environment in the firm, and let nature take its course? This would be heading for the

---

* 'Having the tendency to incentivise criminal behaviour'. An excellent coinage of Bill Black's to describe the state of S&L regulation in the late 1980s.

perfect crime – all of the cash flowing into your pocket is legitimately sourced, while all the fraudulent inflation which drives it would be done by other people. As long as there is no connection that can be found between the creation of the criminogenic scheme and decisions taken by you, this is close to unprosecutable. And given the way in which corporations can work by nods and winks,* it's not hard to manage the set-up of a self-organising scam without leaving any paper trail or even anyone in a whistleblower position.

That's pretty abstract. But there is a level of abstraction even higher than that. What if – stay with me here because there will be examples – what if there really was *no intention to create a criminogenic scheme at all*? If you were lucky enough to set up a company with bad incentives and internal controls by accident, then you would get nothing but positive reinforcement for your decision for quite a while – it would look like the company was profitable, it would grow at a snowballing rate, and in that sort of situation, what senior manager would question whether or not he deserved a big bonus? Hypothetically, it could be possible for a massive control fraud to take place purely by accident, without any criminal responsibility for the overall scheme at all. This would present a really unattractive case; there would be huge amounts of criminality and misrepresentation, but all of it would have been carried out by relatively low-level employees, most of whom would hardly have profited from doing so, and many of whom would be able to credibly claim that they were not sophisticated enough to realise that what they were doing was illegal. Meanwhile, you would have a

---

* Figuratively but also literally; see the discussion of the GE cartel on p.244.

top tier of fantastically rich senior managers, who should
have known what was going on, and about whom everyone
has a strong suspicion that they 'must have known', but no
possibility whatsoever of anyone being able to meet criminal
standards of evidence of them having done so, because they
in fact didn't know. Can you think of anything more likely to
be corrosive to general standards of public trust in the modern
capitalist system? And anything more clearly descriptive of
what actually happened in a lot of cases in the 1990s and early
2000s?

The PPI mis-selling scandal

Many of the cases we have looked at relate to colourful characters with larger-than-life personalities, who aimed to get
rich at the expense of others and ruined people's lives in
doing so. The strange episode in the British financial system
related to the sale of Payment Protection Insurance (PPI) is
in many ways the opposite of these cases, and achieves a level
of abstraction we could hardly have considered possible at
the beginning of our journey into this topic. It was a barely
planned, distributed control fraud, carried out by thousands
of people acting largely independently, none of whom
expected to (or did) get rich from doing so, and was a rare
case of a fraud where the victims generally did significantly
better than the perpetrators. It shows us how an organisation
can become criminogenic without ever really intending to,
simply as the natural result of what happens when a dysfunc-
tional industry meets a weak management structure, under
pressure.

The background to the industry's problem was that, at

the end of the 1990s, British high street banking was both an incredibly competitive industry and an incredibly profitable one. It was in a 'sweet spot' at the end of a period of deregulation which had begun in the late 1980s. The old cartel of the 'Big Four' clearing banks (at the time, NatWest, Barclays, Midland/HSBC and Lloyds; plus the two Scottish banks which were then much smaller and regionally constrained) had seen the threats and opportunities from deregulation, and spent most of the previous decade clearing out excess costs from their high street network – closing down branches, centralising the processing of cheques and payments and taking out entire layers of branch and middle management. They had developed new product lines in the mortgage industry, and were ready to face the threat from building societies moving into their home turf in providing current accounts.

But although the cost base had been slashed, pricing had not yet adjusted, and was still set with reference to norms from the old days of the clearing banks' cartel. Many current accounts did not pay any interest at all, while overdraft, consumer loan and mortgage rates were set a good distance above the Bank of England's base rate. For a few short years, British banks were the most profitable financial institutions in the world.

But this 'sweet spot' could not last. Banks paid dividends and sometimes bought back shares, but investors expected them to reinvest the majority of their profits in growing the business. This year's profits were meant to be added to next year's capital, supporting ever increasing lending. And so it was. But if you're making such a high return on your capital, you simply can't reinvest it all in the same market – there wasn't enough of Britain to go round. Systematically, by the early 2000s, the British banks were trying to make more loans than there could ever realistically have been demand for.

Trying to expand the supply of any quantity beyond the natural demand has one consequence in a market economy – the price drops. The combination of high profitability and large numbers of highly competitive players in a deregulated market isn't sustainable, just like in the textbooks. But life isn't just economics textbooks, and in real companies with human beings managing them, this natural and sensible process sometimes throws up problems that can lead to pathological outcomes.

One thing you commonly see during an episode like this is that the chief executive who took out the costs and gained the plaudits for delivering record returns will often see it as a natural occasion to declare victory and hand the reins on to a successor. Making huge profits and boasting about doing so is fun; watching those profits get competed away and managing your shareholders' expectations back down again isn't. For the kind of ego that gets to the top in large banking businesses, it's very difficult to reduce a target once set, or to admit that a triumphant peak in performance is subject to the normal industry cycles. If you retire, you can preserve your reputation.

But you don't want to choose a successor who will immediately repudiate your legacy and walk away from the targets you set. And in any case, you're a huge ego, so you might genuinely believe that you have created a business colossus that will last for all time. For a variety of reasons, the UK banks saw titans of the industry like Sir Brian Pitman (Lloyds) and Sir Willy Purves (HSBC) head into retirement, to be replaced by successors who were less impressive personally, but who remained publicly committed to unsustainable profit targets. Promotion to the top job in this era was what rugby players call the 'hospital pass' – a ball thrown with such timing that it cannot be dropped, but which effectively ensures that whoever catches it is going to be flattened.

Meanwhile, the next building block in the scandal was the consequences of the cost-cutting moves themselves. By the end of the 1990s, the old-fashioned bank branch manager – patrician, Rotarian or Freemason, pillar of the local business community, feared and respected by all – was a thing of the past. People with that title would, generally, be earning significantly less than the manager of a fast food outlet, and the salaries of counter staff compared unfavourably with petrol stations. Human capital had been systematically sucked out of the retail banking branch network. This meant that staff had less understanding of what they were doing, and less reason to fear the consequences of cutting corners – the job was not one to be scared of losing. All the safeguards associated with the professional status of branch bankers had been taken out of the system along with the professional bankers themselves.

Into this situation, a new product was introduced which had some characteristics which ought to be familiar to us by now. It was a long-dated insurance product in which the premiums were collected up front but the claims paid much later. As always, not all such products are intrinsically fraudulent, but if you are planning on doing something you shouldn't, this is one of the tools you'll want to have in your kit. Payment Protection Insurance was the wrong product, at the wrong time and the wrong price.

The idea of PPI was that if you suffered a shock to your income – by being made redundant, or suffering a long-term illness – the insurance policy would cover the payments on your loan or mortgage. For ferociously technical reasons related to the taxation of insurance premiums and the status of Irish-incorporated subsidiaries, it was cheaper for the banks to structure things as an insurance policy than simply to promise customers that they would let them off a few payments. Versions of the policy had been available for a long time, although they had not been particularly popular with customers.

The version of PPI which was sold over bank branches, however, was a highly toxic example of the genre. For one thing, the coverage was much less comprehensive than one might have expected given the circumstances in which it was sold. Self-employed people could generally not make a claim at all, for example, as despite the name it only replaced salary income. For another, the policies tended to be sold at terms which did not recognise the fact that many loans get paid off early. And finally, the banks realised that by selling it to customers at the same time they took out the loan they had a uniquely strong distribution channel. So they charged vastly too much for it; for most of the period during which the PPI mis-selling scandal was going on, equivalent policies were available from independent providers for roughly a quarter of the price that the banks were charging.

If the product was toxic, however, the way in which it was marketed was something else – like a poorly maintained nuclear power station, it radiated toxicity into the surrounding environment. Branch staff were given aggressive sales targets for PPI, and overall revenue targets which would be impossible to reach without selling it to an absurd number of their customers. It was difficult for the staff to resist this pressure. Compared to previous generations of the same industry, counter staff were less qualified and worse trained. They were also, up until 2004, one of the last sizeable groups of workers to be represented by single-company trade unions.

What happens when you take an undertrained sales force, give them a bad-quality financial product and tell them they will be disciplined or fired if they don't sell enough of it? Nothing good, obviously. But in fact (and without even all that much benefit of hindsight; the unions were complaining about it, albeit ineffectually, from very early on in the process), the specific ways in which PPI went bad were predictable too. Lots of it was sold to self-employed people who could not, even in principle, have made a claim. Lots of it was sold to people who were very unlikely to have been able to claim because of the way their loan was structured. Lots of it was hardly even 'sold' at all – the staff just added it on to the documentation and pricing and handed it over to the customer to sign, hoping they wouldn't notice.

And when it was sold, harassed branch staff had this habit of lying massively about it; over-representing the benefits, concealing the full cost and, to a truly shameful extent, telling the borrowers that it was either a legal requirement or a condition of getting the loan and that they had to take out PPI even if they didn't want to. This was all really a reflection of the fact that the banking industry had, after years of cutting costs, ended up with roughly the quality and experience of staff that they were prepared to pay for.

The sales staff at the bank branches don't make satisfactory villains, though. None of them got rich from this fraud. And they were all under quite unbearable pressure to make their sales numbers. But on the other hand, they did have a genuine moral choice to make, and massively, systematically across the United Kingdom, branch staff made the wrong choice. The bosses of the banks (or more directly, the bosses of the retail networks; in many cases the actual CEOs were too busy doing even stupider things and screwing up even more badly to directly pay attention to sales targets) were responsible for creating the conditions under which the UK banking branch networks become a criminogenic environment. But, as far as anyone can tell, they didn't tell the branch staff to misrepresent the PPI policies and were horrified and took appropriate action on the occasions when they found out what was going on. The problem was simply that they never did find out, because they didn't make enough effort to find out, because, for the most part, they thought that their job was to try and reconcile promises made years ago with the straightforward reality of competition in a deregulated economy.

This is why nobody went to jail over PPI. Prosecuting the small fry and letting off the big bosses is unedifying and leaves a bad taste even in cases like the LIBOR fraud, where the conspirators are aesthetically horrible people who did make substantial personal profits. In the case of PPI, it would have crossed the line from 'unedifying' to 'actually repulsive'. But prosecuting the people at the top of the tree only works in situations when they meet you halfway by committing a crime. To the frustration of all, it is not a crime to set stupid targets for your sales force, nor is it a crime to fail to check up on them. At the time when the PPI scandal happened, it just wasn't a crime to run your bank really badly.*

---

* It has since been made one, in the UK at least. The 2013 Financial Services (Banking Reform) Act provides criminal penalties for a senior executive of a

Although it wasn't a crime, it was a serious regulatory offence. And well it should have been. We have higher standards of seriousness for advice on a £400,000 mortgage loan than for advice on whether a pair of jeans makes your bum look big. As we'll see in Chapter 9 on 'market crimes', culpability is often defined by reference to the legitimate expectations of people taking part in a market, rather than the intrinsic dishonesty of the acts. And while the convention is that fashion retailers tell white lies, estate agents exaggerate and car salesmen come in a varying spectrum, people have high expectations from the sales forces of financial companies, and those expectations have come to be formalised in regulations. This is how the term 'mis-selling' entered the British English language – it is a regulatory term of art, indicating that something has gone wrong in the sales process, that it pretty much looks like a fraud, but that the regulator doesn't intend to go to the trouble of proving criminal intent or liability and instead is going to be handing out sanctions and orders for compensation.

I should probably confess a small degree of culpability here, of the sort that can be summarised by a subheading in the last chapter on 'Auditors, analysts and other disappointments'. I was responsible for analysing banking companies for a stockbroking firm at the time, and the fact that the UK industry was laying the groundwork for a massive cock-up was exactly the sort of thing I should have

---

failed financial institution if they should have known that their institution was being run recklessly. Whether this criminal offence will survive its first contact with human rights legislation is yet to be tested at the time of writing; the corresponding US legislation under the Sarbanes-Oxley Act is regarded by a lot of lawyers to be probably unconstitutional.

been looking out for. I knew it was a terrible product, and I knew that the banks' profit targets were utterly dependent on it, and I said both these things in writing. But I made more or less sure these points would be ignored, because I only made them in the context of my obsession at the time, which was a disagreement with the banks about a technical question of insurance premium accounting. Seeing the wood for the trees is difficult, but even more than this, there are powerful psychological barriers against realising that what you are looking at is not normal business, but is a massive ongoing fraud against the public.

The PPI compensation orders were the cause of the final irony of ironies of the PPI mis-selling scandal. It is the nature of an insurance fraud that it involves time, and the PPI settlements were being made something like ten years after the original mis-selling had taken place. So there was a question of what interest should be paid to compensate victims for the delay. The standard rate for interest in these cases was set by the regulators at 8 per cent, compound, the idea being that this is the rate that the claimant could have earned by putting the money in a reasonably conservative stock market investment, on average.

But the PPI years were not an average period – they spanned the global financial crisis. So while the real stock market plummeted, the hypothetical stock market investment used for calibrating the interest paid on delayed compensation continued to clock up returns at 8 per cent per annum. As far as I can tell, if you were a UK retail customer in 2002 looking to make a decision on a ten-year time horizon, the absolute best investment you could have made was to buy some Payment Protection Insurance that you didn't need.

The scale of the payments was breathtaking. They actually had macroeconomic significance – enough money was transferred from the banks into the hands of retail customers that it needed to be taken into account in the Bank of England's forecasts for consumer spending. The PPI mis-selling scandal was big enough to support *another*, parasitic scandal, whereby high-pressure sales teams persuaded people to let firms of lawyers handle their claims for them, taking an exorbitant proportion of the fees for doing so.*

I worry that the PPI scandal will be under-analysed by students of the banking industry, overshadowed as it was by the global financial crisis. But in its own way it is more worrying than the S&L crisis in the USA. The S&Ls gave us the concept of a criminogenic organisation, and introduced the phrase (if not the abstract concept) of a control fraud. But the PPI scandal shows us that you do not need a bad controlling mind to make a company criminogenic; there might even be a natural tendency toward criminogenesis which needs to be counteracted from the top. It also shows us that control frauds can come into existence even at very low levels of delegation; the important factors are that someone

---

*Another disclaimer required here. Not *all* of these claims management firms were unethical. The initial ones were simply set up by enterprising solicitors who realised there was a huge potential windfall to be gained by chasing up customers who would otherwise miss out due to inertia and laziness. But things spiralled. It is hoped, by the way, that this book will travel far enough in space and time to attract readers who do not know how ubiquitous the PPI claims industry was in Britain. The unsolicited phone calls saying 'You may be entitled to compensation' provided roughly five minutes' worth of material per capita for the country's stand-up comedians between about 2009 and 2014.

has the authority to manage a process, that the process is one which can be subverted to fraudulent ends, and that the psychological conditions of pressure and rationalisation fall into place for that person.

This is uncomfortable for a variety of reasons. It is somewhat unsatisfactory to have to refer to the largely herbivorous and not personally disgusting counter staff as 'fraudsters', but for consistency, it is hard to deny that this is what they were. It is also unsatisfying to be unable to identify a top controlling mind, and to have to accept that the pressures on the employees came from a badly designed control system operating in a competitive market. And finally, it is very worrying to realise that a control fraud with nobody identifiable at the top of it can be industrialised – when employees at the lowest level are empowered, then if the organisation becomes criminogenic then the *whole* organisation becomes criminogenic. There have been a few official studies into the PPI mis-selling scandal, and they make grim reading. But what is needed is for someone to look into a bank which had a massive PPI problem, and find out if there were individual branches which did not mis-sell insurance. If there are any, we need to find out how they resisted the pressure and whether we can build their secret into the whole system. Competition is not going away, after all, and nor are sales targets.

7

THE ECONOMICS OF FRAUD

'I could not think of any man whose spirit was, or needed to be, more enlarged than the spirit of a genuine merchant. What a thing it is to see the order which prevails throughout his business! By means of this he can at any time survey the general whole, without needing to perplex himself in the details.'

J. W. von Goethe, *Wilhelm Meister's Apprenticeship*

Imagine you are managing something – part of a business, an academic department, a government agency or something. Choose something you know a bit about. Now, imagine that you want to defraud someone else. In order to do that, you are going to need to tell some lies in order to gain something of value. What would you try to steal? What would you need to falsify? How would you do it? How would you keep the fraud going over time? How much money could you extract from the fraud?

Once you have written down the list of things you would need to do in order to turn your workplace into a successful fraud, sit down and have a look at it. Isn't this a useful document? It shows you:

- What the key indicators are which show whether your business is doing well or badly.
- What a really good set of numbers (and maybe even

non-numerical performance indicators) would look like.

- How growth and compound interest are expected to affect the legitimate business over time.
- What questions you should ask of a really good set of numbers to make sure that they reflect a good reality rather than someone manipulating them.

In other words, to understand how to defraud something is to understand how to manage it.

That's potentially quite a useful mental exercise – if you're ever in the position of taking over a new operation, or thrust into a consulting assignment, or just wanting to renew your understanding of something you're in charge of, 'thinking like a fraudster' might be a way to generate new insights.* But there's a somewhat more disconcerting aspect to this thought experiment, because it works the other way round too.

Which is to say, if you were to write down a summary of how you manage something, the things you look for and pay attention to, how you expect them to develop and what you check in order to make sure all is as it should be, then you would have the beginnings of a template to carry out a fraud on the same workplace. The information set is the same; to

---

*This way of thinking about things is related to the 'via negativa' advocated by Nassim Nicholas Taleb. The tendency of people like the Medicare administrators to think of fraud as a 'risk' and in general to assume that it is something that can be managed as if it happened at random is also an example of one of Taleb's themes; the mismeasure of randomness and the underestimation of events called 'black swans' because they don't fit into the system that's meant to categorise them.

understand how to manage something is also to understand how to defraud it.

This might suggest a pessimistic conclusion – that anything which can be managed can be stolen from, and that precautions are useless because all manageable entities are equally vulnerable. That would be going too far. It's also true that any lock made by a human can be picked by a human, and that the plans to design a lock are also the template for its vulnerabilities. But that doesn't mean that locks are useless, or that all locks are equally vulnerable.

In fact, we can see that there's almost an inverse relationship between our imaginary pairs of templates (management/fraud and fraud/management). The easier something is to manage – the more possible it is to take a comprehensive view of all that's going on, and to check every transaction individually – the more difficult it is to defraud.

Vulnerability to crime, in other words, tends to scale with the cognitive demands placed on the management of a business. The more things a manager has to pay attention to, the easier it becomes to carry out a commercial fraud. It also gets easier with increasing uncertainty with regard to what a 'normal' or valid transaction looks like; that's why so many big frauds occur in brand-new business lines where there has been no time to establish a baseline of common practice.

We can be even more specific than that. Modern crime is driven by the cognitive demand placed on managers because it *exploits* the *technologies* used in an industrial society to manage that cognitive demand. Fraudsters parasitise the economy by attacking the systems we use to economise on knowledge, information and attention. It's like a stage magic trick – the fraudster has to know where the audience is going to be looking, and make sure that the nefarious action is taking place somewhere else.

A little intellectual history

There are some very deep ideas about economics tied up in that rather glib little phrase 'the systems we use to economise on knowledge'. They are in fact so deep that they have more or less resisted attempts to turn them into mathematical formalisms, with the result that they survived their encounter with academic economists and remain reasonably meaningful. Here then, in appropriately brisk and schematic form, is a history of the techniques used in a modern industrial economy to handle the problem of 'getting a drink from a firehose' – to reduce to (literally) manageable proportions the flood of information thrown up by an even moderately complex economy.

We start with F. A. Hayek. Although the Austrian School of economics is, to be frank, not in very good shape today, nobody can take away their greatest achievement, which is noticing that there was a problem to solve here. It arose in the context of (at the time, very live) debates centred on the London School of Economics in the 1920s over whether a centrally planned (i.e. Communist) economy would be so efficiently managed and productive that it would sweep away all democratic societies. Getting this one right was tougher than it sounds today, simply because Hayek's central insight has been so thoroughly absorbed into our intellectual framework that it seems much more obvious than it was at the time. As Hayek noted, the benefit of a market system is that it economises on information-gathering, by allowing

aggregate production and consumption decisions to arise
organically out of lots of small transactions rather than one
big plan:

> The statistics which such a central authority would have
> to use would have to be arrived at precisely by abstract-
> ing from minor differences between the things, by
> lumping together, as resources of one kind, items which
> differ as regards location, quality, and other particulars,
> in a way which may be very significant for the specific
> decision ... There is hardly anything that happens any-
> where in the world that might not have an effect on the
> decision he ought to make.*

Hayek didn't believe that the information problem faced
by a socialist planner was simply down to a lack of sufficiently
powerful computers. That might be solved by technological
progress. He thought it was insoluble, because most of the
information that you would need to plan an economy was
'tacit' – embodied in personal experience, spread out across
the production units themselves and not available, even in
principle, to any information-collecting authority. Although
this very strong version of tacit knowledge is controversial,
a weaker version of the idea has been very influential indeed.
And that's the concept of *private* information, which the
planner doesn't have, either because it's too costly to collect or
because the people who generate the information don't want
to share it. The great thing about the market economy is that
the information itself can stay private – all the disaggregated

---

* This extract, and opposite, are from *The Uses of Knowledge in Society*.

system needs to know about it can be summarised in its effect on market prices.

It is worth contemplating for a moment a very simple and commonplace instance of the action of the price system to see what precisely it accomplishes. Assume that somewhere in the world a new opportunity for the use of some raw material, say, tin, has arisen, or that one of the sources of supply of tin has been eliminated. It does not matter for our purpose – and it is very significant that it does not matter – which of these two causes has made tin more scarce. All that the users of tin need to know is that some of the tin they used to consume is now more profitably employed elsewhere and that, in consequence, they must economize tin. There is no need for the great majority of them even to know where the more urgent need has arisen, or in favor of what other needs they ought to husband the supply.

So the Hayekian paradigm was one in which the central planner was replaced by a network of small economic actors, each with private (possibly 'tacit') information about their own consumption desires and production possibilities. And this private information was gradually revealed and fed into the overall economy by small transactions at constantly changing prices. As a model, this works well to describe a fish market. But you can't build a cathedral or a nuclear power station* that way.

---

*People who have been lucky enough to stand in the turbine hall of a nuclear power station, or even to see the reactor halls while under construction,

Checking prices is a costly and cognitively demanding process itself. For projects which need to make long-term plans and output decisions over time, it is more efficient to draw together resources on the basis of long-term contracts rather than to keep bidding for them in a brand-new market every day. A large cluster of these long-term contracts is what we call a *firm*, and Ronald Coase's contribution to this strand of intellectual history was to set out the circumstances under which firms would form, and how the economy would tend not to the frictionless ideal, but to be made up of islands of central planning* linked by bridges of price signals.

Of course, bringing the theory of the firm back into the model brings back a lot of the information problems associated with the socialist planning debate. The price mechanism and decentralised markets work to use private information at the firm level, but within the firms, managers are as blind as Soviet central planners ever were. The problem of trying to make sure your desired outcome happens when you can't directly monitor the person responsible for doing it is, in the most general terms possible, known as the *principal/agent problem*, and something

---

often remark that they are the cathedrals of our age. And like cathedrals, they can only ever get constructed by making utterly fanciful promises about abundant riches in some far-off idyllic future state.

* Of course, even if it was possible to organise everything in the economy on the basis of price signals, that would still leave big islands of central planning, because there are organisations like armies which have to organise themselves on a large scale, but which don't have price signals to help them. That said, the idea of an infantry platoon submitting competitive tenders for air support from a variety of providers might make a worthwhile premis for a piece of satirical science fiction. On pages 207–8 we'll get onto the subjects of 'operations research' and 'cybernetics', both of which grew out of the application of scientific techniques to military planning in the Second World War.

like three or four Nobel Prizes in economics (Mirlees, Tirole and at least half each of Meade and Hanson) have been given out for progress in tackling various versions of it.

The basic idea is usually to create something which works a bit like a price signal, to allow the private information to be revealed, and then to design a contract based on this price signal which aligns the incentives of the 'agent' (the employee) with those of the 'principal' (the manager or owner) as much as possible. So if you wanted someone to trade LIBOR futures on your behalf, but you couldn't tell how good they were at it or how hard they were working, you might design a contract based on something you could measure (like their trading profit) and align their incentives with yours (by paying them a bonus based on it). I have picked this example intentionally to warn the reader that the approach often doesn't work very well.*

Not all bonus schemes or incentive contracts are as bad as the ones you see in investment banks. But the prospect of designing perfect performance-based pay schemes which perfectly align everyone's incentives and do away with the need for planning is a chimera; as Coase showed, if this was really possible, there would be no need for the firm to exist. So, while academic economists post Hayek have tended to stay away from the concept of planning altogether, other specialists have stepped in and developed theories about how production and planning systems could be improved.

---

* The English language has an irregular verb to describe the problematic effects of performance contracts, depending on how much sympathy you feel for the person at the sharp end. I respond to incentives / You game the system / He is a crook.

As one might expect, these have typically advanced in the business schools and management consultancies rather than the academic economics departments, and have mainly been directed toward the improvement of techniques of measurement. *If you can't measure something, you can't manage it* is something of a caricature* of modern management science, but it expresses a deep truth; management is an information-processing job, and the development of large corporations has been made possible by the parallel development of reporting structures, quality and output measures and other tools for getting that information from the machines into the offices.

Modern management science could fairly be said to have started with *The Principles of Scientific Management* by Frederick Winslow Taylor in 1911, which first advocated the 'time and motion study' and the scientific analysis of business processes, starting with a famous study of how many rest breaks a man should take while shoveling iron ore onto a truck. And it could almost as fairly be said that a very great proportion of management theory since Taylor has been made up of calls to measure different things, in order to correct for the biases introduced by the previous round of changes. William Edwards Deming, for example, started the

---

* The quotation is variously attributed to Peter Drucker, William Edwards Deming and others. Confusing matters further, the version attributed to Deming is an abbreviated version of a longer but also possibly apocryphal quote to the effect that 'it is completely wrong to say that if you can't measure something you can't manage it'. As always, however, in the context of Deming's whole philosophy of statistical management, the fact that he might have felt the need to say something like that gives you a clue that he was probably protesting too much.

'quality revolution', based on statistical measures of defect rates in manufacturing, and quickly expanded it into a whole philosophy.

Management theory tends to cycle between trying to deliver efficiency, quality and customisation. If you mainly measure cost indicators, quality tends to suffer. If you mainly measure quality indicators, the cost tends to drift up. If you refuse to compromise and demand both low cost and high quality, you tend to find you have concentrated too much on your own production process and not enough on what the customers want. If you try to achieve all three goals at once, you tend to go mad.

The underlying problem is that most of the time, we are trying to manage or administer things which are too complicated to be aware of every detail at every time, so we need to choose what we hope will be a representative subset of all the information that we have.

As well as refining techniques of measurement of inputs and outputs, the twentieth century also saw the beginnings of an attempt to apply scientific techniques to the organisation of the processes themselves. This had always been implicit in the theory of scientific management, but it took a huge step forward with the Second World War, in which 'operations research' began to be recognised as an important field of military planning, with applications from the optimal size of convoys* to the effectiveness of area bombing. The military

---

*A very easy problem to solve *once you realise* that the circumference of a convoy (and therefore the number of ships needed to guard it) scales as the square root of the area of the convoy (and therefore the number of ships being guarded), and that the size of a convoy is so much smaller than the size of the

also began to attempt to systematise techniques of gathering and processing information, such as the 'OODA Loop' (observe-orient-decide-act), which proved highly influential in business thinking after the war.

Variety and control

That's a very brief summary of how thinking developed in capitalist* economics on the question of information and its use in economic systems. But we're not quite done with the intellectual history yet because, at its heart, this is not a purely economic question (as we can see from the fact that the same problem arises in armies, prisons and other non-market areas). At the highest level of abstraction, what we're looking at here is a specific application of a general problem in the field of engineering: the problem of designing control systems, known as *cybernetics*. (Or more often these days as 'control engineering', since the word has gained inescapable connotations of killer robots and sex chatrooms. It was originally coined by Norbert Weiner from a Greek root meaning 'steering'.)

---

ocean that it makes no practical difference to the chances of being spotted by a U-boat. In actual fact, even the Navy's operations research department didn't twig this one until the Battle of the Atlantic was all but won.

* Sadly, an awful lot of the science of management and control systems is probably lost to the modern global economy for the foreseeable future, because it was originally developed in the Soviet Union, published in Russian (if at all) and never translated into English, let alone digitised. The chances of anyone bothering to dig up, translate and reconstruct decades-old debates on planning and management in the absence of price signals are slim, even if, in the opinion of this author, it would be incredibly valuable to do so.

One of the foundational ideas of cybernetics is the 'Law of Sufficient Variety', coined by British management scientist Anthony Stafford Beer. This states that: 'In order to ensure stability, a control system must be able, at a minimum, to represent all possible states of the system it controls.'

This sounds a bit mysterious when written down in the middle of a page, but maybe think of vehicles. A train can go backwards or forwards, so its control system is a single lever. A car can also turn, so it needs a steering wheel as well as an accelerator, to represent this component of its motion state. And an aeroplane needs a joystick rather than a steering wheel, so the control system can represent turns around more than one axis. That's the intuition here.

If the system you are trying to control has more variety than your control system has ability to keep track of, then you have three choices: expand the variety of the controller, reduce the variety of the system being controlled, or give up on the attempt to control. Most management measurement techniques can be seen, cybernetically, as variety attenuators. They're methods of taming the detail and uncertainty of the underlying system, to reduce it to something which can be represented in the head of a responsible manager – to, literally, 'make it manageable'.

This reduction in variety comes with costs attached. One is the thing people mean when they talk about 'managing what you measure'. The underlying variety has not gone away; it's just been hidden under a set of simplified metrics. At best, they maintain the broad structure.* When this hope turns out

* 'Homomorphism' is a useful mathematical term. It has a rigorous definition which is difficult to understand, but if you use it in contexts where you're

not to be fulfilled, or when the underlying system drifts and changes in such a way that the old set of assumptions are no longer relevant, problems happen. Lots of the pathologies of modern managerialism, in business and out of it – 'gaming the system', 'teaching to the test' and indeed 'window-dressing the accounts' – are basically sins against this law of sufficient variety.

And so it might sound sensible to add more features to the control system. But there's only so far one can take this. In the absence, so far, of artificial intelligences capable of running a business, adding more variety to the control system means adding more managers. When you add managers, you add management problems. Some are simple ones of cost accounting: managers cost money, but it's not too hard in principle to decide whether an additional slug of brainpower solves enough problems to justify another salary and expense account. Some are harder ones of cybernetics: adding another manager adds some number of additional communication problems, depending on the network and hierarchical structure of your company.

But the worst thing about adding more managers is that managers are people, and people have their own incentives. A branch of economics called 'public choice theory' is devoted to the question of how people who are embedded in organisations tend to pervert the control systems to their own benefit. At one end of the scale, this shows up as slacking,

---

looking for something meaning 'a simplified summary which loses a lot of potentially material detail but hopefully captures the important structural features', you will be broadly correct and sound like a hell of a science nerd.

taking excessive risks, empirc-building, and so on.* At the other, it shows up as fraud. Adding more capacity to manage a system involves adding more people whom you have to trust.

That's the economic way of thinking about it – crime preys on the systems which make management possible. If something is complicated enough to have more variety than a single individual can hold in his or her head, then this variety needs to be dealt with. There are only two ways of addressing a problem of insufficient variety in the control system. One of them involves reducing the information set, which makes you vulnerable to fraud from the things you are not monitoring. And the other one involves introducing new people to trust, which makes you vulnerable to fraud if they turn out not to be trustworthy.

In other words, the problem of managing fraud is the problem of management itself. It's all about the ways in which you cope with the regrettable tendency of the commercial world to be too big and complicated to deal with all at once.

Fraud and risk

If we look at fraud in a framework of information and control, we start to see it as a problem of sufficient variety; fraud is one of the classes of events which fall outside the

---

*Public choice economics tends to come with a healthy slug of pro-market ideology, as the public choice solution to a planning problem is usually to try to privatise it and generate a price signal to do the work. Because of its jaundiced view of the government sector, public choice has occasionally been caricatured as 'the science of pretending that the whole government works just like military procurement'.

direct information set, and which the control system needs to be able to respond to. The way in which businesses and control systems usually deal with these sorts of events is to treat them as random events ('risks') and manage them on a statistical basis. 'Risk management' is the measurement approach of assuming that your unpredictable events come from a probability distribution which can be guessed or estimated.* Can a risk management model work as a way of understanding fraud?

Well ... some of the time. It is probably necessary to make a distinction between two kinds of fraud. If we consider something like a typical small-time long firm, a drug counterfeiting operation or the usual run of Medicare claims fraud, then the 'random events drawn from a probability distribution' model doesn't look too bad. There is a population of bad people out there, shaking around like the balls in a lottery machine. Every now and then, one of them will bump into your business, and they will try to do something dishonest. The question is, will your control system detect it? Broadly speaking, the answer will depend on the proportion of transactions you check up on.

You can work out, to a degree of accuracy reasonable enough for management, what the cost of a check-up is. You can guesstimate, in the knowledge that your answer might be extremely wrong, what the proportion of bad people

---

* Replacing a large class of events with a probability distribution for their frequency and importance is an example of what we were talking about earlier, when we mentioned how useful a word 'homomorphism' was. It's an example of a variety-reducing transformation which loses a lot of detail but (hopefully) preserves the important structural features.

in your business is. And you can, if you are thinking in a sophisticated manner, form some sort of idea about how the chance of a bad person arriving at your door might itself be under your control – the extent to which criminals are deterred by the frequency of checking. If you get it right, you are managing your fraud risk in the same way supermarkets manage the risk of shoplifting. If you get it wrong, you're on the path to 1980s Medicare levels of losses. That's how the majority of frauds happen, by number, and this model of 'incidental' fraud is one that fits pretty well into a normal risk management framework.

Risk and quality

Quality control is one of the 'planning' disciplines which look like they possibly ought to be part of economics, but which didn't get scooped up into the big intellectual adventure that started with Adam Smith and have therefore remained largely free of ideological and psychological baggage. That's useful, as it's clearly related to the economic concept of risk and return, which has more baggage than a budget flight to a golfing resort. The advantage of a 'quality control' way of thinking over a 'risk management' way of thinking is that it is less dependent on making assumptions about the statistical properties of bad events, so you can apply it to things which are *sui generis* or which haven't been seen before.

Quality control is all about the number of defects, or the accuracy of measurements, and the cost of reducing or avoiding them. While there's no direct relationship or single numerical measure of 'quality', there's a clear definition of what a poor-quality project is going to be: it has inaccurate information, unrealistic or completely unanalysed assumptions and important details unspecified or left to chance.

This is the kind of project that a control fraudster searches out. Fraudsters like low-quality borrowers because they are easier to control. That's partly because they just tend to be lower-quality people, and partly because they don't have alternatives – legitimate lenders won't touch them. If there was a solid real estate development which was willing to refinance itself halfway through for no reason, or to sell a minority stake to a connected party at an inflated value, then control frauds would be delighted to deal with it. But these things don't tend to happen; low-risk projects have fewer things that can go wrong with them, so they have fewer quality control issues and therefore more people are prepared to deal with them.

Although quality control and risk management approaches can encompass the majority of fraudsters in the world by headcount, they certainly don't describe the majority of fraudsters in this book. You wouldn't capture the Salad Oil King in this way, or Artur Alves dos Reis, and definitely not Charles Keating. The very big fraudsters designed their crimes specifically around the weaknesses they had identified in the control system itself. They cannot be usefully modelled as random events or defects; to do so is to *lose* the important structural facts about how they happen.

If American Express had tripled the amount they spent on inspecting Tino De Angelis' tank farm in Bayonne, they would have just dipped into three times as many faked tanks. If Gregor MacGregor's victims had found out more of the truth about the Cazique of Poyais, he would have proliferated more excuses. And as well as being the biggest source of anecdotes, the big, 'entrepreneurial' fraudsters are very likely to account for the majority of financial losses from fraud; one thing we know about the statistical description of fraud losses is that they are dominated by large and rare occurrences,* and that big frauds tend to come in waves, as a particular set of weaknesses in the control system are found and exploited. A normal risk management system is not going to cope well with this sort of attack; what is needed is a meta-management system, one capable of changing its own structure and resolving the paradox of responding to threats from outside its information set. Is that possible? Maybe. We'll come back to it. But we can get some idea of what we are dealing with by looking at how this arms race between controls and deception has played out in the past. And this historic account is an economic one too. Fraud grew up with the modern economy and helped shape it. Lots of our most important economic institutions are shaped the way they are because they had to deal with the frauds which tried to exploit them as they came into being. The history of commerce is also the history of commercial crime.

---

*Some idea of scale here can be given by returning to the question of gender bias in commercial fraud. In the UK, for example, the biggest female fraudster ever convicted was Maria Michaela, responsible for £15m of fake mortgage applications. The biggest male fraudster convicted to date in the UK was rogue trader Kweku Adoboli, who inflicted losses of just under 100 times this amount ($2bn) on UBS. And although Adoboli was the largest single convicted fraudster, his case itself was roughly a hundredth of the size of the LIBOR scandal. It takes thousands of normal-size 'retail' scam artists to match even a single large commercial fraud.

8

COLD CASES

'For as much as many light-hearted and evil disposed persons not intending to get their living by truth according to the laws of this realm [...] have now of late falsely and deceitfully contrived, devised and imagined privy tokens and counterfeit letters in other names unto divers persons [...] for the obtaining of goods, cattels and jewels into their hands and possession, contrary to right and conscience.'

An Act Against Such Persons as do make Bankrupt, from the reign of Henry VIII, quoted in *The Phantom Capitalists* by Michael Levi

A summary of the previous chapter might be that fraud is what happens when you can't check up on everything. And the economics of fraud are all about the best ways to organise the process of checking up on things, given the state of the world you find yourself in. It shouldn't be surprising, then, that both fraud itself and the techniques with which we combat it have grown up and developed alongside the development of the capitalist economy. So having looked at the principles, let's take a quick survey of the practice, starting way back at the beginning. There is only one real commercial fraud in the Bible, but it is a doozy of a public procurement scam.

There are quite a few Bible verses which suggest that there was a background climate in which it was recognised that dishonesty in business existed ('Unequal weights and measures are an abomination unto the Lord', Proverbs 21:23 and 'You shall not have in your bag differing weights, a large and a small', Deuteronomy 25:13). There are also many references to debts and to the different arrangements for forgiving borrowers who were genuinely unable to pay through misfortune, while harshly punishing defaulters; although dishonesty is not specifically mentioned as a motive for defaulting on debt, it is implicit. And there is the story of Jacob and Esau, which (depending on which of the two brothers you see as the villain) might be thought of as an inheritance fraud.

There are also several particular condemnations by Leviticus and Deuteronomy of the practice of hiring labourers and then failing to pay their wages, and the God of the Old Testament is always entering into bargains with people like Jonah who fail to deliver as per contract. But there is one clear case where not only was there a crime of dishonesty, but one which exploited the arrangements of the economy of the time in a reasonably sophisticated way, and where considerable value was transferred and then dishonestly appropriated. It's in the Second Book of Kings, chapter 12, verses 4 to 8:

> Then Jehoash said to the priests, 'All the money of the sacred things which is brought into the house of the LORD, in current money, both the money of each man's assessment and all the money which any man's heart prompts him to bring into the house of the LORD, let the priests take it for themselves, each from his acquaintance; and they shall repair the damages of the house wherever any damage may be found.' But it came about that in the twenty-third year of King Jehoash the priests had not repaired the damages of the house.

Skimming profits from a public sector maintenance contract – it's literally older than Christianity. Jehoash and Jehioda the high priest later dealt with the problem by forcing the priests to place all their offerings into a chest with a hole bored in its lid, and then disbursing the money themselves directly to the masons and tradesmen.*

It is interesting, though, that this is the only real commercial crime in the Bible, and it happens against a public sector institution (and the government has some very distinctive characteristics in its capacity as a victim of fraud, see Chapter 10). This suggests that, despite the existence of a relatively sophisticated economy, fraud in the modern sense was not so common compared to straightforward theft. Fraud is possible to the extent that people are prepared to trust strangers, or to leave valuable objects out of their immediate control; the ancients had much less occasion to do this than we did. There was less to check up on.

Ancient frauds and inheritance

If you take the extreme case of a society of single-family agricultural production, like ancient Iceland, the kind of fraud that was possible was even more circumscribed than it was in the Bible. The Icelandic sagas are perhaps our best record of a literate society in which the main economic unit was still the size of a single extended family (including its

---

* It is noted in 2 Kings 12:15 that they did not require accounts from the tradesmen they directly hired, 'for they dealt faithfully'. I cannot help but wonder whether the writer of the Books of Kings might have been a bit naïve here.

slaves). And the sagas are, of course, full of feuds and conflicts in which dishonesty plays a part;* the importance of oath-breaking in these ancient stories is a clue that people did not always keep their word. But there are also a few episodes in which the dishonesty at the heart of a feud is one which interacts with the economic institutions of the ancient period in a way which is almost recognisable as fraud.

In the *Eyrbyggja saga*, for example, there is a dispute between Thorolf and his son Arnkel, largely over Thorolf's treatment of the freed slave Ulfar:

> Now Thorolf and Ulfar had a meadow in common upon the neck, and either of them at first mowed much hay, and then they spread it, and raked it up into big cocks. But one morning early when Thorolf arose, he looked out and saw that the weather was thick, and deemed that the dry tide was failing, and called to his thralls to rise and carry the hay together, and work daylong all they might, 'for it seems to me,' quoth he, 'that the weather is not to be trusted.' The thralls did on their clothes and went to the hay-work. But Thorolf piled up the hay and

---

* It might be argued that the *Grœnlendinga saga*, in which Erik the Red gave the name 'Greenland' to a windswept ice desert, was an early forerunner of the Land of Poyais. But it's not clear that this was a case of intentionally misleading advertising as opposed to just being something like a branding strategy on the part of Erik. He didn't make many specific claims about Greenland, there were no institutions by which he could buy or sell land, and it appears he just wanted other Icelanders to colonise the north-west island so he would have some company. In any case, the *Grœnlendinga saga* was written several hundred years after the events it describes, so it's not necessarily reliable evidence.

egged them on to work at their most might that it might speed at its fastest.

That same morning Ulfar looked out early, and when he came in, the workmen asked him of the weather, but he bade them sleep on in peace. 'The weather is good,' said he, 'and it will clear off to-day. Therefore to-day shall ye mow in the home-field, but to-morrow will we save such hay as we have up on the neck.' Now the weather went even as he said; and when the evening was wearing on, Ulfar sent a man up to the neck, to look to the hay that stood there in cocks. But Thorolf Halt-foot carried hay with three draught-oxen the day through, and by the third hour after noontide they had saved all the hay that was his. Then he bade carry Ulfar's hay withal into his garth; and they did as he bade them.

Thorolf, in other words, exploits his shared ownership of Ulfar's field to steal its hay. The feud then arose between father and son because Arnkel paid compensation to Ulfar, and later stole seven of Thorolf's oxen to defray the cost of doing so. Thorolf reacted to this badly, and sent six of his slaves to set fire to Ulfar's house in retribution. However, Arnkel saved Ulfar from being burned to death and then entered into a kind of protectorate agreement (*varnadarmadr*) with him in exchange for being made heir to the lands of the childless Ulfar (an agreement known as *handsal*).

Things then got more complicated. Under Icelandic law, if a freed slave like Ulfar dies without children, the lands that were given to him on his freedom are meant to revert to his former owner, in this case another Icelander called Thorbrand. The sons of Thorbrand were angry at the loss of their potential inheritance and believed themselves to be the victims of *arskot*, an ancient Icelandic legal term for the unjust deprivation of an inheritance.

Meanwhile, Thorolf sued Arnkel in the court of Althing, asking for compensation for the six of his slaves that Arnkel killed while protecting Ulfar. In order to influence the case, Thorolf gave a *handsal* to Snorri (the priest/judge) of the right to a valuable forest. But this was meant to be part of Arnkel's inheritance! Arnkel had become involved in two feuds, both of them involving a dispute over *arskot* and one involving a bribed public official. Luckily, the saga was prevented from getting even more complicated by the fact that Arnkel dies a few stanzas later.*

I say that these practices are 'almost' recognisable as fraud because it's clear that it was a lot more difficult to get hold of valuable things just by telling lies in the ancient Nordic world. The most valuable things around were ships, slaves and land, and the currency was barter and precious metal. Ships and slaves were difficult to steal, and land ownership was tied up with families and had considerable restrictions on its sale. There were limited amounts of something which looked a lot like informal credit – you could agree to pay compensation for a field of hay at harvest time by driving oxen to your neighbour several months later. But most transactions were face to face and happened without the necessary dimension of time; there were no real controls over Ulfar and Thorolf's shared ownership of the hay, because it was immediately obvious that it had gone and hardly any less clear who had taken it.

---

* *Feud in the Icelandic Sagas*, by Jesse L. Byock.

The main frauds in the sagas involve things like *arskot*, because the right to an inheritance was one of the first abstract stores of value to emerge as legal systems became codified. Arnkel owned some land, as did the sons of Thorbrand. They also owned rights to take future ownership of land, which is not the same thing as owning a forest, but which is clearly something of value. Land is physical and tangible and hard to steal, but an inheritance right is something different; you can't always tell whether it's been stolen from you and promised to someone else. As soon as the concept of a property right was invented, as soon as ownership got more complicated than simply the ability to control things by fighting anyone else who wanted them, there is a need for a social web of trust that the rights will be respected and not misused. And where there's trust, there's the opportunity for fraud.

Inheritances also have another important property when we look at them as potential locuses of fraud; they were one of the few ways in which abstract property rights over large and valuable things could come to be owned by women. We've noted at various points during this book that the overwhelming majority of commercial fraudsters are men,* and this was even more the case when we look back into the past. It's only comparatively recently that property ownership has been possible for women at all (particularly married women) in most of the world, and

---

* To save a look in the index, the exceptions are Barbara 'Golden Boos' Erni, Sarah Howe of the Boston Ladies' Deposit Company and the unknown originator of the Women Empowering Women pyramid scheme. Maria Michaela, the biggest female fraudster so far convicted in the UK by value, wasn't even a proper commercial fraud; she just applied for false mortgages.

the small number of exceptions to the rule that commerce was a man's game have, for obvious reasons, tended to be exceptional people of extremely strong will rather than the kind of glib, weak, damaged personalities that make up the ranks of the fraudsters. The exception which proves this rule is that in surveys of the great female fraudsters of history, an extraordinary proportion of them ran the same scam – they pretended to be princesses.

Being a phony princess was about the only way a woman could pretend to be rich for much of recorded history, and the social structure of European nobility meant that you could get quite a lot of formal and informal credit based on the assumption that your royal family would pay it back. If nothing else, you might be able to secure a good marriage. So history records the fraud trials of Mary Carleton (1663, pretended to be orphaned Princess von Wolway of Cologne), Helga de la Brache (1876, pretended to be secret daughter of Gustav of Sweden), Mary Baker (1817, 'Princess Caraboo' of the fictitious Indian Ocean island of Javasu) and in the modern age Elizabeth Bigley (1905, pretended to be the illegitimate daughter of Andrew Carnegie). Even as recently as 2004, Lisa Walker extracted substantial amounts of jewellery store credit as 'Antoinette Millard', purportedly a Saudi princess who had converted to Judaism.

There have been plenty of male phoney peers too; the social network of nobility is just the right kind of system for a fraudster as it is robust enough an arrangement to be able to support material amounts of trust and credit, but unsystematic enough to be comparatively easy to use to fool people if you have the pluck and brass neck. It's something of a digression from the development of the modern economy though, except in as much as the correspondence networks of the upper class mirrored similar networks of merchants and traders, which were a very necessary component of the development of maritime capitalism.

Seas of commerce

It was a black day for fraudsters when Archimedes leapt out of his bath; the shout of 'Eureka!' and the invention of the principle of displacement was the beginning of the end for the previously profitable game of alloying silver with gold to skim profits off jewellery commissions. The Greeks had a comparatively advanced economic and political system, and as a result they had some comparatively complex and sophisticated forms of fraud. The kind of white-toga crime* which is best documented is one that is surprisingly little-changed to the present day: various forms of long firm and control fraud related to the ownership and use of ships.

Unlike a land caravan, a ship's cargo is very difficult to monitor in between leaving its point of origin and arriving at its destination – even if the merchant were to personally accompany the cargo or send an agent to do so, he is still wholly at the mercy of the captain. Even in the absence of dishonest dealing, all sorts of bad things can happen to a cargo at sea. It is for this reason that the maritime industry was significantly ahead of the rest of the economy in history, both in the development of mechanisms to handle risk† and

---

* The author requests that all correspondence on whether or not the Greeks wore togas be directed to someone who cares.

† Jonathan Levy notes in his book *Freaks of Fortune* that 'risk', as an

in the parallel development of fraud. Shipowners formed the first syndicates or 'companies' to raise capital and pool their risks. They invented insurance and were the first people to seriously think about forms of financing.

The history of shipping finance is a joy for scholars of a puerile cast of mind, because of the prevalence of the glorious word 'bottomry' (from an old sense of 'bottom' meaning the hull of a ship, naturally), a practice which was in existence from Ancient Greece to the Hanseatic League, only dying out in around the sixteenth century as it was overtaken by more modern forms of insurance. A bottomry was a loan secured against a ship, which had the particular provision that if the ship was sunk, the loan did not need to be repaid. This made it a very unusual kind of credit; for most of recorded history there was no such thing as bankruptcy or limited liability and a loan once agreed had to be repaid whatever the cost. In Athens and Rome, a defaulting debtor could lose his status as a citizen and be assigned to his creditor as a slave; even in the early days of European capitalism the debtors' prison beckoned. Bottomry loans, of course, charged a significant premium over normal loans to reflect the fact that non-payment was a real likelihood.

This practice of bottomry, however, is obviously vulnerable to fraud, and this indeed happened all the time, even in the ancient world. The Athenian orator Demosthenes got his start as a lawyer in marine fraud cases; his speech

---

everyday word to describe the general consequences of uncertain chance, is a relatively modern adoption of a specialist term drawn from the shipping and insurance industries, simply as the name of the commodity which they bought and sold at Lloyd's Coffee House and similar insurance markets.

'Against Zenothemis' recounts the story of two men who borrowed a lot of bottomry money on the basis of a ship with a valuable cargo of grain. They then set sail with an empty ship and scuppered it. The aim was to pretend to their creditors that they had shared the loss, while actually hiding the money somewhere else; one of the conspirators was unlucky enough to drown in the course of the sinking, while the other one, Zenothemis himself, ended up on the receiving end of some top-quality oratory.

It can immediately be seen that this kind of fraud is very difficult to defend against – because ships move from place to place, it was possible for a crooked captain or owner to raise multiple bottomries in different ports. Since news travelled slowly in the ancient world and there were no central registers, even proving that a ship had actually sunk (rather than being hidden in a different port and renamed, a fraud which still happens today) was no trivial task.

But we can also see that it would be really difficult for maritime trade to take place without something like bottomry – the dangers of the sea were very real, and any merchant who borrowed money without the special provisions which made fraud possible would surely end up a slave before long. The only merchants who would be able to trade by sea would be those with sufficient personal wealth to bear the risk all on their own. This would place severe constraints on any society organised so as to be invulnerable to fraud – they would be able to grow only very slowly, as there would be no ability to pool resources together for large ventures. The largest and most advanced human society to have existed without material fraud may have been one of the pre-Columbian American societies such as the Incas, who appear to have organised their economy entirely on the basis of directed labour and shared consumption.*

This comparison suggests another important point: the prevention of fraud is a means to an end, not an end in itself. It is highly unlikely that the optimal level of fraud is zero. Bottomry might have been susceptible to huge amounts of abuse but something like it was a precondition for the development of a modern economy. While the victims of fraud tend to get nasty surprises – remember Mr Gauger – they cannot be anything like as great as when the fraud-free Incas, believing themselves to be the pinnacle of human civilisation at the time, came face to face with Europeans wearing metal armour, carrying firearms and using wheeled vehicles drawn by horses.

So there might be another means for a society to deal with fraud and its prevention – to deal with it by more or less ignoring it and relying on a combination of social stigma and harsh punishment after the fact to stop it from getting totally out of control. Something not far off this experiment was carried out in England in the nineteenth century.

Eminent Victorian crooks

The City of London Convalescent Fund, Pension Society and Savings Bank was promoted as a kind of health and life

---

*They had a relatively advanced accounting system (using knotted ropes called *khipu* to administer their command economy), though; as they developed technologically, they might have developed forms of fraud. The Soviet Union certainly did.

insurance company in 1843, with John Stanley Humphery* as the promoter responsible for selling shares on the Stock Exchange, and a star-studded board of directors. When it was exposed as a fraud shortly afterward, however, these directors escaped public censure. There were a number of reasons why the collapse was not felt to be the fault of one of its directors in particular. First, she was unaware that the company existed. Second, she had not given permission for her name to be used in the flotation. And finally, she was Queen Victoria.†

This sort of thing happened a lot. Corporations had been made legal again in 1825, after a long period following the South Sea Bubble during which you had needed a special Act of Parliament to found one. This facilitated a particular species of fraud – get hold of a worthless company (or found a new one), falsify its accounts and sell shares in it by lying. Investors, however, still needed a little bit of persuasion to take their money out of government bonds and put it into new shares, so it was considered a good marketing tool to get some famous names on the board of directors and make it look like the investors' money would be well scrutinised.

In fact, it often wasn't. Members of the House of Lords were sometimes willing to rent their names out to company promoters, to the extent that the slang term 'guinea pig'

---

* Yes he spelt it 'Humphery'.

† Strictly speaking, Queen Victoria (and her husband Prince Albert) were listed as Patrons of the City of London Convalescent Fund rather than being on the board per se. The Duke of Wellington was a director, though (without his knowledge or permission). These and many other fascinating stories are chiefly taken from *White-Collar Crime in Modern England* by George Robb.

was coined for a company director who received a guinea for every board meeting he missed. Also, people often have the same name; the West Middlesex Life and Fire Assurance Company,* which disappeared after taking £250,000 of premiums, had both 'Mr Drummond' (but not the MP and senior partner of Drummonds Bank) and 'Mr Perkins' (but not London's wealthiest brewer) on its board.

A lot of the problem was that there was only a rudimentary obligation on companies to keep accounts. The 1844 Companies Act introduced a requirement to present shareholders with an annual report and even to have it audited, but did not set out any standards for what that might involve – a company was considered to have been 'audited' if another businessman had spent half an hour looking over its books on the way to one of his other appointments. This was how the accounts of the North Wales Railway Company were passed despite having been written in code to conceal unapproved payments to directors.

And even the extremely weak standards of the 1844 Act were quickly weakened; as laissez-faire economics was also just getting off the ground, the Victorian era saw the ideology of financial deregulation grow up at the same time as, and in many cases faster and more vigorously than, financial regulation itself. In 1856, during a debate over weakening the requirements, the *Times* wrote: 'In the face of all that has been shown of the effect of legislative attempts to keep men prudent ... there are always a number of persons ready whenever any financial disaster occurs to propose measures

---

* Lightly fictionalised in William Makepeace Thackeray's *History of Samuel Titmarsh* as the 'West Diddlesex'.

of control, the fact being wholly lost sight of that a multitude of regulations serves merely to confuse the general public.'

This view of the world carried the day in 1856, and again in 1866 when requirements were further loosened, although the *Times* did have some standards. In 1871, for example, when their financial correspondent went on holiday and left his column in the hands of a stock promoter who used it to advertise a mining fraud, they did at least sack him. Readers of the *Financial Times* who cast their eyes today over its motto 'Without Fear and Without Favour' might not realise that this was in fact an unusual selling point when the paper was launched in 1888. The rest of the financial press was often systematically bribed or even (like the popular magazine *John Bull*, which was launched by Horatio Bottomley to puff his frauds and slander those of his rivals) owned by stock promoters. During his bankruptcy proceedings, Ernest Hooley ('Hooley the Millionaire', who bought companies with borrowed money, 'Hoolified' them by taking on excessive debts and then sold them to the public) complained about the practice: 'I have promoted companies that I have not made a single penny out of, because the newspapers took all the profit ... As soon as it is known that a company is coming out I am besieged by them ... they come quite openly and say "Well, what are we going to get out of this?"'.

Looking back at the era, it is strange to see that repeated episodes not just of frauds, but of waves of exactly similar frauds, took a very long time to result in any measures from the authorities, and that the 'market discipline' which ought to have driven out bad operators and created a demand for professional auditing and verifiable accounts, didn't work. A clue as to why this might have been the case can be gleaned from some of the names given to the fraud waves; there was the Railway Mania, the Finance Company Mania, the Mining Mania and so on. There was, in fact, huge wealth and value being created by mobilising the savings of the British middle class to finance productive industry.

And this was the priority of Victorian England. Fraudsters and crooked bankers are stock characters in Dickens, Trollope and Thackeray, and it has been estimated that as much as one-sixth of the stock market flotations between 1866 and 1883 were frauds. But the other five-sixths were not, and it was generally felt that this was a price (often borne by widows and retired members of the middle class, who were attracted by the possibility of dividends high enough to maintain their social status) which was worth paying. Hypocrisy and turning a blind eye to squalor in the name of progress were, after all, the defining moral characteristic of the age.

Halfway through the century, the limited liability company form was introduced. The Victorians were under no illusions that the limited liability form was a boon to fraudsters, but they wanted it anyway, in order to keep deepening the pool of potential investors. If the Victorians had wanted to crack down on fraud, they could have done. (And they did, finally, toward the end of Queen Victoria's reign, when proper standards of accounting and auditing were enforced in the 1900 Companies Act.) This is a pattern that we can recognise in the modern era too; the controls and technologies of fraud prevention tend to move forward one disaster at a time. The normal state of the political economy of fraud is one of constant pressure toward laxity and deregulation, and this tends only to be reversed when things have got so bad that the whole system is under imminent threat of losing its legitimacy.

Rollo versus the sledge-drivers

The German term for the perpetrator of a long firm fraud is a 'schlitten-fahrer', literally 'sledge-driver', with etymology even more obscure than the long firm itself. The scourge of the sledge-drivers was a Prussian merchant called Stanislaus Reu, who wrote under the pen name 'Rollo Reuschel' as the correspondent on the *Kölnische Volkszeitung* in nineteenth-century London.

Rollo was a born detective. His successful business meant that unlike most journalists of the time he did not have to compromise his principles and he was able to spend time, effort and money on finding sources and completing his investigations. He made it his business to mingle with the lowest orders of the German expatriate community in beer halls and clubs on the City Road where they congregated. On one occasion he had to produce his press card to avoid being arrested for vagrancy when dressed in particularly shabby clothes.

There were plenty of the lowest orders to mingle with, too. As students of the life of Karl Marx will recall, England did not check passports at the time, and was one of a very few nations where foreigners were neither registered nor monitored by the police. This made London the destination of choice for Germans in trouble – a few revolutionaries and political thinkers but a lot of embezzling clerks, disgraced army officers and underemployed, overeducated ne'er-do-wells.* As Rollo put it:

---

* Some overlap here. Rollo boasts of having 'helped to eight months hard labour' a sledge-driver called Popert 'who pleased himself to pose as the leader of the social-democrats'.

England is a free country. Everybody can come and settle here, without being troubled to produce papers, to give notice to the police, to say who he is, where he comes from, what his business. No questions are asked ... Herr Hans Schulz may fly* today from Germany, arrive in the morning as Mr Robinson in London and open in the afternoon as Messrs Dumas, Grosvenor & Co. somewhere in a small back room. Nobody troubles about it, and English liberty becomes this the greatest protection to the swindling fraternity. If Herr Schulz, alias Robinson has occasion to get tired of his firm then a pennyworth of paint is all that is needed and a new grand firm appears in the place of the vanished one.

Rollo was mainly complaining here about the fact that bankruptcy in England at the time was a civil affair; unlike in Germany, state prosecutors rarely got involved in the winding-up of companies and lawsuits against suspected fraudsters could be expensive. This was, however, more of a risk to the merchants of Cologne than to the British themselves, and the reason why sheds a bit more light on our 'Canadian Paradox'. The British merchants were used to the system and dealt on trust and reputation. The sledge-drivers tended not to bother trying long firms against Londoners, because it was too difficult for an impoverished foreigner to get trade credit locally.

It was much easier to take advantage of the longer periods of settlement for international trade and to set one's sights on the folks back home. German manufacturers were (then

---

*Not literally; the book was written in 1895.

as now) always searching for export markets,* and were often sufficiently well-capitalised to extend a lot of credit to their overseas agents. And when the long firm was folded up, they tended to be surprised and appalled that there was no public authority to help them get their money back; the sledge-drivers could take comfort in the fact that few of their creditors felt like throwing good money after bad with an expensive court case. (Those who did tended to end up regarding their British solicitors as worse crooks than the original fraudsters.)

Rollo had fallen victim to a sledge-driver early in his London career, and developed a hatred of the breed. He exposed many of them in his dispatches for the *Volkszeitung*, and did his best to help fellow German merchants get their money back. His most famous battle, though, written about in his book *The Knights of Industry*, was not directly with a firm of long firm fraudsters, but with a crooked credit agency.

Because they were exposed to significant risk in dealing with London merchants on ninety-day credit, German manufacturers would employ the services of 'enquiry-agents' who would, for a few shillings, respond with opinions on the business and standing of merchants, their profitability and stock levels and so on. A typical one might read something like:

---

* And of course, this was the high period of the Empire. London was the first port of shipping for goods to be exported to half the globe. Some manufacturers avoided the sledge-drivers by sending a family member to live in Britain and supervise their interests – Friedrich Engels, for example.

Re: Gustav Opitz, 22 St Mary-Axe, London EC

G. O. is established since 1883 and is exporting goods of all kinds, especially cloth to the East Indies. According to the official shipping-list he exported last year considerable quantities and there is no doubt that his business is a prosperous one ... It is not doubted that he is possessed of means and a short time ago it is said he came in for a considerable amount of money at the death of his father.* Besides he is representing in London one of the largest Manchester firms. It is thought that the mentioned amount of £500 could be credited to him.

Other reports were shorter:

G. O. is rotten. Hands off.

The second of these reports was written by the firm of Stubbs Limited in 1886. Mr Stubbs' clients were surprised to get it, as many of them had been relying on opinions similar to the first one, written by L. Lehnert of 46 Queen Victoria Street. If a merchant wanted a third opinion, they might have gone to Liman & Co. of 23 St Pancras Lane. No such opinion was ever written, but if it had been, it would probably have agreed with the more favourable example above for two

---

* As well as this sort of thing, it was often mentioned in enquiry-agents' reports if the merchant in question had a wife from a good family, or one who might expect to get an inheritance soon. This was, as was normal in the day, naturally considered to be money that was at the disposal of the husband.

reasons. First, 46 Queen Victoria Street and 23 St Pancras Lane were the addresses of two doors of the same building, occupied only by Lothar Lehnert and his business partner. And second, that business partner was not anyone called Liman, but was in fact the convicted fraudster Gustav Opitz. A few months later, Lehnert sent out a circular to his regular subscribers revising his opinion somewhat: 'Re: G. Opitz, 22 St Mary-Axe. This firm has suffered great losses and will hardly be able to overcome the crisis. I should advise not to give any further credit.'

At more or less exactly the time these circulars went into the post, a pennyworth of paint was being applied to change the signage of G. Opitz to that of 'Walter Arnold & Co.', and the creditors lost their money. This was Lehnert's main way of working; he would provide solid references for Opitz and a select crew of friends, then look prescient by tipping off his clients that they were rotten, just at the moment when it was too late to do anything. His reports had very wide currency among manufacturers, partly because he sold them considerably cheaper than his competitors, but also because established enquiry-agents back in Germany would often find it inconvenient and expensive to handle all their London business, and would subcontract either to Lehnert under his own name or to Liman & Co., his other front door. Lehnert managed his own workload by allowing Opitz to sign his name to letters of reference when his hands got tired.

Pretty soon, the firms of L. Lehnert and of Liman & Co. attracted the attention of Rollo Reuschel and were denounced in the *Kölnische Volkszeitung*. As well as detailing his links with Opitz, his many bad references and the double front doors, Rollo made it clear that he expected to be sued for libel if his stories were not true, and that he and the *Volkszeitung* welcomed the challenge in their crusade on behalf of honest German merchants. Lehnert initially retaliated by publishing slanders in other newspapers (mainly anti-Catholic ones), but his reputation and business suffered badly and he realised that he would have to sue or shut up. He then made a series of bad strategic mistakes.

His first mistake was to encourage Gustav Opitz to sue for libel as well as doing so himself. This allowed many of Opitz's past frauds to be read into evidence. His second mistake was to repeatedly misidentify the person behind the pseudonym, and to assume that 'Rollo Reuschel' must be one of his fellow sledge-drivers acting out of professional jealousy. This ensured that the opposing witness box was full of people who had no need to be involved in the case, but who had reams of information about Lehnert's complicity in their frauds. And finally, he mistakenly assumed that Reuschel was an impecunious hack who might be intimidated by the vast expense of the English libel bar, rather than a very successful businessman who was not only able to finance his own defence, but to pay the costs of his employer as well. Rollo's barrister showed up in court with over a thousand items of correspondence between Lehnert and various sledge-drivers, but the jury were asking to end the trial before he had been cross-examined on the first two. Because of the award for costs, Rollo briefly became a creditor of both Lehnert and Opitz; he didn't expect to get paid and indeed he wasn't.

The escapades in *Knights of Industry* make fine reading, but the overall perspective of the book underlines something we have been emphasising since the first introduction to the frauds of Leslie Payne – that the pattern of credit and

information in a trading economy reflects a pattern of trust
and power. All through the book, Rollo continually asserts
that trade credit is overused and manufacturers made the
victim of sledge-drivers because other forms of financing
are very difficult to obtain. As a description of what financial
conditions were like in Victorian London, this is very much
counter to the normal view; it was a time of reckless financial
expansion. What Rollo is describing though, of course, is
the state of financial affairs *as seen by the German expatriate
merchant community* at the time. English merchants and
manufacturers dealt with each other on credit all the time,
but they did it by a system of IOUs and of 'acceptance
houses' which exchanged them for ready cash. The German
merchants, apart from the very biggest and best, were almost
entirely shut out of this system.*

Rollo's book ends with a set of recommendations for
licensing and regulation of the enquiry-agent system, to
govern conflicts of interest and to ensure that shoddy or
dishonest agents cannot drive good ones out of the market by
underselling them. It is fascinating and disturbing to notice
that not only were none of his recommendations adopted,
but that with only small updates to the language, all of them
could have been published in the last ten years as a critique of
the credit rating agencies who gave AAA recommendations
to worthless mortgage-backed securities. To a large extent,
what society gets in terms of large-scale commercial fraud is
determined by what it is prepared to legislate for.

---

* Some of the very best ones, of course, had found their way to the heart of
the City and its merchant banks – names like Schroder, Kleinwort and
Baring.

9
MARKET CRIMES

'The final cause of law is the welfare of society.'

Benjamin Cardozo, *The Nature of the Judicial Process*

There is a kind of investment banker who likes to work in a friction-free, first-class-all-the-way world of high finance. It is an exhilarating feeling to concoct schemes and advise the titans of industry on mergers and acquisitions, changing the face of capitalism with every phone call and PowerPoint slide. The day-to-day reality is more prosaic though. Even the masters of the universe depend on the staff in the print room – the graphic designers, typesetters and editors whose efforts are needed to make the magic happen.

John Freeman was one such worker bee,* labouring as an agency temp for banks like Credit Suisse and Goldman Sachs. He was a stock New York character, trying to keep his head above water with multiple dead-end jobs; he had also waited tables at the Brasserie Les Halles and done data processing for Philip Morris. It was 1997 and John's lifestyle was kind of working; he had even, as so many Americans did at the time, begun to play the stock market. It didn't go too

---

*Forgive the digression, but the phrase 'corporate drone' is meaningless. Drones don't do the work in beehives. Worker bees do. A 'corporate drone' would be someone whose only purpose was to fertilise the corporate queen and I can't think of a single company that's managed that way.

well though, and so he found himself logging on to an AOL chat room where investors in a company called 'Headstrong Group' (it made safety helmets) gathered to bemoan the poor performance of their investment.

At some point, while other netizens were inventing the acronym 'LOL' and the concept of cybersex, the conversation in the Headstrong Group stock chatroom turned to John's temp job. Possibly with a winkie emoticon, possibly not, it was suggested that since he was designing the PowerPoint slides used by bankers in negotiations over corporate takeovers, he might share the names of the companies being taken over with his pals on AOL, who could buy the shares ahead of the good news.

John Freeman didn't invest in the stocks himself – he thought the market was too risky after Alan Greenspan had talked about 'irrational exuberance' and besides, he was broke. But he was willing to help out his cyber pals in return for a commission of 10 per cent of the trading profits. Before long, in response to increasing demand for tips, he was wandering through the building late at night, looking on people's desks and rifling through shredder bins. He expanded his network beyond the chatroom, to include some of his former colleagues from the restaurant.

The chatroom network were not exactly subtle about it. Stock exchange staff, and securities regulators, tended even in those days to react to a takeover announcement by having a quick look through the previous few days' trading records to see who was buying ahead of the news. When no fewer than twenty-three consecutive takeovers had significant buying from a single stockbroker's office in Bowling Green, Kentucky, it raised some red flags. It turned out that one of the chatroom crowd had started passing on tips to friends and relatives in his home town. It didn't help matters that some of Freeman's syndicate had decided to name their trading account 'Blue Horseshoe Investments', after the code name used by Gordon Gekko in the film *Wall Street*. By 2000, the whole network had been rolled up.

The interesting thing here is that this sort of insider dealing is a relatively modern crime. In the USA, it was banned in 1934, but it remained legal in the UK until 1980 and was only banned in New Zealand in 1998 (and even then, the Kiwis only got round to making it a criminal, rather than civil, offence in 2008). Not only that, but the criminal authorities are not even able to make their minds up as to who it is a crime against. In most of the world, it is regulated as a crime where the victim is the uninformed investor who buys or sells stock from the insider. But in the USA, it is treated as a theft of the intellectual property of the company; information can only be illegal to trade on if it has come from a closely defined 'insider' and has been acquired in exchange for some sort of payment.* Even quite experienced investors can sometimes fall foul of this, because it means that information which is OK to act upon in America is utterly illegal if you are trading stocks in London.

The non-US concept, which tends to be more restrictive, is the version of the crime that has been outlawed in nearly all of the world's stock exchanges, usually in response to pressure from large global investors who don't like feeling at a disadvantage. But it is clear on looking at the historical

---

* Oversimplifying mightily here of course, and US courts often disagree on their interpretation in specific cases.

development of these laws that, for all that they are passed under the rhetoric of 'investor protection', they actually look much more like straightforward commercial decisions taken in order to improve a country's market share of global investment.

The gradual decline of the principle of 'caveat emptor' from the days of the Victorian railway promoters to the Sarbanes-Oxley Act is not a story of the improving moral development of the Western world; it's a reflection of the gradual understanding on the part of capital market operators that investable wealth was becoming a mass market phenomenon, and that if you stopped robbing people blind with stock pools and takeover rumours, you would attract more of them into the capital markets, to make more money overall by robbing them through trading commissions and management fees.

Small investors in the stock market legitimately expect that they're going to have a chance to make a profit; if, instead, they're systematically going to be filled up with the duds, then they're going to find something else to do with their savings and/or gambling money. And even in the modern world of huge fund managers and high-frequency robot traders, retail investors are more important than you might think.

Retail investors have one hugely attractive property when considered by a professional – they're dumb money. Not only are they unlikely to have private information, a lot of the time they haven't taken care to consider all the public information. When the party on the other side of the trade is a small investor (or a lot of orders from small investors all over the country, 'bundled' by a retail stockbroker), you can be reasonably sure that you're not taking too big a risk that the person selling stock to you knows something about it that you don't.

This makes retail orders very valuable to the market. One of the reasons why stockbrokerage commissions are so cheap these days is that retail brokers have finally realised how valuable they are. They charge a quite substantial fee to players like the high-frequency traders for the privilege of dealing against their order flow, and they rebate some of this fee to their customers. But the retail orders would eventually dry up if the customers lost too much or felt that they weren't being given a fair chance. And without a steady flow of 'dumb money' lubricating the wheels, the professionals would find it a lot harder to trade, as they'd always suspect each other's motives for buying or selling.

So the prohibition on insider dealing has grown up as a result of changes in the market itself which tended to emphasise the importance of retail investors. It's the rough equivalent of letting race horses walk round the parade ring, to demonstrate to the punters that none of them have been hobbled.

In a way, the moral intuition that the stock market in some way ought to be a fair battlefield of supply and demand between equals might actually be a back-formation from the fact that insider dealing is against the law. There's no consistent ethical standard here – nobody who buys underwear seriously objects to the fact that Calvin Klein has a better understanding of the fair price than they do.* It's not so much that the law creates

---

* And indeed that Calvin Klein sets the price of underwear in order to maximise their own profits and changes that price from day to day and in different stores for reasons to do with their own advantage rather than 'true'

the crime, as that the defining characteristic of market crimes is that they're crimes against people's legitimate expectations, and that means that context matters a lot. A large part of the work of competition regulation, for example, is in setting out the legitimate expectations for each industry, and deciding whether they have been breached. That's why cartel cases go on for so long and employ so many experts. And it's why it's comparatively difficult to find a clear-cut example of a fraudulent cartel agreement.

Cartels

It is actually quite difficult, as the senior management of a large company, to communicate to your middle managers that you don't want them to break the law when it comes to illegal price fixing. John Brooks, in his book *Business Adventures*, tells the story of a hapless Mr Ginn, a manager at General Electric responsible for making sales of electricity generating equipment to the Tennessee Valley Authority, in competition with Westinghouse and a number of other equipment manufacturers.

Mr Ginn was required to sign a GE policy document, declaring that he understood the company's rule that employees should not enter into any understanding with competitors about pricing, nor even share information. Having signed it, he asked a senior manager (Mr Paxton) whether he ought to comply. Mr Paxton told him that he

---

supply and demand conditions from the manufacturers. Basically all the practices of the garment industry would cause a LIBOR regulator to spontaneously combust with rage.

should, and (surprisingly to Mr Ginn) did not wink as he said this. Mr Ginn enquired whether Mr Paxton had intended to wink, and was told that he had not, that he greatly disapproved of GE's culture of winking when giving instructions about important policies, and that Mr Ginn should definitely obey the policy.

Confused by these mixed messages, Mr Ginn went to two of his other senior managers, Mr Fairman and Mr Erbin. They both told him that Mr Paxton was being naïve, and that Mr Ginn should continue to attend the regular meetings that GE held with representatives of its competitors. Confident that he had understood company policy correctly, Mr Ginn proceeded to several meetings at which bids were agreed, minimum pricing was enforced and competitors who had failed to respect agreements were held to account in special 'griping sessions'. A few months later, he confessed to Mr Paxton who told him he was a damned fool and promoted him.

With his new promotion, Mr Ginn was invited down to New York, for a meeting with Ralph J. Cordiner, the chairman of the board of GE. Mr Cordiner took the opportunity to clearly instruct Mr Ginn that there was to be no ambiguity and the policy on price fixing had to be respected. The message was established so forcefully that there was little Mr Ginn could do other than walk straight to Mr Erben's office to have it clarified. Mr Erben explained that the true meaning of what the chairman had said was 'Keep on doing what you have been doing, but be sensible about it.'

All of this story came out in the course of some congressional hearings, during which GE and its lawyers maintained that the company had a strong culture of compliance and a deep respect for the Sherman Antitrust Act. This point of view did not carry the day and Mr Ginn's career at GE ended with a few weeks in jail.

GE's behaviour (and that of its competitors) cost the US public purse* millions of dollars, by raising the price of vitally needed generation equipment above the level that it reached in 'normal' competitive periods (this was quite easy to ascertain, as the price-fixing system was not well organised and frequently broke down). But did the customer really have a right to that money? The legal point of view is clear that it did, but the law in question is relatively recent; the Sherman Act was passed in 1890, well into the industrial period.

It had been recognised much earlier that collusion between business people tends to raise prices at the expense of the general public. Adam Smith's *Wealth of Nations* has a famous passage that 'People of the same trade seldom meet together, even for merriment and diversion, but the conversation ends in a conspiracy against the public, or in some contrivance to raise prices.' These days, the intellectual battles of the Progressive Era have been so comprehensively won by the anti-cartel side that it's hard to convince ourselves that there hasn't always been a sense of moral odour hanging around the practice of price fixing.

But it's surprisingly recent. The famous passage from Adam Smith is immediately followed by one saying 'It is impossible indeed to prevent such meetings, by any law which either could be executed, or would be consistent with

---

* And, in principle, any other customers in the market, although the vast majority of the equipment for which prices were being fixed were sold to state and municipal buyers.

liberty and justice.' And in identifying anything problematic at all in collusion between tradesmen, Smith was right on the cutting edge of moral thought in his day. For centuries earlier the intuition had been opposite – that a shopkeeper who undercut his fellow merchants was doing a shameful thing. Marx's *Capital*, nearly a century later, still refers to 'full-priced' bakers denouncing their 'underselling' rivals to a parliamentary committee of inquiry. The prohibition of cartels really is an example of a market crime as distinct from any other type of fraud; it is a rule passed in order to make the overall economy work better, which draws its legal force from a general interest of society rather than a specific right of the injured party.

Another characteristic of the crime of cartel-forming is that the boundaries between legal and illegal behaviour are blurred and arbitrary. Mr Ginn and his friends gathered in hotels to decide who would be the lowest bidder for a coming tender and at what price, and so he went to jail. But more subtly organised methods of communication are either entirely legal, or enforced as civil matters by specialist competition authorities rather than as crimes.

British petrol stations, for example, were found by the UK's Monopolies Commission (as it was called in the 1980s) to converge on a single price in any given geographical area by a means of implicit signalling through their pricing; one station might raise by a penny, then the others would either follow suit, or cut by a penny to indicate disapproval. A station owner who wanted to take market share might cut the price by a few pennies a gallon, but if his neighbours felt unable to match this, they would cut even more, 'punishing' the excessively competitive player for his ambition. The oil

companies which supplied the retail petrol stations were even
in the habit of providing 'selective price support' to facilitate
this game, which seems to have been played in a way oddly
reminiscent of the ACOL system of bidding in bridge. This
practice of selective price support was eventually banned, but
it was not considered a criminal offence.

The reason why companies inexorably tend to collaborate
with their competitors can be explained in terms of elementary
economics. One of the first things one learns to prove in price
theory is that in a competitive market, the price of a single unit
of output will tend to equal the *marginal* cost – the cost to an
established producer of increasing output by one more unit.*
But the marginal cost rarely equals the *average* cost of producing
a unit of output, because there are fixed costs, overheads and
the like. This is a rare example in which elementary economics
works, by the way; companies in industries with high fixed
costs and low marginal costs (like airlines, and media) go bust
a lot because they can't resist competing prices down to levels
which don't cover their overheads.

Even in industries where the problem isn't so drastic, there
is always a huge, unbearable tension between objectives of
market share and profitability. It's not really all *that* much of
an exaggeration to say that managing the trade-off between
these two objectives is at least half of the skill of strategic
management. And one of the clearest ways to ease the trade-

---

* There are various ways of expressing this, and the level of mathematical
rigour you find in textbooks runs the gamut from ludicrously simple to
simply ludicrous. But the intuition is not hard. If you can produce an extra
unit for $x, then you're obviously not going to sell it for less than $x. But if
you try to sell it for more than $x, someone will be able to undercut you. So,
the only consistent price is exactly $x.

off is by doing something which decreases the tendency for competition to reduce pricing. You can do this in numerous ways; the most productive and socially valuable one is to make an improvement to the product or get more efficient, allowing you to earn profits. At the other end of the scale, it's secret meetings and price-fixing. The point at which the line is drawn between legal and illegal behaviour – and the point at which a second line is drawn between merely prohibited behaviour and an actual crime – is a political-economic decision, made in the perceived interests of the system as a whole. This is true of cartels, even though the cost inflicted on consumers can be very large. It's also true of another area of corporate criminality, which has to be thought of as a market crime (and is typically tried as a civil offence) even though it's another example of a case where fraud becomes a crime of violence.

Toxic waste dumping

Fifteen miles from the site of Tino De Angelis' Bayonne facility, and four miles from the Harbor Tank Company where Tino's expansion fraud did business under Joe Lomuscio, there was another oil-storage tank farm in Edgewater, New Jersey, belonging to the Hudson Oil Refining Corporation. This company was run by Russ Mahler, one of the most important producers of recycled petroleum products in the USA. For a number of years, he had been responsible for taking oil and fuel from US military aeroplanes and ships, re-refining and purifying them and selling them as engine lubricants.

It was a good business for many years; in the period when

the Salad Oil King was his near neighbour, there was no evidence that Russ Mahler was doing anything wrong. But as the 1970s went on, business got tougher. The problem was that engine oil was becoming more sophisticated; additives were being used to improve the performance of brand-new motor oil. Not only did this reduce the value of non-premium recycled oil, the additives themselves caused problems in the purification process and made things uneconomic.

As a re-refiner, you gradually ended up with a large quantity of substandard, hard-to-sell lubricant, and a small quantity of incredibly toxic industrial waste, including cyanides, PCBs and heavy metals. The small amount of money you could make selling the oil to the few remaining customers willing to buy it would hardly pay for the cost of disposing the industrial wastes safely. And that was before the regulations started to tighten.

In 1976, the Resource Conservation and Recovery Act was passed, mandating the Environmental Protection Agency to establish national standards for waste oil, among other things, tightening up the regulations and establishing a federal standard set at a somewhat higher level than the patchwork of existing state regulation. Disposal of re-refining byproducts was about to become a lot more expensive. And shortly afterward, nasty things started showing up in the sewage system.

Russ ran another tank farm in Syracuse, New York. The sewage-pumping plant immediately downstream from this tank farm started to notice that the monitoring equipment on their outflow was consistently being tampered with by Russ Mahler's employees. When they installed tamper-proof sensors, they discovered that around 40,000 gallons of cyanide, benzene, toluene and xylene had been dumped into the sewage system over the course of a week. Russ had even been importing cyanide from plants in Canada and flushing it down the drain in Syracuse.

This scandal cost Russ his permit from the New York State Department of Environmental Control, but hardly stopped him. About a hundred miles down the road from the main Hudson plant in Edgewater, there was an abandoned mine shaft in Pittston Pennsylvania. Russ's employees put a total of three million gallons of toxic waste into this hole, which then spent the next few years seeping through watercourses until in 1979 it was found polluting the Susquehanna River. While the three state agencies of New York, New Jersey and Pennsylvania struggled to close down dumping grounds faster than Russ could find new ones, Ronald Reagan was elected, and Russ got a stroke of luck.

Congress passed a law (in 1980) exempting oil wastes from EPA regulation 'pending further research' into whether they were really all that bad. After paying fines and closing down the Pittston hole, Russ Mahler started a new oil company called Quanta Resources, and somehow convinced the New York authorities that despite having the same owner, employees and assets, it was nothing to do with the serial polluter that they had banned in 1976.

Meanwhile, heating oil prices were on the rise, particularly in New York City. While the re-refining of lubricant oil was a tough business and getting tougher, the heating oil business was potentially a real money-spinner. You could get waste oil very cheap – because of the cost of safe disposal, people would practically pay you to take it away, particularly if they had been dealing with their own PCB and dioxin problems by sticking the toxic waste into their barrels of used lubricant. If you then just relabelled it as heating oil, the profit margin could be huge. All you needed to triple your margins was a robust attitude to any qualms you might feel about sending barrels of dioxins, carcinogens and heavy metals to be burned and pumped into the atmosphere of one of the biggest and most densely populated cities on earth.

The scam was made even easier by the fact that, although New Jersey had strict regulations treating used lubricant as hazardous waste, Pennsylvania didn't. So it was possible to make a three-cornered trade; take waste oil into your system in New Jersey, complying with all state regulations, ship it a three-hour drive to Pennsylvania and relabel it, then export the heating oil to New York under its Pennsylvania labelling, without mentioning that it had ever been considered dangerous in New Jersey. Not all of the oil was burned, though. Several hundred gallons of dioxin-contaminated heating oil were spread across dirt roads in Times Beach, Missouri to reduce annoying dust clouds, as a result of which the EPA had to buy up every single house in Times Beach and leave it as a ghost town.

Eventually, Russ Mahler's exploits caught up with him. He served a year in prison for polluting the Susquehanna River, and Quanta Resources went bankrupt after newspaper and television reporters got a tip-off that they ought to commission tests on some of the fuel oil he was supplying. He remains one of a comparatively small number of people to have done jail time for an environmental crime.

The illegal dumping of toxic waste hardly seems like a minor or technical offence — it's one of the most serious corporate crimes of violence that there is, and given the orders of magnitude of people affected, it almost certainly significantly exceeds the worst excesses of the Mafia in terms of the number of deaths caused.* But it is a kind of fraud (and one which often involves other frauds in counterfeiting safety certification), and as a kind of fraud, it is essentially a market crime. If anything, the inclusion of this category of corporate violence under this heading ought to disabuse the reader of any sense that market crimes are 'technical' or 'victimless'; they include some of the most callous and despicable actions ever to be carried out under the heading of crimes of dishonesty.

As we all know, even when carried out entirely legally, the production, use and disposal of many modern products kills people in large numbers. The automobile industry, for example, causes thousands of avoidable deaths every day, but it is only guilty of a crime when something like the Volkswagen 'defeat device' scandal occurs and an attempt is made to avoid a specific regulation passed by the bodies whose job it is to decide on the trade-off between economic benefit and human cost. In fact, the decision as to what might constitute an acceptable level of risk to the public is a political one. It is made differently in different places depending on different assessments of the costs and benefits – a defining characteristic of a market crime. Russ Mahler benefited from the fact that there was no federal regulation of waste oil dumping and the state authorities did not co-operate with one another.

---

* With a large amount of overlap, of course, as disreputable waste management companies have often turned out to have significant cross-ownership with organised crime families in the USA. There's a degree of vertical integration if you often have bodies to dispose of.

The temptation in looking at crimes of industrial pollution is to assume that the only victims are the people who are actually physically harmed. In fact, the population affected does not stop at the edge of the toxic cloud. The market crime inherent in a pollution case is an attack on the overall framework by which we trade off environmental costs against economic benefits. It's a crime against the control system of the overall economy, the network of trust and agreement that makes an industrial economy liveable.

A fraudster of any kind is someone who has managed to subvert that network and operate without the normal constraints of civil society. And the 'snowball' property of fraud tends to ensure that once those controls are escaped, the enterprise will tend to grow at a compound rate, as dishonest profits are reinvested in more dishonest business. In biological contexts, a part of the system which has escaped the normal self-regulatory mechanisms and begun to grow without constraint is called a *cancer*. Unless they are controlled, fraudulent business units tend to outcompete honest ones and drive them out of business. In doing so, they generate profits, and those profits can be redirected into financing the corruption of the whole system. Runaway corruption is something which does happen, and which can undermine entire societies.

A more typical example of a market crime, though, is something that feels a bit more victimless. There's not much disputing that there ought to be *some* regulation of the dumping of toxic waste, but more in regards to where the line should be drawn between interference in commerce and the rights of consumers. Only very intellectually pure libertarians indeed would think that the market could regulate air and water quality. But there can be situations in which a market crime is committed and your instinctive sense of outrage isn't engaged anything like as much. Sometimes it can even be the case that the rules made by the market to protect its own integrity involve pretty palpable injustice to the people who end up on the wrong end.

The Piggly Wiggly Corner

Clarence Saunders of Memphis, Tennessee, knew as well as anyone did that there's a trade-off between the precautions you take against being the victim of theft, and the amount of business you lose by making things less convenient. He was the inventor of the modern self-service supermarket with his Piggly Wiggly chain, dispensing with the clerks and counters and allowing customers to put things in their own baskets. He used to run advertisements, praising his customers for their honesty and rhetorically asking 'why the downtrodden innocents are marked with suspicion', although his manual for shopkeepers devoted seven pages to the detection and reduction of shoplifting. His key insights were that theft was only one of the costs involved in running a grocery store, that it was by no means the largest one, and that by reducing the price below that of the competition, Piggly Wiggly would attract enough customers to make the overall economics work out.

Rather than losses from 'shrinkage' (as the industry came to euphemise the problem of shoplifting*), his biggest problem

---

* Techically, 'shrinkage' covers all losses from theft, both shoplifting by customers and pilfering by employees. Clarence Saunders, of course, had less of a problem with the latter.

was making the Piggly Wiggly shops convenient enough that customers would accept that they did not make deliveries, and to keep the shelves filled with popular products and manage the ordering system in the absence of clerks who would naturally notice when stocks were running low as they went to fetch orders. His ergonomic and managerial inventions to solve this problem attracted admirers all over the world – among the people who visited his stores to understand his doctrines of lean inventories and 'just in time' ordering were Sakichi and Kiichiro Toyoda, the founders of Toyota.

It was not surprising that when Piggly Wiggly Stores Inc. listed on the Chicago Stock Exchange in 1919 it was a sensation. Three years later, it issued more shares and transferred to the New York Stock Exchange, and the problems began almost immediately. Piggly Wiggly Stores Inc. started trading in June of 1922, got into trouble in November and by 1923 Clarence Saunders had made enough bad decisions to cost him his company.

As we mentioned when looking at accounting fraud, stock markets like clean narratives; it's their way of managing the almost infinite variety of the information they have to deal with every day. This often means misfortune to companies which look like they ought to have a simple story ('Buy Piggly Wiggly, the chain of self-service stores that's growing across the country!') but actually don't.

Piggly Wiggly Stores Inc., the company that people could buy shares in, didn't own the Piggly Wiggly name or the patents on Saunders' innovations. Those were all owned by the Piggly Wiggly Corporation, which in turn was owned by Clarence Saunders and a group of investor friends. The Stores Company owned the right to create new Piggly

Wigglys, which it sold to separate investors in different geographical territories. And it owned just under half of the 300 Piggly Wiggly shops which had been franchised by Clarence Saunders before 1919. So when a stock market investor walked down his own Main Street to buy coffee or bacon, he would not necessarily know whether the Piggly Wiggly he went to was one of the ones he had a share in, or one of the ones he had an indirect interest in via a licensing arrangement, or one of the ones that he had no ownership of at all, but which paid the same royalties to Clarence Saunders as his company did. As long as things went fine, of course, this was a happy state of ignorance with few consequences.

Things didn't go fine. Elliott Business Builders Inc., a company which franchised Piggly Wiggly shops in New York some years earlier, went bankrupt on 18 November 1922. The generation of headlines combining the name 'Piggly Wiggly' with the word 'bankrupt' spooked investors greatly, and the share price started to tank. At this point, Clarence Saunders started to do things which no doubt seemed sensible at the time.

Shares are bought and sold on credit. When you make a deal on the stock exchange,* the buyer has a few days to deliver the cash and the seller has a few days to deliver the shares. This arrangement is quite like trade credit, isn't it? And trade credit is both a necessary administrative convenience, and an opportunity for all kinds of misbehaviour, as readers

---

*If you are a broker or large investor who can make special arrangements with your broker, that is. You or I (unless you are a lot richer than I) pay cash on the nail, and our broker gets the benefit of the free credit. Note also that they've considerably shortened the settlement period since 1922.

will have noticed. In the case of the stock market, buying a share that you don't have enough money to pay for is called 'trading on margin', and selling a share that you don't own is called 'short selling'. In both cases, the expectation is that you will be able to scrounge up either the cash or the share before the 'settlement date'. You scrounge up cash by borrowing it or selling something else, of course, but how do you scrounge up a Piggly Wiggly share?

The answer, and the source of Clarence Saunders' misfortunes, is that the brokerage community maintain a pool of shares available to be borrowed,* and make them available to scrounge up by people who have made short sales. Since, on any given day, buy and sell orders in any given share tend to more or less even out,† the pool of shares available to borrow tends to be a reasonably constant quantity from day to day. Unless something unusual happens.

Something unusual, like professional traders launching a 'bear raid' on a company which is fundamentally sound, perhaps because of headlines combining its name with the word 'bankrupt'. Short-sellers jumped onto the Piggly Wiggly share, borrowing stock from the pool. Their aim, of course, was to wait until the price was much lower, then buy back the shares and return them, meeting their obligations to deliver the shares.

On its own, a bear raid does not affect the size of the pool of shares available to borrow all that much; when short-

---

*Because clients are always being annoying and putting in orders to buy a share that the broker didn't happen to be holding in his inventory, among other reasons.

† And if the orders are not evening out, you move the price until they do!

sellers sell their borrowed shares, they sell them to the same brokers who maintain the pool. All that happens is that the same pool of borrowable shares has more IOUs written against it – more obligations to, at some point in the future, deliver a share back to the borrowing pool. What does reduce the size of the pool is if someone – say Clarence Saunders – starts *buying* shares, and instructing his brokers not to make them available.

When this happens, you can get a situation where the stack of IOUs obliging short-sellers to deliver a share is greater than the pool of shares they can borrow to meet them. If you push things really hard, the pool can be totally exhausted and shares can no longer be scrounged up. When that happens, a short-seller is in a very nasty place – he has obligations to deliver the shares, but no way of doing so. Rather than borrowing the share, he has to buy it, and the holder of all the shares that used to be in the pool can literally name his price. This is called a 'corner', the fairly obvious metaphor being for the one that the short-seller is trapped in.

Clarence Saunders recruited the advice of Jesse Livingstone, the most celebrated stock exchange speculator of the Roaring Twenties. Of course he didn't have enough money to buy all the Piggly Wiggly Stores Inc. shares on his own, so he used the funds of the Piggly Wiggly Corporation which he controlled. He also borrowed on his own account, and authorised the Corporation to take out new debts as well. Finally, he sold more shares to the general public, on a 'layaway' plan which allowed them to be bought in instalments over ninety days.

It worked brilliantly. The shopkeeper from Memphis took on the New York sophisticates at their own game and won.

Having initially been as low as $30 a share, the Piggly Wiggly share price rose to a peak of $124 by 20 March 1923, when the shares were suspended because there were none of them left to trade.* Clarence announced that people who had sold shares to him in the previous week would have to come to him in his office at three o'clock with either the stock certificates or $150 in cash.

And then the regulatory authorities of the New York Stock Exchange started to get involved.

From this point on, the reader might start to think 'poor Clarence Saunders'. In many ways he was treated quite scandalously by the financiers. But it is worth looking at things from the perspective of other parties to this affair, and based on the information they had at the time. Using the corporate treasury of Piggly Wiggly Corporation to buy shares in Piggly Wiggly Stores and drive their price up for the benefit of Clarence Saunders is not really great behaviour; frankly it looks like the sort of thing that a control fraud would do. Nor is it really all that ethical to sell shares to the public in order to raise funds to inflate their price, but to do so on a 'layaway' plan which ensures that those members of the public can't sell their shares until the corner has finished and the price has fallen back again. And in general, as with the rules against insider dealing, it is not all that good for the image of stock market investment in general for the prices of popular shares to be pushed about by secret plans made by rich insiders.

It was for this reason that the Exchange had passed a rule

---

* That is, there were none left with the brokers to buy or sell; all the shares were either with Saunders, or with everyday investors who were happy to hang on to them.

in 1922 empowering it to take measures to prevent market corners. And Clarence Saunders was the first person to fall foul of this rule. It was not a criminal charge that tripped him up, or even a civil lawsuit. It was a simple extension of the settlement period. The Exchange announced that rather than having to deliver the shares to Saunders by 3 p.m. on the 20th, settlement in Piggly Wiggly would take place on the 26th, at 5 p.m. The short-sellers had another week.

A week is a long time when the majority of the shares are being held by small investors all over the South and Midwest, and when the brokerage houses have regional offices which allowed them to scour the country from Albuquerque to Sioux City. Customers who had bought the shares for $50 on 'layaway' found brokers knocking on their doors willing to pay $80 for the same shares, before they had made the second instalment. Clarence realised the game was up as share certificates flooded back into the brokers' pool from all over America, and dropped his cash price to $100. At this price, he had made a profit of half a million dollars, but this was not enough to cover the interest and fees on the money he had personally borrowed. He ended up having not only to sell the Piggly Wiggly Stores shares he had cornered, but his own stake, and his shares in Piggly Wiggly Corporation. Even this was not enough, particularly as the other directors started asking pointed questions about the use of corporate funds, and Clarence Saunders ended up in bankruptcy. He had played the game and won, but they had changed the rules.

These days, a corner like that would never have been allowed to get started; as soon as it became clear that you were manipulating the share price, the regulators would step in and require you to stop, then start to look through the books to decide which specific charge they were going to bring against you. This is the quintessence of a market crime; all Clarence did was buy shares at the going price, and everyone who dealt with him did so willingly and transparently. He did not deceive anyone; he literally took out advertisements in the newspapers saying what he was doing. But the market wanted to protect itself, and his conduct was disruptive to a set of economic institutions that other people rely on. So tough luck, Clarence. He found other investors and came back with other ideas in convenience retailing; at his death in 1953 he was halfway through patenting a fully automated grocery shopping machine called 'Keedoozle'. But he died a lot poorer and less happy than if he'd never borrowed $10m to teach Wall Street a lesson.

DEFRAUDING THE GOVERNMENT

'Some cases are humorous, some sad, and all are real. Some will anger you as a Federal employee and some will anger you as an American taxpayer.'

From the introduction to the US Department of Defense's
Encyclopedia of Ethical Failure

Bradley Birkenfeld had driven to the chalet up winding roads in his bright red Ferrari. Taking the perfectly chilled champagne from the fridge and putting it into an ice bucket, he threw open the blinds and saw the Alpine vista spread out before him. He turned to his Brazilian supermodel girlfriend and smiled, pointing out to the mountains. Then he did an Austin Powers voice and said 'Does it make you *Matterhorny,* baby?'

He really did. He even wrote about it in his autobiography as if he was proud of it. Although these days he has gone straight and lives a life of quiet philanthropy, the character of Birkenfeld in *Lucifer's Banker* is definitely one on whom the reader gets a sense that the finest things in life were a bit wasted.

I preferred his earlier work. His contributions to a piece of theatre called *United States Internal Revenue Services vs UBS AG*, played out in the Southern District Court of Florida,* were spot on. It even had a happy ending, as

---

* This is the IRS' home court, where big federal tax cases are usually tried.

Bradley Birkenfeld managed to get $75m transferred into his pocket, free, clear and legal. Some of the people in this book got away with the money and some went to jail; by a quirk of the system, Bradley did both.

The source of the money in this case was indeed the US tax authorities. The government has one attractive property as a target for someone aiming to commit a fraud – it is prepared to take on nearly anyone as a customer. While most private sector businesses can refuse you credit terms or turn away your business just because they don't like the look of you or they heard a rumour, the government usually feels like it has to give a reason. In very low-trust societies, government corruption is even more rife than you might expect, precisely for this reason; it is the economic actor which cannot, by definition, be part of a small personal trust network, but which has to, also by definition, get involved in the economic life of nearly everyone.

Some qualifications are needed to this sweeping statement. In cases where the government deals with private companies simply on a normal commercial basis – as a purchaser of paperclips or janitorial services, say – it is not necessarily more vulnerable to crime than a similarly sized and equally well-managed private company. Not *necessarily*, that is, but in fact public sector organisations usually are a bit more vulnerable, because there are no private companies of similar size and organisational style to an industrialised country's government. Public sector bodies are usually very big, and they have senior management functions delegated to non-specialists who were usually elected to office for reasons unrelated to their competence in financial control.* This

---

* They also, without wanting to make too much of this, tend to have people

tends to matter more in big defence contracts than in paper-clip procurement.

But if you spot these disadvantages, there's no reason why the purchasing and commercial departments of a public sector body shouldn't be able to control fraud almost as well as their private sector counterparts. They can choose who they buy from or supply; they can decide who gets terms and who pays cash, which of their contractors get cash up front and which are paid on completion. In these parts of the government, which do the same sorts of things as normal businesses, the government doesn't *have* to deal with crooks, it's just a bit more likely to.

Where the government can't turn away business, though, is in its involvement with the rest of us through the tax system. Everyone pays tax, so everyone has an opportunity to avoid tax, and the only way that the tax authorities can avoid dealing with someone is through the counterproductive means of letting them off their tax liability. And tax fraud is big business.

The distinction between tax avoidance and tax evasion is a commonplace – 'avoidance' is usually taken to be the (usually legal) use of technicalities and corporate structures to minimise a tax liability, while 'evasion' is the (usually illegal) act of providing false information to the tax authorities in order to conceal the existence of a liability in the first place.

---

in senior positions with major financial responsibility, who have become used to a lifestyle totally out of proportion from what they might be able to enjoy if they were not an elected representative. Government corruption is probably another book all of its own, but yes, in a lot of cases the subversion of systems and breaches of trust are coming from inside the public sector organisation, not outside.

Of course, the two categories overlap. If you are a really aggressive avoider, you may believe you have no tax liability to declare, but the taxman may disagree and consider you to be an evader.

Some countries (most importantly Switzerland) have recognised a third category of offence – that of 'tax fraud'. The distinction is between a mere neglect to inform the tax authorities of a source of income, and the actual presentation of a fraudulent document. Although it might be thought that this is a distinction without a difference (and in general, the tax collectors of countries which are home to holders of Swiss bank accounts have tended to be scathing about it), this has on occasion had considerable legal importance. Under Swiss law only felonies (like tax fraud) are extraditable offences, and minor peccadilloes like 'mere' tax evasion were until quite recently not considered to be important enough to outweigh the constitutional protection of bank secrecy.

This distinction was the basis of Bradley Birkenfeld's crime. He was an employee of UBS, the big Swiss bank, who had responsibility for finding American clients. And he was very good at it, which is why the usually rather staid Swiss tolerated his exuberant pursuit of cars, girls and mediocre sex comedies. His modus operandi was really simple: find a rich person, pal up to him and promise him that you can achieve the 'three zeroes' (zero income tax, capital gains tax and inheritance tax). Then get your new friend to send his money to Switzerland, tell the Swiss authorities that he is a US citizen and so won't be paying Swiss tax and don't tell the US authorities anything about him at all.

Having stuck the money in Switzerland, Birkenfeld's

clients had the problem of what to do if they wanted to spend it. Although there were some attractively spy-ish solutions attempted, like small-carat diamonds hidden in tubes of toothpaste, the most efficient method turned out to be a simple one – the bank which had the deposit, because it could take cash as collateral, would be prepared to give the customer a loan, charging interest on it equal to the interest that the deposit was earning, plus a fee for the service. This not only allowed the tax evader to bring the money onshore in a legal account with an ATM card and all the other useful payment technologies, it even generated an interest expense that could be set off against income on the client's declared onshore investments.

Everything was going fine until Bradley Birkenfeld fell out with his Swiss bosses. In his book, he suggests that this was the result of motiveless malice with an element of jealousy at his talent (it's also possible that they just got sick of his jokes). In any case, he resigned and shortly after showed up in Washington DC with a lawyer and a determination to talk to the authorities about tax evasion facilitated by UBS. The IRS, it is fair to say, hit the roof. They immediately demanded that UBS provide them with a full list of all their clients who were US citizens. UBS, in a decision which presumably seemed sensible at the time, said no.

Telling Uncle Sam to get lost is usually a bad move, and indeed it turned out to be, but it was not as crazy as it seemed. The old order was changing, and not everyone had realised it.

In the aftermath of the Second World War, it was understandable that many people, particularly in Europe, would want to hold some of their wealth away from possible confiscation by the government,* particularly in countries close to the Iron Curtain. The Cold War itself created many situations in which the diplomatic and intelligence communities were glad of the existence of a world of secret money and unaccountable transactions. And the gradual decolonisation of places like the Dutch Antilles and the Cayman Islands left many small countries with few natural economic advantages other than a set of tax treaties and a legal structure familiar to First World bankers. It was only in 2003 that the Organisation for Economic Co-operation and Development made it any sort of priority at all to do something about tax havens.

Over the following years, the US authorities had got tougher and tougher on tax crime (in particular, Swiss-regulated bankers like Birkenfeld were absolutely not meant to be touting for business in the USA, and they were instructed to tell immigration authorities that they were only on pleasure trips). But bank secrecy was still a core principle of Swiss law, and that distinction between 'evasion' and 'fraud' made all the difference. Not only did UBS expect to have the full diplomatic weight of their government behind them, they were possibly in a situation where they could not comply with the US request even if they wanted to; handing over bank account details was against Swiss law outside of very tightly drawn exceptions. This was the point where I began to take an interest.

---

* Although perhaps less understandable that they trusted the Swiss banks to keep it for them – the scandal related to the Swiss banks' attempts to take possession of 'dormant accounts' of the victims of the Nazi Holocaust is its own story.

At the time, I was an investment analyst with a specialty in making enemies at UBS by writing nasty things about the outlook for their business after the global financial crisis. I was also one of only a few people in the City of London who subscribed to the PACER US court records system. So I saw it all happen, in slow motion. There are a few cases in this book where I was peripherally involved but failed to see the wood for the trees. This is not one of them – I had my eyes entirely open, and it was not a pleasant experience. Denial, when you are not part of it, is actually quite a terrifying thing. One watches one's fellow human beings doing things that will damage themselves, while being wholly unable to help. It's even more acute if, as was the case for me, you have to write about it every day and get your facts checked by people who disagree with you.

During the few weeks of *IRS vs UBS*, I spoke to bankers with twice my experience, executives with decades more experience and professors of Swiss tax law who had literally drafted the treaties governing their relationship with the USA. All of them told me that it was inconceivable that the names would be handed over. Sooner or later, the IRS would realise that it could not bully a sovereign state, and give up. They started to change their minds at about the time when Raoul Weil, their Head of Global Wealth Management, was declared a fugitive from justice.* Within the year, Switzerland and the USA had a new tax treaty and UBS had agreed to pay a fine of $780m to the USA.

For his part, Bradley Birkenfeld did not have a happy

---

* He was found not guilty in the end, in 2014, but something like that tends to concentrate the mind.

experience with the IRS. He had been unwise enough to start providing them with information before ensuring that he had immunity from prosecution. Unsportingly, the IRS investigators effectively used the information he had given them as a lever to get more; he had effectively confessed to aiding and abetting tax crimes in the USA, and the agents on the case did not feel like using their discretion to do Bradley a favour. In his book he claims that the IRS guys just simply hated him, a believable hypothesis. He was sentenced to forty months in prison and served thirty-one of them before being let out for good behaviour.

On his exit, though, he picked up a big cheque. While he was in jail, the courts had ruled that, although he had admitted his own crimes, he was entitled to whistleblower status for informing the authorities about the crimes committed by his employer. And the relevant whistleblower statute entitles an informer to between 15 per cent and 30 per cent of the money collected as a result of their information. Of the UBS fine, some had been paid to securities and banking regulators and was ineligible for the program, but there was enough left for the IRS to make an offer of $104m. Net of tax (which Birkenfeld actually whined about having to pay), that left $75m.

There was no particular reason why the offshore tax evasion franchise collapsed – it wasn't a cumulating, snowballing fraud like most of them. It was just not useful any more. The Cold War was over, and so the governments of the developed world had less interest in maintaining plausibly deniable boltholes with which one could fund shady things. Top rates of tax had been falling for decades, so there was less urgency felt by the global elite. And so tax evasion is a bit of a boring business these days; there are hardly any Birkenfelds left, to the chagrin of Ferrari dealers and the joy of people who like peace and quiet in restaurants.

There are not very many countries left where you can deposit money in a bank and feel sure that its concealment from your domestic tax authorities is guaranteed by the force of law. Secrecy is forced to work through obscurity: layers of trusts owning trusts owning companies which own companies, making it more and more difficult for the taxman to establish the true owner of an asset, and creating uncertainty and legal expense for anyone wanting to prove that tax is due, and due to them rather than to another country. In this way, the whole field drifts into the hands of lawyers and accountants and starts looking more like avoidance than evasion. The creation of reasonable doubt over the existence and magnitude of a tax liability tends to move the whole operation in the direction of the civil rather than criminal courts, and to make the question one of what steps it is reasonable for the public purse to take to guard its tax revenues. Modern tax evasion, then, occupies a borderline between a market crime and an old-fashioned long firm against the government, with the credit extended by the fact that tax is paid in arrears.

There is one kind of tax fraud, however, which is worth special consideration, as it very much lies on the 'long firm' end of this spectrum.

Carousel fraud

There's a temptation to think of tax evasion as distinct from other kinds of fraud – if the tax you're avoiding is calculated as a percentage of the profits on a legitimate business, surely you have to be in a legitimate business to start with. But this is less a case of being sophisticated about fraud than it is of being naïve about tax. For one thing, the old adage is true that a penny saved is a penny earned. Tax is one of your input costs as a business, and if you can avoid it, then you can undercut competitors and expand your business at a rate unconstrained by the normal realities. Sometimes the government will even give you a chance to steal cash, for example when it delegates the collection of some of its tax revenue to private companies. This happens most frequently with sales taxes (which have to be collected at the point of sale), and is the basis of one of the biggest fraud segments in Europe – the so called 'carousel fraud'.

Explanations of carousel fraud tend to melt the brain. Defence lawyers for people accused of the crime absolutely love to draw tricky diagrams and watch the jury's eyes glaze over. The best way to understand it is to build up from the basic component: the mechanics of VAT collection. Keep your eye on the fact that the traders are meant to be collecting a consistent percentage of their mark-ups* (the difference

---

*Americans and readers in other countries that don't have a VAT might be scratching their heads a bit here. Why, why do this, rather than just charging sales tax on the final price? Basically, because when sales taxes get higher than about 8 per cent, people start making strenuous efforts to avoid them, and retail customers don't report their accounts to the government but business customers do. So by charging the VAT stage by stage through the process of distribution, you get a series of automatically generated checks; when Freddy claims a refund of £200,000 it triggers a check that Jim-Bob has paid the same amount. As well as facilitating checking, the system of refunds for VAT already paid on inputs ensures that the tax doesn't 'layer' – you don't want the eventual tax rate on the final sale to depend on the number of different companies and wholesalers involved in the process.

between cost and selling price – hence 'value added') and sending it to the tax authorities.

So, the basic component of the fraud is that the first trader (let's call him Jim-Bob) makes a widget out of scrap metal. He sells the widget to the second trader (let's call him Freddy) for £1m plus 20 per cent VAT. Freddy sends £1.2m to Jim-Bob's bank account, and Jim-Bob has an obligation to pay £200,000 to the UK taxman.

Freddy then sells the widget to the local donkey sanctuary, which is a charity registered for VAT. Assume he sells it at widows-and-orphans rates, for the same £1m plus VAT that he paid for it. The donkey sanctuary sends £1.2m to Freddy. Freddy has, in principle, an obligation to give the UK taxman the £200,000 of tax he has collected on their behalf. But set against this, he is due a refund of the £200,000 tax he has already paid, to Jim-Bob. Freddy has no net VAT obligation.

The donkey sanctuary, as a VAT-registered charity, is allowed to claim a refund of the VAT it has paid. So the government sends a cheque for £200,000 to them. If Jim-Bob then pays the £200,000 he owes, this transaction is all square – as things turned out, there was no mark-up on Freddy's part of the deal, and the eventual final sale was to a party that doesn't pay VAT, so the government ended up getting zero tax revenue. If Jim-Bob disappears, though, the government has made an unplanned donation to a donkey sanctuary, the counterpart to which is the writing-off of Jim-Bob's debt. By pretending to collect the tax and then not remitting it, Jim-Bob has managed to extract a cheque for £200,000 from the taxman.

To be honest, making a widget factory disappear is not a convenient thing to do, and setting up a fraudulent donkey sanctuary is an eccentric way to launder money. So let's switch things up a bit to get something more clearly profitable. To do so, we'll take advantage of the *other* crucial detail of VAT collection – because tax is collected on final sales in the country where those sales are made, in the European Union imports and exports are carried out on a VAT-free basis. That means that importers don't get charged VAT on their purchases, and exporters, like the donkey sanctuary, can apply for a refund of the VAT that they have already paid to domestic suppliers.

The VAT-free status of imports and exports comes into the picture twice. Rather than producing his widget – in fact, since we're adding realism, let's be explicit. It's no longer a widget, it's a mobile phone SIM card, the preferred vehicle of carousel fraudsters because they're valuable for their weight so you have less leakage to shipping costs. So instead of producing a widget, Jim-Bob imports £1m of SIM cards from a supplier in France, called Jean. He sells them to Freddy for £1.2m, recording his obligation to pay £200,000 of VAT to the British taxman. (Jean, of course, is an exporter, so he neither charges VAT to Jim-Bob, nor records any liability to the French taxman.)

Freddy then sells the SIM cards to a French customer, called Pierre. He sells them at mate's rates, for £1m, and since he is an exporter, he reclaims the £200,000 of VAT he paid to Jim-Bob, getting his cheque from the government. Now, here comes the 'carousel' bit. We can close the loop by assuming that Jim-Bob's supplier Jean, and Freddy's customer Pierre are the same person (called Jean-Pierre). Jean-Pierre has now got his SIM cards back, and has neither gained nor lost on the deal – he received £1m cash from Jim-Bob and paid it to Freddy. What has happened in the UK, though, is that the tax authorities have sent £200,000 to Freddy, on the understanding that they will be receiving the same sum from Jim-Bob.

Now we set the carousel in motion ... Let's presume that the tax authorities allow Jim-Bob to pay in arrears.* Say ninety-day terms. And we know that every time the SIM cards move from Jean-Pierre, to Jim-Bob, to Freddy and back to Jean-Pierre, Freddy gets a cheque for £200,000 and Jim-Bob records a tax debt of the same amount. How many times can we move those SIM cards round in a circle in ninety days? Even given the laziest drivers and warehousemen, you'd have to guess that the answer is at least ten. So by the final day of the quarter, Freddy has received refund cheques totalling £2m, while Jim-Bob has a bill from the VAT authorities, also for £2m. It is now time to give the taxman the bad news – Jim-Bob is nowhere to be found and has disappeared. Meanwhile, Jean-Pierre comes into his office on the first day of the new quarter and is happy to see he has a new order for £1m of SIM cards from a new customer, called 'Bob-Jim'.

These frauds are tough to bust. In this example, I can let you in on the truth, that Jim-Bob, Freddy and Jean-Pierre were all conspirators and they split the £2m between them. But of the three of them, Jim-Bob is the only one who is going to be easy to make a case against,† because he's the

---

* As they do, although with substantially more checks and balances than they used to in the early days of the VAT-free treatment of imports and exports before they realised they were losing literally billions to carousel fraud. They are also substantially tougher when it comes to checking up on things before sending Freddy his refund too, which causes significant cash flow problems for innocent exporters.

† Even the case against Jim-Bob might not be open and shut, if instead of literally scarpering he had the sense to put his company into bankruptcy and

one who piled up a big debt to the government and didn't pay it. Freddy has done everything right – he paid the bills from Jim-Bob and then applied for VAT refunds to which he was legally entitled. And Jean-Pierre hasn't done anything wrong – he has bought and sold SIM cards at the market rate, and how are you going to prove he knew that his British customers were connected?

In fact, it's quite easy to see how parties could be brought into this fraud who really were innocent, and it's likely that some innocent people have gone to jail as conspirators for the crime of not being picky enough about who they do business with. Since over the course of ninety days, this syndicate is making a 100 per cent return on their initial investment of £1m, they have plenty of scope to make a loss on their SIM-card trading business if it incorporates a few more 'buffers' into the system, clouding the trail by offering attractive prices to entice honest traders to insert themselves into the chain. You can also (this is called a 'countertrading' fraud), send another packet of SIM cards round the system in the other direction, so that some of the stages in the middle have no net liability to report and therefore no automatic reports to the taxman are made. And it helps for everyone to have bank accounts with an offshore bank that isn't very reliable in responding to inquiries from the tax authorities. In other words, all of the obfuscatory arsenal of the fraudster is available to conceal the bad intentions of the party who is planning to carry out a

---

make it look like a normal case of trading losses where the VAT man was sadly just one of a set of unlucky creditors. It was not uncommon in the heyday of carousel fraud for failing companies to be taken over by crooks simply for their potential as a vehicle for this crime.

classic long firm fraud against the government – to build up a big trading debt and then not pay it.

The reason why VAT fraud has been so difficult to stamp out, though, is the one that we stressed to begin with – most of the defences that private companies use to defend themselves against fraudsters are not available, or only available in very restricted form, to the taxman. Everyone pays tax; you can't just refuse to register a firm for VAT without reason. It's important to export trade that the VAT can be reclaimed, and so law-abiding taxpayers have a reasonable expectation that their refund claims will be processed promptly and not unduly held up by fraud investigations. The tax authorities have enough political unpopularity as it is, without sending honest traders into bankruptcy. And the nature of VAT is that it has to be paid in arrears and on a net basis – a trader who both pays and collects VAT can't be expected to finance a £200,000 timing gap just because they sold some inventory to a domestic client when they were expecting to sell it to a foreigner.

By way of a digression, this is a perfect example of why frauds are difficult to prosecute. The description of a carousel fraud above took me about five attempts to write, using every possible trick I could think of to make it comprehensible and keep the reader's interest. It is still quite difficult; I have to go back and remind myself from time to time how it can work. And this is a simplified and cut-down version of the real-life frauds that revenue officers have to explain to a jury; in real life the criminals will actually try to make it more complicated and harder to keep track of. As a specific crime, carousel fraud is hellish to understand and only real specialists can keep all the details of one in their heads at once. But the underlying

principle is as simple as you like. By taking advantage of the
way that the tax is collected, someone creates a situation in
which the government has advanced them some money, in
the anticipation that it will be paid back. The person who has
run up the liability disappears without paying for it, leaving
the person who borrowed the cash dishonestly the richer. It's
a long firm fraud. If you need to understand one, keep your
eye on a) who it is that is holding the cash, b) who it is that has
the liability that's going unpaid and c) whether there's reason
to believe that there's a relationship between the two of them
that makes it likely that Jim-Bob would do something to put
cash in Freddy's pocket.

Money laundering

As well as its power to tax, the government can get things it
wants and provide benefits to the community it serves by
enacting and enforcing laws. One of the key advantages
enjoyed by people who obey the law is that (as well as avoiding direct punishment), they can use the legitimate market
economy to make and spend their money and get rich. If your
main source of income is from criminal activity, however,
then there is a sense in which your money is as dirty as you
are.

Crime, or at least crimes other than the ones which are
the subject of this book, is a cash business. Banking records
can be subpoenaed and used to identify parties to an illegal
transaction.* Criminals tend to prefer a more anonymous

---

*Stealing something, of course, is not a transaction. But it is hard to steal
bank deposits without leaving some trace of having done so. If you haven't

means of payment. However, precisely because the ownership of large piles of cash is associated with criminality, it can be inconvenient if you want to make large purchases or investments – people tend to notice and investigate. The inability to conveniently use the modern banking and payments system is a huge disadvantage for criminals when compared to the legitimate economy.

So the government's ability to use the banking system and its records as a tool of law enforcement is an important part of its overall power to enforce its laws. It is also, to return to a theme, a significant check on the growth of criminal enterprises; a drug ring cannot grow faster than its cash-handling capability. Undermining this system and trying to make dirty money appear clean is a fraud against the government, and the name of the crime is 'money laundering'.

Money laundering tends to carry harsh penalties because the nature of the crime is to erase evidence of other crimes, and the assumption is that anyone willing to go to the trouble of laundering their cash must be trying to avoid investigation for something very serious indeed. This presumption is also born out by the typical loss rates in a money laundering operation; the initial pile of cash can shrink by up to 50 per cent in the process of being converted into clean-looking bank deposits. This is also a measure of the extreme usefulness of the electronic payments system compared to having to do everything in cash, of course.

Like so many other offences, money laundering relies on

---

got the skills to carry out a fraud, and to persuade someone to voluntarily transfer money to you, you're better off trying to steal cash or directly realisable valuable goods.

the fact that once the circle of trust is penetrated, there are few or no further checks to pass. In the context of money laundering, the objective is to get cash transformed into a deposit held with a reputable bank. Once that objective has been achieved, the money is effectively 'clean' and can be spent or invested; a criminal may have other problems in explaining to the authorities how he is able to support a lifestyle well out of proportion to his honest income, but the payments system will not generate red flags.

And the example of money laundering also demonstrates one way in which systems of mutual trust break down. Call it the 'Trainspotting Problem', after the novel and film in which heroin addicts shared needles and therefore ended up catching the same diseases. If the purpose of a trust system is to avoid the need for checking, then you need to take into account that when you allow a new entity into the circle of trust, you are also, implicitly, making the decision to trust everyone that they trust. The way this works for money launderers is that good banks don't accept large deposits of dirty cash. They also tend to check up on transfers from banks which are known to be 'high risk' (in context, a euphemism for 'probably crooked'). But there is a tier of mediocre banks, who are not so bad as to be the subject of aggressive checking by the good banks, but neither are they so good as to be unwilling to deal with the bad banks. Plotting a path through a chain of financial institutions from one which is prepared to take a suitcase full of cash to one which will allow you to conveniently use the money is a big part of the skill of money laundering. (Of course, there are also short cuts, especially when good banks have corrupt branches. In 2011, HSBC was fined $1.9bn for not properly supervising its Mexican subsidiary. Branch managers had made special adjustments to the windows at their counters to accommodate the metal briefcases that the drug cartels favoured for carrying cash.)

The other crucial component of a money laundering strategy is a list of the ways in which something valuable can be owned, bought and sold without the identity of its owners being a matter of public record. This is particularly important when you are laundering payments not because their source is dirty (proceeds of crime) but because their eventual destination is (terrorist financing, for example). The list seems to shorten every year, as the international authorities crack down on the last remaining secrecy jurisdictions, and as reputable banks get more and more frightened of the consequences of money laundering convictions and reduce the size of their circle of trust.* But it is still possible to find small (and not-so-small) countries which allow the creation of companies with nominee directors and no register of shareholders, places with no land registry and so on. Anywhere that you can find lawyers who are prepared to conceal the names of those who pay them, and a legal system that allows them to get away with it, you will find money laundering.

And in many cases, a jurisdiction where the verification of ownership is really difficult and inconvenient can do a lot

---

*The relevant regulations are called 'KYC rules', for 'know your customer'. The principle is that as a bank (or lawyer, real estate broker, etc.), you are not meant to do any transactions where you are not sure of the true identity of the 'beneficial owner' (as in, not a lawyer's office or a front corporation) on both sides. That's hugely inconvenient, but every year the extent to which the regulators and cops are prepared to accept excuses seems to diminish.

of the work of one where the information is not available at all. It slows down any eventual criminal investigation, and the time gained can be used to create further and further layers of obfuscation, until the criminal is adding layers of concealment faster than the authorities can peel them away. But more than this, a jurisdiction where verification is difficult or time-consuming is one that changes the trade-off between checking and trust, the trade-off which is at the centre of the crime of fraud. The decision as to whether to process a particular transaction is always one of risk against return, and the aspirant money launderer can search around until he finds a financial institution which is willing to take the risk. Once that step has been achieved, the process of navigating up the quality spectrum can begin.

Money laundering is basically a market crime. It has been decided that, because the global financial system is so ubiquitous, it makes sense to use it as a tool of law enforcement. That decision having been made, the creation of a new set of crimes was an inevitable consequence. Airlines are not prosecuted for helping criminals flee justice* and the sellers of guns and balaclavas are not held liable for robberies, but financial institutions have, in return for their many privileges in the wider economic system, been delegated certain investigative tasks. Failing to meet those obligations, and gaining market share by allowing bad actors to use the honest economy's financial system, is a crime of dishonesty against the government.

---

* Although sometimes freight companies are held responsible for failing to take precautions against illegal immigration and people-smuggling.

THE BOTTOM LINE

'See they conducted experiments on convicts … I don't know on
what grounds they reason a man in jail is a bigger liar than one
out of jail … The chances are telling the truth is what got him
there.'

Will Rogers

I have to confess, I generally find commercial fraud pretty
amusing. There's something about the fantasy of it all that
appeals to me; the game of wits involved in creating an illusion of something, then choosing the right moment to whisk
everything away, and disappear somewhere warm with the
hot money. And you're stealing generally from rich people,
without using violence. It's got a bit of the appeal of Robin
Hood, with less danger of an arrow in the vitals. Leslie Payne
once said* that, if you have no convictions or bankruptcies on
your record, that 'everyone gets one free shot at a long firm',
and I'd be lying if I said I'd never daydreamed.

I have two friends who spend a lot more time than me
looking at the subject, though, and they don't share this
outlook at all. One is a hedge fund manager who augments
his returns by short-selling the shares of fraudulent stock
promotions, and the other is a computer expert who writes

---

* And Michael Levi the criminologist agreed, after looking through
conviction data and speaking to police officers.

programs to trawl through email archives and to catch online poker cheats. Both of them independently confirm something which you can check up yourself by randomly choosing a first-person account from the bibliography; the more time you spend trying to get inside a criminal's head, the less attractive you find them. They're cheats, is what they are, and like people who cheat at sports, they spoil the game for the rest of us. There's very little real art to the illusion; as we saw in Chapter 7, all there really is to it is to find a weakness in a system of management and control, and then to exploit the fact that lying is easier than telling the truth.

It's not by any means a victimless crime, either. Long firm frauds often end up bankrupting their suppliers, who then often have insult added to injury by being suspected of complicity in the fraud. Stock promoters steal people's lifetime savings and pension funds. Pyramid schemes victimise people who can't afford to lose the money, and tear apart communities and affinity groups in the process. Even when the immediate victim is someone like American Express Field Warehousing, who really look like they deserved to meet a Tino De Angelis, there are other victims we don't hear about. How many perfectly honest traders in agricultural commodities were unable to get working capital because all the lenders were scared of the next Salad Oil scam? There are too many of these parasites, and they don't get caught or sentenced nearly enough.

It's a sad fact, as my friends confirm, that if you want to find frauds, your best asset is a list of existing fraudsters. You might have noticed that comparatively few of the case studies we've looked at were first offences. There's something about commercial fraudsters that keeps them coming back to the same pattern of behaviour. And there's something about the modern economic system that keeps giving fraudsters second chances and putting people back into positions of responsibility when they've proved themselves dishonest. This is 'white-collar' crime we're talking about after all; one of its defining characteristics is that it's carried out by people of the same social class as those responsible for making decisions about crime and punishment. We're too easy on people who look and act like ourselves.

But beyond that, are there things that can be done? Looking at the frauds in this book, and in particular at some of the economic principles that underlie them, I think there is potentially a Golden Rule that can be extracted from looking at the way Bill Black busted the S&L fraudsters, or the decline of Artur Alves dos Reis, or the failure of Barings to stop Nick Leeson. Let's start thinking, one last time, about how frauds are made.

The fraud triangle

In passing at the end of Chapter 8, we started thinking about the extent to which frauds could be thought of as random events that happen when a bad person bumps into a structural control weakness. Things can be made a little more psychologically and sociologically complex than that. But not too much: Donald Cressey's model of the 'Fraud Triangle', set out in his 1972 classic *Other People's Money*, has never been surpassed.* The fraud triangle model is the equivalent of the

---

* Although in the typical way of management consultants looking for 'proprietary' solutions to sell, there have been all sorts of proposals for

classic murder triangle beloved of detective novelists. Rather than means, motive and opportunity, it suggests that a fraud happens when the following conditions are simultaneously met:

Need. Bankers commit acts of dishonesty for the same reason that heroin addicts do; they have been put in a position where they need to come up with larger sums of money than they can generate by honest means. This side of the triangle is agnostic as to the reason for the need; simple greed, institutional pressure, fear of admitting failure or whatever underlying cause, the first component of a fraud is someone who needs the money.

Opportunity. An opportunity to commit fraud is a weakness in a control and checking system – either one which exists because of the way in which the intrinsic variety of the system has been reduced to make it manageable, or one that the fraudster himself has created by exploiting a position of control.

Rationalisation. White-collar crime is committed by people who have been trusted with something, and there are psychological barriers to breaking a trust. Usually, before an opportunity to commit fraud is exploited by a person with a need, the fraudster will have to come up with a way of overcoming these barriers. This is a 'rationalisation' – a way of redescribing the crime so as to make it less emotionally repellent. Something like 'It's only a temporary measure

---

Fraud Squares, Double Triangles and all manner of other polygons. By the way, at the time of writing, *Other People's Money* could not be ordered to the reading rooms at the British Library, because their copy had been 'mislaid'. That's *one* possible explanation …

to put trades in this 88888 account', or 'If I get enough colonists to Poyais there will be a viable community'. Once the capability to rationalise is in place, it's there for good, seemingly; this accounts for the propensity of fraudsters to keep coming back to the well.*

We can think, as we did in Chapter 8 when we were talking about risk management and quality control, of the overall climate of fraud as being made up of little bits of the triangle, floating about. And that can begin to explain how things like the 'Canadian Paradox' come about. Places like Greece have lots of needs and a high propensity to rationalise. As a result, they need to run in a way that creates very few opportunities; in a low-trust society, you don't do business with strangers. Places like Canada can afford to provide lots of opportunities because a prosperous and egalitarian society creates fewer needs, and a high-trust economy is one in which the propensity to rationalise is low.

Time and size

But the fraud triangle model only takes us part of the way. It's a good basis for a risk management system, but we've already noticed that risk management solutions tend to miss the kinds of frauds that we have mainly been talking about. The fraud triangle does not distinguish between 'incidental' frauds launched against targets of opportunity, and 'entrepreneurial' frauds which are designed against specific targets by 'fraud

---

* The failure to come up with a convincing rationalisation is also presumably the reason that my own designs at a long firm have never got beyond the pipe dream stage.

entrepreneurs'. And, related to this, it is a model of the *incidence* of fraud rather than one of its *severity*.

The amount of money you lose in the event of your becoming a victim of a crime is dependent on two things: how long it takes you to discover the fraud, and the rate at which the fraudster can extract value from you while the crime is going on.* These two factors are why entrepreneurial fraud, as opposed to incidental fraud, is such a difficult management problem. It's hard to make estimates of how long it will take you to find out that someone's deceiving you and it's hard to guess what will go on in the meantime. (If it wasn't, nobody would get married.)

There are some things that you can say about the likely properties of a fraud though. First, that it will grow over time, and that it will probably grow quickly, because most frauds have the snowball property. And second, that if it is an entrepreneurial fraud, it will be something which bypasses all of the processes and controls that have been set up to prevent it so far.

That's the basis of my proposal for a Golden Rule: *Anything* which is growing unusually quickly needs to be checked out, and it needs to be checked out in a way that it hasn't been checked before.

Nearly all of the frauds in this book could have been stopped a lot earlier if people had been a bit more cynical

---

* If this was a formal mathematical model, there would need to be a bunch of other parameters. Most obviously, that if the fraud goes on long enough to drive you bankrupt, the amount lost also depends on how much is available to steal in the first place. Not having to bother with pedantry like this is one of the key advantages of an institutional approach to economics.

about growth. The S&L crisis, for example, was crystallised and brought to an end when the regulators passed a blanket rule limiting the rate at which an S&L could write new loans. The Medicare frauds were finally brought under a degree of control when computer systems were brought in which were capable of identifying providers which had rapidly expanded the claims they were making. And it's a fairly general principle of cybernetics or operations research. Whether you're looking at the temperature of an engine, the cell division of a tumour or the memory usage of a computer program, runaway growth is a sign that things have left the domain of the existing control system and need to be dealt with at a higher level of organisation.

It's more complicated than that

However, this isn't the end of the story – not quite. The Golden Rule might help to protect us from ongoing frauds, but we've seen from chapter 9 on market crimes that frauds can be defined retrospectively; there can be cases where the decision that needs to be made is not how to check transactions against a set of standards, but about what those standards themselves ought to be.

And that decision has to be a pragmatic one. We always face the same dilemma that the Victorians did: do you want to reduce fraud to a minimum, or do you want to be rich? If you're not going to take the risk of Poyais, you're not going to end up like Canada. The decision about what market crimes to create is not so different from the decision about how strictly to enforce laws against unambiguous crimes of dishonesty. The cost of eliminating dishonesty is much more to do with the amount of legitimate business that never gets done. The cost of dishonesty itself is inseparable from the extent to which bad actors drive out good. The trade-off that we need to make at the level of society is between these two quantities. Perhaps the best that we can do is to accept that fraud is an inevitable part of society, bring up our children to be honest, and adopt a sceptical – but not too cynical – attitude to things that seem too good to be true.

BIBLIOGRAPHY AND SOURCES

As mentioned on a few occasions in the text, stories of frauds often make amusing reading, once you have overcome the miasma of self-pity and exculpation. Criminological, sociological and economic works on financial crime tend to be somewhat less exciting reading, and the selection is not very wide; it is a subject that the academic literature tends to shy away from. This is something of a pity, given the actual importance of white collar crime, when compared to the relatively minor forms of social deviance which make up the run of the mill of criminological research. A highly honoured exception is Michael Levi, whose book on long firm fraud, *The Phantom Capitalists* (Routledge, 1981) is essential reading and one of the only really satisfying treatments of crime as an economic phenomenon. His *Regulating Fraud* (Routledge, 2014) is also well worth reading.

The other classic – if you can find it – is Donald Cressey's *Other People's Money* (1954), which introduced the fraud triangle psychological model. Since this one is out of print and widely stolen from libraries, it might be easier to read *Why They Do It: Inside the Mind of White Collar Criminals* by Eugene Soltes (PublicAffairs, 2016). *The Economics of Innocent Fraud* by J. K. Galbraith (Houghton Mifflin, 2004) provides some clues to the location of the boundary between criminal deception and the ordinary operation of a capitalist economy, while the novel *The Shipping Man* by Matthew

McCleery (Marine Money Inc, 2011) is a lightly fictionalised account of how trust and deception work when hedge fund managers try to get involved with Greek ship owners.

On specific frauds, most of the stories in this book come from crimes big enough to have at least one good book written about them; it is a genre with something of a short shelf life as the progress of economic growth tends to render the amounts of money involved in scams from ten years ago almost quaint. On The Land of Poyais, I read *The Land That Never Was* by David Sinclair (Da Capo Press, 2004), and the accounts in *Forging Capitalism* by Ian Klaus (Yale University Press, 2014), and *The First Latin American Debt Crisis* by Frank Griffith Dawson (Yale University Press, 1990). I also found the book review in the 1822 *Quarterly Review* which showed that people were on to 'Thomas Strangeways' early on.

Leslie Payne's *The Brotherhood: My Life With The Krays* (Michael Joseph, 1973) is almost pedagogic in its detail on medium-sized long firms, while the definitive account of 'The Great Salad Oil Swindle' is the book of that name by Norman Miller (Coward McCann, 1965) (contemporary newspaper accounts of Tino De Angelis also demonstrate the extent to which he generated anecdotes, and the *Life* magazine interview on his release from prison is a classic). A similar laugh-a-minute account of the OPM Leasing affair is given in *Other People's Money* by Stephen Fenichell (Anchor Books, 1985), although *Bad Business* by Robert Gandossy (Basic Books, 1985) gives a somewhat more sober account of the way that Mordy and Myron managed to bypass all controls that people should have put on them. Readers who don't want to plough through countless Reddit pages on dark markets might prefer to read about them in *DarkMarket* by Misha Glenny (Vintage 2012).

Malcolm K. Sparrow's *License to Steal* (Basic Books, 2007) is the definitive work on Medicare fraud, and the source of the alarming statistic that up to a third of the program was stolen at the peak in the 1990s. His analysis of the methods of Medicare fraudsters is also invaluable in general application to the relationship between controls and the crooks who work around them.

On pyramid schemes, Charles Ponzi's own autobiography, *The Rise of Mr Ponzi* (Public Domain, 1936) is a detailed if slightly disturbing read; he appeared to believe that he could allay suspicions simply by asserting that he was honest immediately after detailing an obviously dishonest act. Patrick Halley's *Dapper Dan* (CreateSpace, 2015) gives a lot of the necessary background on how the city of Boston worked at the time, in the form of a biography of Ponzi's lawyer. The depressing reality of small-ticket pyramid schemes is brought home by *False Profits* by Robert Fitzpatrick and Joyce Reynolds (Herald Pr, 1997) and by *Ponzi Schemes in the Church* by Dr Sidney Stewart (Independently published, 2017). Guy Lawson's book on Sam Israel, *Octopus* (Oneworld publications, 2013) includes a lot of fascinating detail on Bayou Capital and on the prime bank guarantee fraud community which was not available in contemporary newspaper coverage. The story of Pigeon King International was covered from start to finish in *Better Farming* magazine, although Jon Mooallem's 2015 story in the *New York Times* magazine is more fun to read. The Federal Reserve conspiracy books promised on p. 112 are *The Secrets of the Federal Reserve* by Eustace Mullins (Bridger House Publishers Inc,

2009), and *The Federal Reserve Conspiracy* by Anthony Sutton (Dauphin Publications Inc., 2014), but really, don't bother. Cheri Seymour's *The Last Circle* (Trine Day, 2010) also, unfortunately, fits into this category although as an account of someone whose life was badly affected by coming across Robert Booth Nichols it has some value.

Murray Teigh Bloom's *The Man Who Stole Portugal* (Secker & Warburg, 1967) is the best work in English on the Banknote Affair, although Thomas Gifford's novel *The Man From Lisbon* (McGraw-Hill 1977) seems to get all the key facts right in exploring Alves Reis' psychology. Of the many corporate histories of the Bre-X scandal, my favourite is *Bre-X* by Jennifer Wells (Orion Business, 1999); on drug counterfeiting and Vioxx I would choose *Poison Pills* by Tom Nesi (Thomas Dunne Books, 2008) and *Dangerous Doses* by Katherine Eban (mariner Books, 2006), although there are many excellent retrospectives on what went wrong in medical journals.

For most of the accounting and stock market frauds, I watched them happen in real time and had my own records. *Confessions of a Wall Street Analyst* by Dan Rheingold (Collins, 2006) gives an excellent summary of the 00s telecom frauds, as well as a clear portrait of why analysts are such weak protection; it should be read alongside Bethany McLean's business classic, *The Smartest Guys in the Room* on Enron (Portfolio Trade, 2003). I cannot bring myself to recommend *The Wolf of Wall Street* by Jordan Belfort (Bantam Books, 2007) but it is out there. As a description of how the stock market works, *Supermoney* by the pseudonymous 'Adam Smith' (actually George Goodman) (Michael Joseph, 1972) is much better.

Bill Black's *The Best Way to Rob a Bank is to Own One* (University of Texas Press, 2005) brought the concept of a control fraud to us, although the book is very much from Black's own perspective within the Federal Home Loan Bank system. Charles Keating's biography, *Trust Me* by Charles Bowden and Michael Binstein (Random House 1993) gives the other side of the picture, and *Inside Job* by Stephen Pizzo (McGraw-Hill, 1989) is a fair history of the S&L disaster. *Rogue Trader* by Nick Leeson (Little, Brown & Co, 1996) is another example of the fraudster autobiography genre, and really needs to be read alongside a more objective history such as *All That Glitters* by John Gapper and Nick Denton (Hamish Hamilton Ltd, 1996). There is no really good history of the PPI scandal yet, but *Chain of Title* by David Dayen (The New Press, 2016) describes a distributed control fraud in the USA.

Mike Freeman's *Clarence Saunders & The Founding of Piggly Wiggly* (History Press Inc., 2011) gives the bones of the market corner, while the GE cartel is described in *The Great Price Conspiracy* by John Herling (R.B. Luce, 1962), and the unique management style which supported it in John Brooks' *Business Adventures* (Hodder & Stoughton ltd., 2014). The John Freeman insider dealing ring was put together from contemporary newspaper reports which are easily available online and Russ Mahler's crimes are summarised in 'Crime in the Waste Oil Industry', a journal article by Alan Block and Thomas Bernard (1988).

As a former employee of a Swiss bank myself, I received a comprehensive and tedious series of training courses in money laundering and tax fraud (how to avoid it, rather than how to do it!), and how to recognise some of the key phrases, as demonstrated in Bradley Birkenfeld's *Lucifer's Banker* (Greenleaf Book Group, 2016) – he clearly did some of the same courses. On money laundering in general, *The Laundrymen* by Jeffrey Robinso (Arcade Publishing, 1997) is still relevant, while Rachel Ehrenfeld's *Evil Money* (HarperCollins, 1992) is slightly more up to date.

For historical crimes, Jonathan Levy's *Freaks of Fortune* (Harvard University Press, 2012) and Frederick Martin's *The History of Lloyd's and of Marine Insurance* (MacMillan, 1876) give a lot of the background on how capitalism developed to the point of being able to support really big frauds. David Kynaston's history *The Financial Times* (Viking, 1988) gives some detail on the milieu of the Victorian financial market, although George Robb's *White Collar Crime in Modern England* (Cambridge University Press, 1992) is really irreplaceable. Rollo Reuschel's *The Knights of Industry* (Public Domain, 1895) is still available in an electronic edition.

GLOSSARY OF FINANCIAL TERMS

Accruals, in accountancy contexts, the practice of trying to make profits, costs and revenues match up to the time period in which the transactions happened rather than when the cash was paid or received.

Actuary, a specialist accountant for insurance companies. The author will not enter into correspondence with outraged actuaries who want to tell him it's more complicated than that.

Affidavit, a public record that someone has affirmed something to be the case.

Audit, the act of checking over a company's set of accounts to make sure that everything is both true and properly accounted for.

Bond, a tradeable loan. Bonds have standardised legal documentation so they can be bought and sold by people who haven't met the original borrower.

Cartel, a price fixing arrangement between companies.

Cash on delivery (COD), as it says, a commercial transaction carried out without credit, on the basis that payment is made at the time goods are delivered.

Collateral, something that the bank can take if you don't pay the loan back. Usually they will try to get a legal claim on more collateral than the value of the loan.

Credit risk, the risk that a borrowed sum of money won't be paid back.

Creditor, opposite of a debtor. The one the debtor owes the money to.

Equities, shares in a company. Part ownership of the profits and losses of a company.

Escrow, the practice of giving payment to an independent party, to release once the goods have been satisfactorily delivered or the service carried out.

Five forces, buyers, suppliers, competitors, substitutes, entrants. A way of describing the structure of an industry, invented by Michael Porter and beloved of management consultants.

Flotation, the process of selling securities to the public.

Fraudulent conveyance, the practice of transferring assets out of a company in the anticipation that it is about to go bankrupt. This might be done in order to keep the company trading when it shouldn't, or it might be done to move assets to a connected party and effectively steal from the creditors.

Interbank, when one bank deals with another.

Joint-stock corporation, a company with lots of shareholders, the implication being that most of the shares are owned by people who don't have any involvement in the day-to-day management.

Limited liability, most modern companies. You can only lose what you put in; if it goes bankrupt, the company's creditors can't pursue you personally for money that the company borrowed. Seems uncontroversial now but was a very big deal when the principle was first invented. Obviously highly convenient to corporate fraudsters.

Maturity, a bond 'matures' when the principal is paid back. 'Maturity' can also refer to the date on which this happens, or the amount of time left before that date.

Mens rea, literally 'guilty mind'. The state of knowing that what you're going to do is dishonest and intentionally doing it anyway. Very difficult to prove in cases of fraud, particularly long firms where the crook is claiming he was just unlucky.

Notary, a kind of lawyer specialised in the certification of documents. Notaries (and lawyers) wanting to argue it's more complicated than that, see 'actuaries' above.

Pledge, what you do to collateral. To give someone the right to repossess it. You should only do this to one lender at a time per piece of collateral, but if you're a fraudster you might to it two or three times.

Promote, the practice of marketing a company to the public, often by making exaggerated claims about its potential and profitability.

Secured, the status of a loan which has some collateral.

Securities, generic term covering both bonds and equities. Tradeable financial claims, sold to the public.

Sovereign, in the context of bond markets, a borrower which is a country.

Strict liability, of criminal and regulatory offences, the property that you can be guilty of it just by doing the bad thing, whether or not you had *mens rea.* On civil liberties grounds, democracies tend to not like to have too many strict liability criminal offences, but they often have to be created (sometimes as non-criminal regulatory sanctions) as protection against fraudsters because it is so difficult to prove *mens rea.*

SWOT (strengths, weaknesses, opportunities, threats), another consultant's tool for looking at competitive position.

Term, in the context of borrowing money, the period for which you borrow it.

Terms, in the context of paying for things, the amount of time you have to pay a bill and sometimes the interest rate you pay for not settling immediately.

Unsecured, the status of a loan with no collateral. Entirely dependent on the borrower making the payments.

ACKNOWLEDGEMENTS

Fraud is a slightly touchy subject for people who want to maintain a commercial career, so there is an element of 'no names, no pack-drill' to these acknowledgments. The head of forensic data analysis at a leading accountancy firm helped me out a great deal with suggestions, as did several senior bank regulators, all on the condition that I kept their names out of it. Thanks very much.

I owe a lot to my colleagues from when I was a banking analyst; Tom Rayner is mentioned in the introduction but I'd also like to thank Andreas Hakkansson for explaining the history of Swiss banking to me and Guillaume Tiberghien for allowing me to spend so much of my career doing obscure research into quirky little areas rather than doing something about the disgraceful state of my earnings models. Jonathan Pierce and Hugh Pye taught me everything I know about UK banks, although I would have been considerably richer if they had taught me everything *they* knew. Darren Sharma was a constant source of encouragement.

Henry Farrell read an early draft and, along with my superb editor Ed Lake, helped considerably in arranging a collection of fascinating facts and in-jokes into something resembling an actual book. Tess Read viewed the very earliest drafts of many of the sections and helped me keep the digressions under some semblance of control. Hilary Davies, my beloved mum and Glendra Read, my mother-in-law, both encouraged me during occasional dark moments.

The dedication at the front of the book is to Tess, as it should be, but this book is also dedicated to all the many victims of commercial fraud, over the years. As I hope it makes clear, we are all in debt to those who trust; they are the basis of anything approaching a prosperous and civilised society.

INDEX

3–6–3 banking 175
88888 account 167–8, 170–71
9THWONDER (online scammer) 43, 49

A
accounting scams 66, 97, 106, 113, 142, 149
accounts receivable *see* credit control
accruals principle 152
actuaries 114
Adoboli, Kweku 165
affidavits 9
affinity groups 90, 92, 94–5, 116, 284
Against Zenothemis 226
Alves dos Reis, Artur Virgilio 120–25, 214, 285
American Continental Corporation 177, 182
American Express 54–61
Amway 95
analysts, securities 130–31, 159–62, 194
AOL 240
appraisal fraud 179–80, 182
dead-horse-for-dead-cow 180–81
cash-for-trash 181
arbitrage 170
Archimedes 224
Arizona 113, 177–80
Arizona State Attorney General 113

Arnkel (saga character) 218–22
Arthur Andersen 154, 157
audit, auditors 17, 21, 56, 62, 66, 90, 99, 105–7, 109, 113–15, 132, 136–7, 149–52, 155–61, 171, 176, 179, 182, 189, 194
in the Victorian era 229–31

B
Baker, Mary 223
Bank of Angola and Metropole 124
Bank of England 1, 9, 14, 122, 188, 196
inquiry into failure of Barings 168
Bank of Portugal 121–5
bankers 4, 19, 38, 39, 286
nineteenth century, British 5, 7, 231
investment bankers 65, 68, 143, 144, 239–40
nineteenth century, American 89, 117
twentieth century, American 174, 268, 269
twentieth century, British 190
see also Charles Keating, Bradley Birkenfeld, Artur Alves dos Reis, Bob Diamond, Sir Brian Pitman, Sir Willy Purves
banknotes Escudo 120–25
Poyais dollars 13

printing, security features 121

bankruptcy 30, 33–6, 59–60, 71, 78,
    80, 101, 105, 216, 225, 233, 283
    in ancient history 34, 225

banks 2, 5, 12–14, 45, 52, 55, 65, 71,
    81, 88–9, 97–8, 111, 122, 151, 161,
    170, 174, 188–96, 205, 239, 268,
    280–81

Barclays 1–2, 188

Baring Brothers 17, 165–72, 238,
    285

Baring, Peter 170

Bayou Capital 105–13, 115

bear raid 258

Beer, AS 209

bees 239

Belfort, Jordan 145–7

Better Farming magazine 102

Bible 92, 122, 125, 216–18
    Ten Commandments 14, 23

Big Four, accountancy firms 157

Bigley, Elizabeth 223

Birkenfeld, Bradley 263–6,
    269–70

Bitcoin 44–9

Black, Bill 180–81, 185, 285

Blockbuster Video 153

Bloomberg 3

Bonnefoy, Philippe 172

bonuses 22, 165, 172, 184–6, 205

Boston 37, 84–90, 117–19
    thriftiness of citizens of 117

Bottomley, Horatio 230

bottomry 225

Brazilian straddle 163–4, 171

Bre-X 126–33
    as stock market promotion 129,
        132, 148

bribery 27, 65, 79, 89, 106, 221, 230,
    264
    of professionals vs laymen 114–15,
        179

British Bankers Association 12

Brooks, John 244

Busang 130–32

Business Adventures 244

Byock, Jesse 221

C

Calvin Klein 243–4

Canada 3, 11, 16, 84, 101, 126–130,
    251, 287, 289

Canadian Paradox 10–11, 116, 233,
    285

Capitalism 6, 96, 187, 208, 216, 225
    maritime 224

Cardozo, Benjamin 239

Carleton, Mary 223

Carnegie, Andrew 223

carousel fraud 271–8

cartels 23, 188, 244–9
    euphemism for drug gangs 46,
        281

cash flow 20, 27–8, 29, 31, 32, 34, 46,
    65, 67, 82, 88, 90, 102, 155
    fictitious profits vs 97, 148, 151,
        152, 154, 171
    government and 265, 272

Central banks see Bank of England,
    Bank of Portugal, Federal
    Reserve, 111, 120, 123,125

channel stuffing 159

chatroom 240

chief executives 1, 79, 189

circles of trust 113, 114, 116,137, 280,

Citizens for Decent Literature 178

City of London Convalescent Fund,
    Pension Society and Savings Bank
    227–8
Coakley, Dapper Dan 90
Coase, Ronald 204–5
collateral 36–9, 54–5, 61, 69, 143,
    151, 179, 267
    fraudulent appraisal of 179, *see*
        appraisal fraud
communism 183, 201, 204, 208, 227
Companies Act 1844 229
Companies Act 1900 231
compound growth 91, 96–9, 99–101,
    104–108, 195, 199, 254
compound interest 84–119, 195, 199,
    254
consolidation (accounting principle) 155
conspiracy theories 110
control engineering *see* operations
    research
control fraud 22, 23, 90, 163–97, 214,
    224, 260, 265
    distributed 184–97
'cooling out the mark' 78
Cordiner, Ralph J. 245
Cornell, George 26
counterfeiting 21–2,23, 61, 120–41,
    145, 148, 212, 216, 253
    of banknotes 120–24
    of drugs 135–7
countertrading (VAT fraud method)
    276
credit rating agencies 238
Credit Suisse 239
credit, trade 20–22,27–9, 33, 35, 37,
    46, 50, 72, 73, 80, 82, 164, 233, 238
    patterns reflecting commercial
        power 29, 46

financial system and 29, 257–8
    credit control 30–32, 38, 45, 47,
        80, 233–7
bottomry 225
government and 264, 271
Cressey, Donald 63, 285
criminogenic systems 22, 185–7,
    196–7
criminologists 11, 63, 283
    apology from author for misusing
        jargon of 23
cybernetics *see* operations research

D

dark markets *see* evolution, Silk Road
Davies, Dan
    anecdotes from career of 1–4,
        160–61, 195, 269, 284
de Angelis, Tino 51–62, 249, 284
    bicycle racing 51
    post-criminal career 61
de Guzman, Miguel 128–30
    theories of diatremes 129
    eaten by pigs 132
De la Brache, Helga 223
de Niro, Robert 51
Deming, W. E. 206
Demosthenes 225–6
Department of Justice (USA) 2
Deregulation 174–5, 188, 229, 231
Diamond, Bob 1
DiPascali, Frank 113
directors, company 31–3, 35–6, 89,
    150, 228–229, 261, 281
Dirty Rotten Scoundrels 17
distributed control fraud 184–97
doctors 75, 134–5, 140–41, 161
    vulnerability to biotech stock

frauds 146
drugs
  illegal 44–8, 110, 117, 145
  pharmaceutical, counterfeit
    135–7
  pharmaceutical, not counterfeit
    137–41

E
economics 48, 83, 125, 174, 198–215,
  229, 248
  unsatisfactory treatment of fraud
    by 20, 174, 189, 208, 288
Elliott Business Builders (Piggly
  Wiggly franchisee) 257
enquiry agent 234–6, 238
Enron 17, 142, 153–7, 160
entrepreneurial fraud vs incidental
  213, 215, 287, 289
Equilibrium 16, 49, 61, 133, 137,
  157
Erik the Red 219
Erni, Barbara 36–8
Escrow 45–9
European Exchange Bank
  (Bahamas) 40
Evolution (online market) 43, 49
exhaustive list of women in this
  book 122
exit fraud 43–50, 137

F
faster the speed, the bigger the mess
  172
FE payments 45–9
Federal Home Loan Bank, San
  Francisco 178, 180
  Board 180, 182

Federal Reserve 70, 110
  warning against getting too
    interested in 122
Feud in the Icelandic Sagas 221
Financial Times 230
Fitzgerald, Ella 138
fraud triangle 285–7
fraudulent conveyance 105
Freaks of Fortune 224–5
Freeman, John 239–41
Freeport McMoRan 132
Friel, Anna 165
fronts 79–81

G
Galbraith, Arlan 101–3
gas stations see petrol stations
Gauger, Mr 5, 6, 12, 227
Gekko, Gordon 241
gelang firma 73
General Electric 244–7
geologists 127–30
  presentations at investor
    conferences 128
Global Crossing 150
Goethe, J. W. von 198
Goffman, Erving 78
gold
  alluvial 130
Golden Boos see Erni, Barbara
golden rule of fraud detection
  288
Goldman Sachs 65, 68, 11, 239
Goodfellas 80
Goodman, George 142
Goodman, Myron 63–72
goodwill (accounting) 176
government

in general 53, 76, 174, 211, 218,
    263–82
South American, possibly
    fictitious 7, 8
USA 51, 57, 91
Portugal 121, 122
secret global, definitely fictitious
    110
Indonesian 132
Gowex 150, 154
Grant Thornton 106
Greece 10–11, 116, 208, 224–6, 287
    Ancient 34, 225–6
Greenspan, Alan 240
'guinea pigs' 228–9

H

Hanseatic League 225
Hasin, Sidney 66, 69
Hayek, F. A. 201–3, 205
Henry VIII 216
high-net worth investors
    tendency to have time on hands
        109
    tax strategies of a proportion of
        266–8
Hippocratic Oath 134
hire purchase scam (Leslie Payne)
    36, 39–40
homomorphism 209, 212
Hooley, Ernest 'The Millionaire' 230
hotel bills 37
House of Commons 1
Howe, Sarah 90, 116–19, 222
HSBC 188, 189, 280
Hudson Oil 249, 251
Humphery, John Stanley 228

I

IBM 64–8
Iceland 218–22
Inca Empire 226–7
Incentives 13, 22, 62, 74, 115, 135,
    159, 165, 174, 185–6, 205, 210
incidental fraud vs entrepreneurial
    213, 215, 287, 288
Infinity Game 92–9
information 24, 71, 199–208, 211–15,
    238
    control of by fraudsters 41, 65, 71,
        115, 173
    insider, securities fraud 23, 239–
        42, 260
inheritance 117, 217, 218–22, 235,
    266
insider dealing 23, 106, 129, 241–43,
    260
insurance 36, 39–40, 65, 163–4, 171,
    225, 228
    medical 74–7, 84
    Payment Protection Insurance
        (PPI) 187–97
insurance scam (Leslie Payne) 40–41
International Reply Coupons see
    Ponzi, Charles
investors 1, 16
    in OPM leases 65–7, 69–71
    Charles Ponzi's 86–9
    hedge fund 96, 104–9, 113
    in pigeons 100, 103
    institutional 104
    nineteenth century female 118–20
    mining 126–30
    reliance on accounts 142–54
    expectations of UK banks 188
    Victorian 228, 231

Retail 240–43
in Piggly Wiggly 256–61
IRS *vs* UBS 263–4
Israel, Sam *see* Bayou Capital
drug habit of as potential indicator
something was wrong 116

J
Jehoash (high priest) 217
John Bull 230

K
Keating Five 182
Keating, Charles 177–83, 214
Kennedy, John Fitzgerald 61
Kerviel, Jerome 165
King, Don 163
Knights of Industry 234, 237
Kolnische Volkszeitung 232, 234, 236,
237
KPMG 150
Kray, Ronnie and Reggie 26–7, 31,
36, 39, 41
Kutz Method 152–3
KYC (know your customer)
281

L
Lab fraud anaemia 74
Ladies' Deposit Bank (Boston)
116–19
lawyers 19, 27, 33–4, 39, 45, 71, 115,
117, 161, 180, 182, 194, 196, 225,
267, 271, 272, 281 (they're usually
in the background even when not
specifically mentioned)
professional qualifications of 114
extreme expensiveness of 234

leasing
tax advantages of 64
see also OPM Leasing
importance of residual value 66
accountancy issues 152
Leeson, Nick 17, 165–73, 285
Lehman Brothers
collapse 13
relationship with OPM Leasing
65, 71
Lehnert, Lothar 235–7
Lernout & Hauspie 150
Let's Gowex *see* Gowex
letterhead 31, 70, 80, 122
Levi, Michael 81, 216, 283
Levy, Jonathan 224
libel 77, 236–8
LIBOR 1–4, 12–16, 193, 205, 215, 244
Liman & Co 235–6
limited liability 34, 225, 231
Lincoln Savings & Loan 177–8, 180,
182–3
livestock 100
Livingstone, Jesse 259
Lloyd's of London 164, 225
Lomuscio, Joe 59
Long firms 21, 23, 27, 29, 35, 41–2,
43–50, 61, 63, 72, 73–5, 77, 79–82,
96, 141, 142, 163, 164, 212, 224,
283, 284
'sledge-drivers' 232–4
against government 271–4
Lucifer's Banker 263

M
MacGregor, Gregor 5, 8, 9, 17, 77,
78, 214
dubious knighthood of 7, 162

military career 7
  previous frauds 18
Madden, Steve 147
Madoff, Bernard 96, 104–5, 113
Mafia 41, 253
Mahler, Russ 249–53
management
  scientific 19, 200, 206–12, 215
  risk management 212–13, 287
  strategic 248
  public sector 264
marginal cost pricing 248
Marino, Dan (fraudster) 107–9, 113,
  115
Marino, Dan (quarterback) 107
maritime capitalism 34, 224–6
market corner 259
market crimes 23, 24, 58, 194, 239–
  62, 271, 282, 289
markets
  general characteristics of 23, 197,
    201–4, 208, 278, 289
  financial 3, 4, 8, 13, 26, 58–60, 99,
    100, 107–8, 129, 132, 142–5,
    147–8, 149, 150–56, 161, 163,
    166, 171–2, 176, 195, 230–31,
    239–40, 242–4, 256–61
  pharmaceutical, 'grey' 136–7
  drugs, illegal 43–50
  prime bank securities 110–11, 184
  real estate 179–80
  supermarkets 213, 255
Marx, Groucho 66
Marx, Karl 84, 232, 247
McGregor, Ewan 165, 173
McVitie, Jack 'The Hat' 26, 41
Medicare 73–6,134–5, 199, 289
Merchant of Venice 34

Merck Pharmaceuticals 138–40
Michaela, Maria 215, 222
military planning 204, 207, 211
Milken, Michael 177, 183
Miller, Norman 52
mis-selling 194–6
money laundering 278–82
Monopolies Commission (UK) 247
mortgages 38, 77, 101, 175–9, 188,
  191, 194, 215, 238
multi-level marketing 94–5

N
New England Journal of Medicine 139
New Zealand 9, 172, 241
newspapers 9, 125, 152, 230, 237,
  252, 262
Nichols, Robert Booth 110–12
Nikkei index 170–71, 173
nobility Scottish 7
  phony scottish 5–9, see Gregor
    MacGregor
  phony 223
North Wales Railway Company 229
notaries 114, 125, 133
  indiscriminate stamping of
    documents by in 1920s Portugal
    121–2

O
ODL Securities 112–13
OECD 268
oil recycling 249–54
OODA loop 208
operations research 204, 208–10, 289
OPM Leasing 63–72
  snowball effect of interest expense
    98

accounting trick 152–3
options markets 163–4, 171–2
Optitz, Gustav 235–7
Opus Dei 53, 57
Original Dinner Party 92
Other People's Money 63, 285

P
Paddington Buys A Share 20, 43
Parmalat 155
Patsies *see* fronts
Payment Protection Insurance (PPI)
    187–97
Payne, Leslie 26–8, 30, 33–6, 39–42,
    67, 73, 98, 163, 237, 283
petrol stations 190, 247–8
pharmaceutical industry 133–41
    track and trace 136
Philadelphia Savings Fund 70–71
Pigeon King International *see*
    Galbraith, Arlan
pigeons, racing 100–103
Piggly Wiggly 255–61
Ponzi, Charles 84–90, 96, 109, 116
    trial of 90
    takeover of Hanover Trust 88–9
    launch of scheme 86
Portuguese Banknote Affair 120–25
Powers, Austin 263
Poyais 5–9, 15, 78, 121, 162, 215, 219,
    287, 297
prime bank securities 110–13, 122, 184
Prince 135
Prince Albert 228
Princess Caraboo *see* Baker, Mary
Princesses 6, 223
Principles of Scientific Management
    206

Prison 18, 61, 112, 119, 125, 173, 208,
    252, 270
    debtor's 34, 225
private equity 144
psychology 17, 87
public choice theory 210–11
pump and dump 147
pyramid schemes 91–5, 116, 184, 222

Q
Quakers 118
quality control 184, 207, 213–15, 287
Quanta Resources 251–2
Quarterly Review 162
Queen Victoria 228
Queenan, Joe 10
Qwest 150

R
Rabelais, Francois 120
Railway Mania 176, 231
Ranbaxy Laboratories 137
Reagan, Ronald 174–5, 251
real estate 89, 177–81, 214, 281
Reddit 48
regulators
    financial 2, 4, 14, 18, 99, 165,
        177–83, 194–5, 240, 260–61,
        280–81, 289
    softness of in 1960s London 40
    environmental 250–51
    pharmaceutical 136, 137, 140
Reuschel, Rollo (Stanislaus Reu)
    232–8
    libel case 237
Richmond-Fairfield 107
Robb, George 228
Rockwell Industries 66–71

Rogers, Will 283
rogue traders 98, 165–73, 215
Royal Canadian Mounted Police 129

S
salting (mining fraud technique) 127
Sarbanes-Oxley 194, 202
Saunders, Clarence 255–61
Savings and Loans 174–84, 185, 196,
    285, 289
    economic theories of failure 174
    business model 175
settlement, securities 60, 107, 108,
    112, 163, 257, 261
Sherman Antitrust Act 246
shipowners 10, 116, 117, 164, 224–6
ships 164, 207, 221, 224–6
    US Navy 89, 249
short firm 73–5, 93
short selling 147, 258–9, 261, 283
shotgun/rifle technique 76–7, 134
signatures, forged 67, 123
Silk Road (online market) 44, 47–8,
    50
simplified summary which hopefully
    captures the important structural
    features see homomorphism
Sketch of the Mosquito Shore 8, 162
Skilling, Jeff 17, 142, 153
slaves 34, 219–21, 225
'sledge-drivers' 232–8
SLK Securities 108, 115
Smith, Adam 11, 213
    on cartels 246
snowball effect see compound
    interest
societies, high and low trust 10, 16,
    62, 125, 166–7, 264, 287

Soviet planning 204, 208, 227
Sparrow, Malcolm 74, 76
St Joseph (fictitious city) 5
stock exchanges
    Alberta 11, 129
    Toronto 129
    Vancouver 11, 126
    London 9, 117
    New York 59–60,147, 228–31,
        256–61
    Chicago 59–60, 256
    Singapore 170–72
    Osaka 170
    Tokyo
    in general 142–5, 147, 163–4,241–2
    NASDAQ 240
Strangeways, Thomas 162, see also
    Gregor MacGregor
Strathclyde Genetics see Galbraith,
    Arlan
Stratton Oakmont 145–8
Sufficient Variety, Law of 209
Sullivan, Scott 154
Susquehanna River 251, 252

T
tacit knowledge 202–3
Tarantino, Quentin 105
tax 32, 64, 69, 98, 155, 159, 177, 191,
    263–71
    value added see VAT
Taylor, F. W. 206
Taylorism 206
Ten Commandments 14, 23
Tennessee Valley Authority 244
Thackeray, W. M. 229
The Economist 125
The Great Salad Oil Scandal 52

The Sting 17
The Uses of Knowledge in Society
    202, 203
The Wolf of Wall Street 145–7
Thomas Jenkins & Co 5
Thorolf (saga character) 218–22
Times, The (newspaper) 230
Times Beach (polluted town) 252
toxic waste 249–54
Toyoda, Sakichi and Kiichio 256
traders, financial 2–3, 59, 98, 107,
    116, 163, 242, 258
    rogue 165–8, 172–3
Trainspotting 280
trust 10–12, 15–17, 20–24, 38–9, 49,
    62, 75, 125, 131, 134, 141, 180, 211,
    222, 233, 254, 264, 286
    circles of 113–16, 137, 280–82
Tupperware 95
TVA *see* Tennessee Valley
    Authority
Tyson, Mike 101

U
UBS 263, 266–70
    Kweku Adoboli scandal 215
UK banking sector
    unusual conditions of at end of
        1990s 188–90
Ulfar (saga character) 218–22
unprotected females 117

V
VAT 271–8
Victorian era 117, 176. 227–31, 232
VIGOR (research study) 138–40
Vioxx 137–41
Volkswagen 253

W
Walsh, David 128–9
warehouse lending 54
Waterlow & Sons 121, 123–5
Wealth of Nations 246
Weil, Raoul 269
Weiner, Norbert 208
Weissman, Mordecai 63–72, 153
West Diddlesex *see* West Middlesex
    Life and Fire Assurance Company
West Middlesex Life and Fire
    Assurance Company 229
Westinghouse 244
*White Collar Crime in Modern
    England* 228
women 91, 94, 118–19, 122
Women Empowering Women 94,
    222
World of Giving (pyramid scheme)
    92
Worldcom 152, 154–5
wrongful trading 35–6